Apple Inc.

Apple Inc.

Jason D. O'Grady

Corporations That Changed the World

GREENWOOD PRESS
Westport, Connecticut • London

Library of Congress Cataloging-in-Publication Data

O'Grady, Jason D.
   Apple Inc. / Jason D. O'Grady.
       p. cm. — (Corporations that changed the world, ISSN 1939–2486)
    Includes bibliographical references and index.
    ISBN 978–0–313–36244–6 (alk. paper)
  1. Apple Computer, Inc.   2. Computer industry—United States.   I. Title.
    HD9696.2.U64O676   2009
    338.4'70040973—dc22   2008038757

British Library Cataloguing in Publication Data is available.

Library of Congress Catalog Card Number: 2008038757
ISBN: 978–0–313–36244–6
ISSN: 1939–2486

First published in 2009

Greenwood Press, 88 Post Road West, Westport, CT 06881
An imprint of Greenwood Publishing Group, Inc.
www.greenwood.com

Printed in the United States of America

The paper used in this book complies with the
Permanent Paper Standard issued by the National
Information Standards Organization (Z39.48–1984).

10 9 8 7 6 5 4 3 2 1

This book is dedicated to my wife Elizabeth, my daughter Ginger, and my family for their unwavering support.

Contents

Preface

Few companies can claim the successes that Apple Inc. can, from practically inventing the personal computer to creating an entirely new market for portable media players to re-inventing how we purchase and enjoy music. A case can be made that Apple took personal electronics to an entirely new level, surpassing even Sony, largely considered to be the original pioneer of consumer electronics. Apple is the little company that could. Starting out as the minority player in an industry crowded with larger and better-capitalized competitors, Apple turned the industry on its ear.

Two guys named Steve, working in a garage in 1976, created a prototype computer designed to be different in a way no one thought possible: It would be easy to use. Those two Steves not only succeeded with that product, but they also broke ground in the business world in a new and different way: They proved you could not only have fun at work, but that pursuing a capitalist dream could be hip.

Starting with the Macintosh—a niche machine at best—the company slowly built upon its successes; from the iMac to the iPod to the iPhone, there's no denying the impact of the Cupertino company on the computer industry and the larger consumer electronic world as a whole. Apple began by revolutionizing once-complex machines into easy-to-use "personal" computers by pioneering technologies like the Graphical User Interface (GUI) and the mouse and taking them into the mainstream. The Apple II put the concept of personal computers into the consciousness of the average consumer. Computers were no longer relegated to scientists and PhDs; they had become accessible to the average consumer.

The second coming began with the return of Steve Jobs to Apple in 1997. Jobs ushered in the next generation of Apple with the iPod media player and then the iPhone—two devices so revolutionary that Apple dropped the "Computer" from its name, changing the official corporate name to Apple Inc. Apple metamorphosed from a little company that made computers to a company that made a difference. Critics have written Apple off time and again, yet it rises from the ashes to astound its detractors and delight its customers. That's not luck or happenstance—it's vision, dedication, and persistence.

In addition to pioneering in computer technology, Apple single-handedly changed the way we consume music. The company's svelte media player (the iPod) has sold more than 160 million units[1] and a music service (iTunes) has sold more than 5 billion songs[2] and both continue to climb.

iPod and iTunes work so seamlessly together that it's hard to imagine how we used to listen to music before them. Almost no one could have predicted that Apple would have revolutionized music, consumer electronics, and culture in the way that it did. The Macintosh and its successors captured the hearts and minds of computer users so deeply that being a "Mac person" makes you a member of a special club.

How did the company do it? Let's find out.

ACKNOWLEDGMENTS

Steve Wozniak, Owen Linzmayer, Leander Khaney, John Greenleigh, Dan Farber

Ian Page (Mac Tracker), Glen Sanford (Apple-History.com)

Mack and Manco's pizza and Toll House chocolate chips during those late nights, Pandora.com and its dub reggae station for providing the soundtrack.

Introduction

Apple Inc. is one of the most influential companies in technology today, but it wasn't always that way. What started out as a one-off hobby machine that a talented electronics wiz built for himself (and to show off to friends) became the core of one of the largest and most successful computer companies of all time. Apple turned the hobbyist's tool of choice—the computer—into an essential life tool that we can't live without today.

When the computer became personal and within the reach of the average consumer, worlds collided. What was originally intended as a high-tech device reserved for scientists, mathematicians, and intellectuals suddenly became the domain of an average person with an average salary. Suddenly, computing power that was previously reserved for elite members of the aerospace and defense industry was within the reach of you and me. Processing power never before imaginable was now not only within reach but fit neatly on the top of a desk.

But what could you do with a tool like that? When Steve Wozniak and Steve Jobs created the Apple I, there was no software available for it. Everything had to be hand coded into the machine. Later the Apple II ushered in the era of the cassette drive for saving and loading programs, which opened all kinds of doors. What they built was more than simply a tool; it was a platform for others to build upon. Soon hundreds of programs followed. Apple had started a cottage industry in software to go along with its amazing personal computer.

Fast forward a few years and computers are starting to crop up everywhere. A market for software applications thrives, as do sales of ancillary equipment like peripherals, upgrades, and accessories. All the while a community of like-minded individuals congregate to discuss their successes, exploits, failures, and questions. People are attracted to more than just technology; they enjoy the social and community aspects that are associated with it. Being close to a particular technology, like computers, puts you in contact with others that share your interests. This type of community fosters learning and intellectual discussion and slowly develops into a unique culture unto itself.

Apple had an amazing impact on technology, society, and the world. And it continues to innovate to this day. Using the personal computer as a foundation, Apple has turned technology into an essential tool of our daily lives. Today computers provide information, communication, and entertainment in ways that we never could have imagined back in 1976. Thanks to the Internet and the graphical user interface, a person with a computer today has access to more information at his or her fingertips than rulers of the land had only a century ago.

Now information is getting faster and the devices are getting smaller. It once took a large bulky computer and a slow dial-up modem to access the Internet. Now it can be called up with a few taps and pinches of a finger on a touch screen that fits into your pants pocket.

Apple is a revolutionary company in many ways. This book will examine several ways that Apple changed the world:

1. Inventing the personal computer (PC)—Apple started the personal computer revolution with the Apple II in the 1970s and made computers even more easy to use in the 1980s with the Macintosh.
2. Making the computer easy to use—Innovations such as the mouse, the GUI, trackpad, and click wheel gave us easy, intuitive ways to access our digital content.
3. Developing software that was extremely user-friendly—Apple created a low barrier to entry by creating software that is usable and intuitive so users can begin without reading the manual. A consistent and predictable user interface across applications, interoperability, and a built-in help system make us productive right out of the box.
4. Making the Internet easy—The iMac and iBook allowed customers to get online within 15 minutes of opening the box and set a new standard for Internet access that is still the envy of the industry. Apple then made it equally easy to post movies and photo galleries on the Web. AirPort wireless access cut the cords.
5. Introducing digital media management—iTunes, iPhoto, and iMovie spearheaded the digital media revolution and made it easy to manage all of our digital content.
6. Introducing digital media playback—iPod, iTunes, and iPhone set the standard for listening to music, watching television and movies, and making phone calls too.
7. Saving digital media commerce—Apple single-handedly rescued the music industry from the perils of peer-to-peer file-sharing networks. Digital entertainment that was headed for certain death thanks to pirates thrives today on iTunes.
8. Helping advance computer technology—Apple popularized technology, like FireWire for high-speed data access and Wi-Fi for

wireless Internet access, making data move faster and without the clutter of wires.

9. Making communication easier—iPhone revolutionized mobile phones and iChat AV made it easy to videoconference with family and colleagues across the globe.

In the first chapter we'll take a fun and historical look at how Apple came to be and delve into the background of one of the world's most interesting companies.

Chapter One

Origins and History

There's a certain romance about the history of Apple; people often refer to it as being founded in a garage and while it sounds great—everyone loves the story of the underdog making it—it's not entirely true. The two Steves started out building Apple computers in Steve Jobs's parents' living room and they later moved their production operation into the garage when they ran out of room.

HP's Garage Roots

Apple wasn't the only company to have roots in a garage. Hewlett-Packard founders William R. Hewlett and David Packard got their start by developing an audio oscillator in a garage at 367 Addison Avenue in Palo Alto—not far from where Steve Jobs grew up in Los Altos. The HP Garage was registered as California Historical Landmark #976 on August 13, 1987.[a]

[a] California Office of Historic Preservation (OHP), "Birthplace of Silicon Valley, Historical Landmark #976," http://ohp.parks.ca.gov/listed_resources/default.asp?num=976.

Apple began in the Santa Clara Valley vicinity of California—known for its fruit orchards—when Stephen Gary Wozniak (Woz) was introduced to Steven Paul Jobs by Woz's neighbor Bill Fernandez. Woz and Fernandez built their first computer out of parts that were discarded by local companies for cosmetic reasons. They called it the "cream soda computer" after the beverage they loved to drink while building computers in the Fernandez family garage.

The problem with computers of the time was that components were prohibitively expensive. Woz was relegated to designing computers on paper where he focused on trying to minimize the amount of components required—which would keep the electronics as clean as possible. In June 1971, after withdrawing from college, the 16-year-old Jobs was introduced to 21-year-old Wozniak by Fernandez. Jobs eventually convinced Wozniak to mass produce and sell his computer design. The synergy between the two was undeniable. Woz was the engineer and Jobs was a marketing maven; between them they had the skills to build and promote computers in a way that no one had discovered yet.

When Jobs needed computer parts for a class project, he looked up Bill Hewlett (of Hewlett-Packard fame) in the telephone book and called him at home. Hewlett gave Jobs the parts that he needed and, because he showed such initiative, a summer job at HP assembling frequency counters.

In the fall of 1971 Woz returned to academics, enrolling at the University of California at Berkeley, and got into business with Jobs shortly thereafter. Wozniak was skeptical at first but was later convinced by Jobs to do it because, regardless of what happened, they could tell their grandchildren that they started their own company.

Wozniak built "blue boxes" (see the sidebar) from instructions his mom showed him in a 1971 issue of *Esquire*. Jobs purchased the parts and sold the devices in the dorms for $150 each under the alias Oaf Tobark and split the profit with Woz (a.k.a. Berkeley Blue), whose main job was building the devices.[1]

Anatomy of a Blue Box

A blue box is an early phone-hacking tool that emulated phone company tones and signals. By placing the speaker of the blue plastic box (hence the name) up to a standard telephone receiver, the owner could essentially route his or her own calls, circumventing the phone company's billing system. At the time, long-distance calling could be very expensive, and it was very desirable to be able to make free calls—especially for someone with family and loved ones on the other side of the country.

APPLE I

In 1975, Wozniak attended meetings of the Homebrew Computer Club, an early computer enthusiast group that met in Silicon Valley. Several famous Silicon Valley pioneers (both ethical and unethical) had been members of Homebrew at some point or another. It was a perfect venue to both hone their technical chops and demonstrate their technical prowess.

One of Wozniak's first major projects was the Computer Conversor. A friend that ran a computer time-sharing company, Alex Kamradt, solicited Woz's help in developing a video-teletype machine that could be used with his firm's minicomputers. But a teletype was only the beginning; Woz was motivated by a new generation of microcomputers like the Altair 8800 and he got the idea to incorporate a dedicated microprocessor into his lowly teletype and turn it into a fully functional computer.

Central Processing Units (CPUs) like the Intel 8080 ($179) and the Motorola 6800 ($170) were out of his price range, so Woz instead designed computers on paper while waiting for prices to drop. Wozniak was working for Hewlett-Packard (whose bread and butter were calculators) and tinkering with computers like the Altair at night. "All the little computer kits that were being touted to hobbyists in 1975 were square or rectangular boxes with non-understandable switches on them," claimed Wozniak.[2]

After Woz discovered that microprocessor and memory prices had fallen dramatically, he realized that he could purchase everything he needed to build a computer with one month's salary from HP. In 1976 MOS Technology released the 6502 processor for only $20 and Woz adapted his 6800 paper designs to run on it. Wozniak completed the Apple I, and took it to a Homebrew meeting to show it off. Jobs was in attendance and immediately saw the potential of producing and selling the computer to hobbyists.

The Apple I was notable because it used a standard television as the monitor, whereas many computers at the time had no display at all. Although it was faster than teletypes of the day, the Apple I was no speed demon. It was, however, pioneering in terms of design. Woz was a master at minimizing the amount of chips that his designs required. This reduced both price and complexity—making his machines easier to debug if something went wrong. It was Woz's chip reduction strategy that endeared him to fellow engineers at Homebrew. This was the feature for which his peers respected him the most.

One nice feature was that the Apple I had all of the boot code on a Read Only Memory (ROM) chip, which allowed it to boot up relatively fast. At the urging of Paul Terrell, owner of the Byte Shop in Mountain View, Woz included the ability to load and save programs to a cassette drive, which used standard audiocassettes.

After seeing the design of the Apple I in action, Terrell immediately gave Jobs an order for 50 units (at $666.66 each). Jobs took his first purchase order to Cramer Electronics, in an attempt to leverage it for the parts he and Woz needed to actually build the first batch of computers. When the massive parts distributor balked at Jobs's lack of credit, he flashed the purchase order from the Byte Shop for 50 computers and showed that the payment terms were COD.

Jobs requested net 30 day terms so that he could deliver the computers to the Byte Shop and pay Cramer Electronics on time. Once the credit manager verified the Jobs purchase order, he extended credit terms. Jobs, Wozniak, and a small crew worked day and night to deliver the original 50 Apple I kits. Jobs and Wozniak's friend, Ronald Wayne, helped to build the machines in Jobs's living room. The group borrowed, scrounged, and even sold prize items (like Woz's calculator and Jobs's VW bus) to pay for the parts needed to assemble the Apple I kits. Jobs secured the parts while Wozniak and Wayne, who bought into the company, built the first batch of 200 Apple Is.

The Name *Apple Computer*

There has been a lot of speculation over the years about the name *Apple Computer* and its origins. Many speculate that it was homage to Apple Records, The Beatles music label, as both Jobs and Wozniak were big fans of the Fab Four. Others believe that Apple was chosen because it would fall before Atari in the phone book—Atari was a major Silicon Valley company at the time.

Steve Jobs decided on *Apple Computer* in 1976 because he had grown fond of visiting a small apple farm owned by his friends. Jobs would spend time helping out at the farm, and he told Woz about his idea to use *Apple* as the name. The pragmatic Woz immediately recognized the conflict in using a name so similar to The Beatles' record label, but they couldn't think of anything that was better so they ran with it.

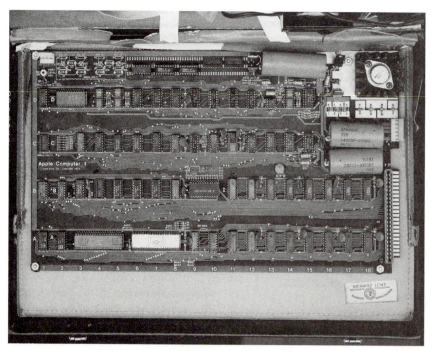

The machine that started it all—The Apple I motherboard. Image © John Greenleigh, www.flipsidestudios.com.

Apple went through several phases in its ascent to tech glory and had its share of bumps along the way. After the Apple I was complete, Woz already had something better in mind. Like most good engineers, he was always thinking about ways to make his designs better. He wanted to optimize them, use fewer chips and less expensive materials, make them faster, more powerful, and colorful. Since Apple was just a couple of entrepreneurial guys that didn't have the luxury of a large staff or an R&D (Research and Development) budget, they had to persevere and struggle to keep it alive, but they had fun doing it.

APPLE II

Wozniak used proceeds from sales of the Apple I to start construction of its successor, the improved and enhanced Apple II. The Apple II featured a much better television interface that allowed it to display graphics, and eventually color. Jobs insisted that the Apple II have an improved case and built-in keyboard so that the new machine would be instantly usable, unlike the Apple I models that required assembly.

All the improvements Woz wanted in the Apple II were starting to add up, and Jobs knew that he needed to secure outside funding if the Apple II was going to become a reality. Daunted by the task of raising money for the Apple II, Wayne, who had a previous failed venture, dropped out of the company and sold his stake back to Jobs and Wozniak. Jobs ran into many roadblocks in his attempts to raise capital for the project. Banks

At the forefront of the personal computer revolution—The Apple IIe. Image © John Greenleigh, www.flipsidestudios.com.

were reluctant to lend the pair money because they had doubts about the marketability of a computer for the average user.

A major breakthrough occurred when Jobs met Armas Clifford "Mike" Markkula Jr., who agreed to co-sign for a bank loan for $250,000. Having secured seed money from Jobs's angel investor, the three had enough working capital to produce the Apple II and formed Apple Computer on April 1, 1976.

Read more about Mike Markkula in Chapter 2, "Founders and Key Players."

The trio used their bank loan to manufacture an entirely new Apple II case, designed by Jerry Manock, and the complete Apple II debuted on April 16, 1977. The machine was a smash hit, and the Apple II eventually took credit for what we now know as the personal computer. The Apple II was wildly popular, selling millions of units and spawning a number of successors, including the Apple IIe and IIGS.

APPLE COMPUTER INC.

Apple was incorporated January 3, 1977, and had its Initial Public Offering (IPO) on December 12, 1980. The stock opened at $22 per share on December 12, 1980, and closed at $29. More than 40 employees who left Apple on December 11 as working stiffs came back to work the next day as millionaires. The Apple IPO raised more money than any IPO since Ford in 1956. The first Apple shareholder meeting was held at the Flint Center, in January 1981.

APPLE III

Competition from long-established computer makers like Commodore and IBM began to pick up in the early 1980s because they saw the Apple II and VisiCalc's spreadsheet software as a threat to their lucrative business computer market. Apple decided that the next Apple computer, the Apple III, would be designed for business users and would challenge the mighty Big Blue, IBM.

Launched in May 1980, the Apple III ended up being a commercial failure for several reasons. For starters, at $4,340 to $7,800, it was far too expensive compared to competitors and its software catalog was limited. Although designed to be compatible with the Apple II, this feature was intentionally hobbled.

The real time clock chip in the Apple III, manufactured by National Semiconductor, was prone to failure after long periods of use. Since Apple was soldering the chips directly onto the motherboards, they were impossible to replace, requiring soldering or a complete board replacement. To make matters worse, Jobs wanted the Apple III to be designed without a cooling fan (or vents) so that it would operate silently. He thought that the case could be engineered so that the electronics would cool by convection and that heat would dissipate through the chassis. This turned out to be incorrect and the chassis wasn't able to adequately cool the system, and the Apple III became prone to overheating and crashing. When it would overheat, some of the Integrated Circuits (ICs) would become disconnected from the motherboard.

Almost all the original Apple III computers were recalled, and Apple had to replace as many as 14,000 of the first Apple IIIs for free. They were replaced with brand-new machines with twice as much memory (256KB RAM, or Random Access Memory) and new circuit boards that fixed most of the problems. Apple released the Apple III Plus, which sold for $2,995 in December 1983. The revised model fixed most of the hardware problems and included 256KB RAM, video interlacing, an Apple IIe keyboard, and a built-in clock, but the damage was already done.

One year after the Apple III, almost as if it smelled blood in the water, IBM unveiled its Personal Computer (or PC for short), which featured a newer 16-bit design that opened up the market to a wide range of inexpensive IBM clones. After the Apple III became known for poor reliability, business users fled for the comfort and familiarity of IBM. Apple discontinued the Apple III in September 1985 after selling only 65,000 systems. Steve Wozniak said that the Apple III failed because Apple's marketing department designed it, unlike Apple's previous engineering-driven projects.[3]

LISA

While one team was busy building and selling the Apple III, another, separate group was designing Apple's next computer, which would mark a departure from Apple's original text-based computers. This new computer would truly revolutionize computing and popularize terms like *mouse, icon,* and *desktop.*

After a tour of the Xerox PARC (Palo Alto Research Center) laboratories in December 1979 and a demonstration of its Alto computer, Steve Jobs decided that the Graphical User Interface (GUI) was the future of computing. Apple traded $1 million in pre-IPO Apple stock for three days at PARC to study its machines. Apple engineers came away from the experience with the foundation of their first computer based on a GUI, called Lisa. According to legend, the project was named Lisa after Jobs's first daughter, but Apple claims that the name is an acronym for Locally Integrated Software Architecture. Lisa was launched in 1983 at the sky-high price of $9,995, which is what most likely doomed it to failure. Success notwithstanding, Lisa was a forbearer to a much more successful Apple project—Macintosh.

The precursor to the Macintosh—The Lisa. Image © John Greenleigh, www.flipside studios.com.

MACINTOSH

Jobs was diplomatically removed from the Lisa project to prevent a replay of the Apple III fiasco and instead focused his attention on Apple's next computer, the Macintosh. Jef Raskin came up with the idea for the Macintosh in early 1979 and formed a small team in September to make it a reality. His concept was to produce an easy-to-use, low-cost computer that included everything an end-user could want in a complete package.

In September 1979, Raskin got a green light from Apple for his Macintosh project, and began to assemble his team. Bill Atkinson from Apple's Lisa team recommended Burrell Smith. Raskin assembled his hardware and software team that included Atkinson, Smith, Chris Espinosa, Joanna Hoffman, George Crow, Jerry Manock, Susan Kare, Andy Hertzfeld, Daniel Kottke, Bud Tribble, and Brian Howard.

The first Macintosh—The Mac 128k. Image © John Greenleigh, www.flipside studios.com.

Read more about Jef Raskin and the rest of the Macintosh team in Chapter 2, "Founders and Key Players."

The first Macintosh board was designed with a 5MHz Motorola 6809E microprocessor and 64KB RAM. Bud Tribble suggested that they use the Motorola 68000 processor from Lisa in the Mac, and by December 1980 Smith had succeeded in implementing the 68000 and even increased its speed from 5 to 8MHz. The new board was able to support a larger 384 × 256 pixel display and reduced production costs.

When the Macintosh was in the early development stage, a slightly miffed Jobs adopted the project and was determined to make it better than Lisa. Raskin led the Mac team until leaving after a personality conflict with Jobs in January 1981, ultimately leaving Apple in February 1982. According to Andy Hertzfeld, "Jef did not want to incorporate what became the two most definitive aspects of Macintosh technology—the Motorola 68000 microprocessor and the mouse pointing device. Jef preferred the 6809, a cheaper but weaker processor which only had 16 bits of address space and would have been obsolete in just a year or two, since it couldn't address more than 64Kbytes. He was dead set against the mouse as well, preferring dedicated meta-keys to do the pointing. He became increasingly alienated from the team, eventually leaving entirely in the summer of 1981."[4]

How the Mac Was Almost a Bicycle

The name *Macintosh* was originally selected because it was Jef Raskin's favorite type of apple, but the Mac almost wasn't an Apple at all. When Raskin took a leave of absence in February 1981, Steve Jobs and Rod Holt made the decision to change *Apple* to something else. They felt that the name *Macintosh* was just a code name and that a name change was in order to reflect the change in regime.

Holt decided on *Bicycle* as the new name that would replace Raskin's *Macintosh* for the duration of the project and presented it to his design team. When they balked, Holt insisted that all references to *Macintosh* be changed to *Bicycle*, telling them that it shouldn't really matter "since it was only a code name."[a]

The *Bicycle* name originated from an ad that Apple had placed in *Scientific American* magazine. The ad featured quotes from Steve Jobs about computers, including one about how personal computers were "bicycles for the mind." The logic was that humans could run as fast as other species, but a human—on a bicycle—could beat them all.

Rod's edict was never obeyed. Somehow, Macintosh just seemed right.

[a] Andy Hertzfeld, "The Father of the Macintosh," http://www.folklore.org/StoryView.py?project=Macintosh&story=Bicycle.txt.

Macintosh shipped on January 24, 1984, and was revolutionary because of its innovative mouse input device and easy-to-use graphical user interface (GUI). The Mac design was unique because it shipped with a 9-inch, 512 × 342 pixel monochrome monitor and 128KB of RAM—better specs than the original designs. Although the memory was soldered to the logic board, it could be upgraded to 512KB with a steady hand by soldering in new, higher-capacity chips—a popular upgrade that many people had done to their machines.

Jobs led the Mac team until a battle erupted between him and new Apple CEO, John Sculley, in 1985. The Apple board took Sculley's side in the dispute, and Jobs was removed from most decision-making processes—a move that didn't sit well with Jobs, who later resigned.

After leaving Apple, Jobs founded NeXT, a company that built futuristic computers based on the NEXTSTEP operating system. NeXT computers didn't sell well due, in part, to their high cost. In 1986, during his departure from Apple, Jobs purchased the computer-graphics division of LucasFilm from George Lucas, who was in the midst of a divorce, for

$10 million, and renamed the company Pixar. Jobs returned in 1997 after Apple bought NeXT in December 1996 for $429 million.

Apple went through several phases after the successful launch of the Macintosh and in the absence of Jobs.

1985–1997: THE SCULLEY, SPINDLER, AMELIO ERA

While Apple marketed the Macintosh to college teachers, graphic designers, and professionals, the inexpensive and expandable Apple II targeted home users and public schools.

Apple released a compact and less expandable version of the Apple II called the IIc in April 1984. In September 1986, Apple released the fifth and most powerful Apple II, the Apple IIGS, featuring a 16-bit architecture, mouse-driven operating system, amazing color graphics, and top-shelf sound capabilities that surpassed those of most other computers, including the black-and-white Macintosh. The "GS" in the name stood for Graphics and Sound.

When Steve Jobs left Apple after a dispute with new CEO John Sculley, a new era of management was upon Apple. Sculley, a former vice president of PepsiCo, was selected to be CEO of Apple on April 8, 1983, with a mission of applying his marketing skills to the personal computer market, especially the Macintosh. Sales of the Lisa tanked, and although the Macintosh was a bona fide success, it couldn't beat the IBM PC. IBM was selling more units, thanks to a competing GUI in Microsoft Windows 3.0. The Amiga and Atari ST platforms were also formidable competitors during this period.

For more on Apple's competitors, see Chapter 9, "Competition."

Part of Sculley's strategy was to push the Mac by releasing dozens of major models with hundreds of configurations. Sculley raised the initial price of the Macintosh and used the additional money to increase profits and spend more on advertising.[5] Apple responded to competition from the IBM PC with the Performa, Centris, and Quadra product lines, but they were marketed poorly. Apple's dizzying array of configurations and model numbers didn't fit with Apple's reputation for simplicity, and sales suffered. Sculley was removed by Apple's board, and Michael Spindler was named President and CEO in 1993.

Spindler surprised everyone in 1994 when Apple announced that it was switching to new PowerPC chips from longtime rival IBM. The new PowerPC processors required a partial rewrite of the Mac operating system so that older programs could still run in emulation on the new machines. Although Spindler presided over several successful projects, like the introduction of the PowerPC, he was also responsible for his share of failures, including the Newton and the Copland operating systems. Spindler was replaced by Gil Amelio as Apple CEO on February 2, 1996.

Gil Amelio, a veteran of National Semiconductor, identified several reasons why Apple was failing, which included a lack of cash, a lack of quality hardware and software, a lack of focus, and an out-of-control culture. Amelio laid off one-third the Apple staff, discontinued the Copland OS, and shipped Mac OS 8. Amelio eventually negotiated the purchase of Steve Jobs's new company NeXT Inc. for $427 million, which he later admitted was too much. NeXT Inc.'s NEXTSTEP operating system would become the foundation for Mac OS X, which became a runaway success. Despite Amelio's initiatives, Apple sales continued to tank and the company lacked direction. Amelio said:

> Apple is a boat. There's a hole in the boat, and it's taking on water. But there's also a treasure on board. And the problem is, everyone on board is rowing in different directions, so the boat is just standing still. My job is to get everyone rowing in the same direction so we can save the treasure.[6]

Apple's stock price was the lowest it had been in 12 years under Amelio, and market share continued to plummet due to quality problems and confusion about the product line. After a $740 million loss in the second quarter of 1997, Amelio was removed as Apple CEO by its board of directors. Jobs returned to Apple in December 1997 as part of the acquisition of NeXT Inc. and later became the interim CEO.

For more on Apple's CEOs over the years, see Chapter 8, "Apple Leadership."

1998–2001: RECOVERY, RENAISSANCE, AND RESURGENCE

Recovery

When Steve Jobs returned in 1997, he had his work cut out for him. Jobs inherited a company at its bottom, its stock and market share were at historical lows, quality was dismal, and the company lacked direction. Jobs took the reins as interim CEO and began Apple's recovery phase, raising needed money and restructuring the company's product line.

His first effort to right the ship was to repair the massive hole in its hull that was leaking money. In 1997 Jobs announced a $150 million investment from Microsoft in exchange for the company agreeing to continue to develop and release its popular Microsoft Office for Mac suite. The deal provided much-needed cash and the commitment that Office would continue to be developed, a vote of confidence in the platform and critical assurance needed for businesses to continue buying Macs.

Jobs then discontinued licensing the Apple ROMs and Mac OS to the clone makers, who he described as "leeches." Rather than growing Apple market share, as originally planned, cloners instead took Mac sales away from Apple. Next, Jobs created the machine that would save Apple, the iMac. iMac was an all-in-one computer with a handle, similar to the original "toaster" Mac he designed, except that it now came in a curvy translucent blue case.

Apple started a marketing campaign around the new iMac design called "No Beige," aiming to distance its design from every other beige box computer of the time. The iMac was more than a savior for Apple; it also invigorated the entire computer industry with its bright, eye-catching design. Soon everything from Windows PCs to household items like irons were being redesigned in transparent color schemes that emulated the iMac's design. Then just when everyone caught up, Apple released the iMac in five new colors. They looked like Lifesavers candies, which Jobs referred to as "lickable," and consumers ate them up.

The iMac was nothing short of a runaway success, selling more than one million of the colorful all-in-one Macs per year. But the iMac was more than simply another computer, it was a symbol of Apple's return to viability and a turning point for computer design as a whole. Arguably the most influential person in the early stage of the Apple renaissance was Jonathan Ive, the principal designer of the iMac, iPod, iBook, and iPhone.

Renaissance

During the renaissance, Apple also pioneered in the area of wireless networking technology, which would become a pervasive technology in just a few short years. In 1991 Apple unveiled the iBook, its first consumer notebook computer and also the first Mac to support wireless networking and Internet access. The renaissance continued as Apple reinvented its professional desktop computer line with the Power Mac G4, which shipped with a fast Motorola PowerPC processor that utilized a new 128-bit floating point instruction set called "AltiVec."

Resurgence

Apple's resurgence began in 2001 with Apple's launch of three key strategies:

1. Mac OS X—Apple's first multi-threaded, protected memory operating system,
2. Apple retail stores—which were a huge gamble at the time, and
3. iPod—the diminutive music player that literally changed the music business.

Apple released its first truly modern operating system in 2001 as a result of its purchase of NeXT. Mac OS X was built on NEXTSTEP and the

FreeBSD kernel and was the perfect synthesis of stability, reliability, and security—three things that the Mac OS lacked. The OS X (pronounced OS *Ten*) featured a completely overhauled user interface, a Classic environment that allowed customers to run their legacy Mac OS 9 applications.

Apple's launch of a line of retail stores in 2001 was met with great skepticism but turned out to be one of the crowning achievements of the resurgence. Gateway Country Stores had cropped up in suburban areas across the United States but were faltering and retail, in general, was a gamble. When Gateway announced the closure of all its stores in April 2004, Apple had opened 53 stores. Apple reinvented the retail store from the ground up by hiring the best. It built a prototype store in a warehouse near the Apple campus to test the concept and arranged it around interests: photos, videos, music, and kids. In it Apple borrowed a concept from the Four Seasons Hotel: the concierge desk. The Apple Store's "Genius Bar" was born.

Apple's gamble has made it one of the most successful retailers in America. Apple opened its 200th retail store in October 2007. The Fifth Avenue location in New York City attracts 50,000 customers per week and Apple Store sales are tops in the industry, averaging $4,032 per square foot. In 2004, Apple reached $1 billion in annual retail sales, faster than any U.S. retailer. What's more, sales recently topped $1 billion per quarter.[7]

The third prong of Apple's resurgence occurred in 2001 when the iPod revolutionized the world of music playback and, arguably, the music industry as a whole. Music is widely regarded as the universal language of mankind and its appeal and romance are undeniable. iPod provided a compact and convenient way to carry thousands of songs in your pocket. More important, Apple made vast amounts of music easily accessible via an innovative scroll well and hierarchical menu system. Just about anyone, young or old, could take an iPod and figure out how to use it without ever touching the manual—a testimony to its unmatched simplicity.

After Napster and other peer-to-peer file-sharing services had decimated the prerecorded music business from 1999–2001, iPod arrived just in time to give people an easy way to enjoy their massive digital music libraries. It was a perfect storm for iPod, and it easily became the most significant consumer product of 2001, maybe even the decade. After Apple's huge hit with the iMac in 1997, the iPod was a home run. Lightning had struck twice at Apple.

2002–PRESENT: THE NEW APPLE

After 12 devastating years in his absence, Steve Jobs returned to Apple in 1997 and not only resuscitated the company he co-founded but completely re-engineered everything about it. After things stabilized, he pulled off one of the biggest turnarounds in business history with the introduction of iMac, iPod, Mac OS X, and a chain of retail stores. With a new wind in its sails, Apple was determined not to rest on its laurels. In addition to keeping flagship products current and fashionable, Cupertino continued to innovate, pushing the stock price higher and higher.

After simplifying its hardware strategy to two major markets (consumer and professional) and two product lines (notebook and desktop), Apple was ready to branch out. In 2002, it released the Xserve, its first serious attempt at a server. Then in 2005 it announced the Mac mini, the smallest and least expensive Mac ever. In 2007, the company launched the Apple TV set-top box and the revolutionary iPhone. In 2008, it released the thinnest notebook in the world, the MacBook Air. And after shipping millions of Macs with G3, G4, and G5 chips from IBM and Motorola, Apple announced a switch to Intel processors in 2005 and completed the changeover by 2006.

Apple marketed the Mac as the hub of the digital lifestyle and designed it to manage the flood of electronic gadgets and gizmos that were coming to the market. The original iMac was promoted as a digital hub and Apple expanded the concept with the iPod, iTunes Store, and Apple TV, and tied it together with Mac OS X and the iLife suite of software. Apple's brilliant jigsaw puzzle pieces were falling right into place.

Building on the success of iTunes and iPhoto, Apple bundled them with iMovie, iDVD, iWeb, and GarageBand and packaged it as "iLife." iLife came bundled with every new Mac and was critically acclaimed as a major benefit of buying a Mac. While Windows PCs came loaded with useless trial software, bloating the hard drive, Macs came with useful and powerful production and entertainment software that worked out of the box. In 2005 Apple released iWork, an office suite that included a word processor (Pages), spreadsheet (Numbers), and presentation software (Keynote). That was the perfect complement to iLife. iWork provided a simple and inexpensive ($79) office suite that was compatible with Microsoft Office.

In 2003, Apple launched the iTunes Store, the first true alternative to downloading music illegally from file-sharing networks. The iTunes Store offered digital music downloads for sale for 99 cents each and full albums for $9.99 each. Apple's foray into digital music downloads was nothing short of a revolution. For the first time, consumers had the option to purchase a single track instead of having to buy an entire album. Consumers embraced the concept with open arms and made Apple the number one music retailer, online or offline.

Apple expanded the offerings, once mostly limited to music, at the iTunes Store to many other categories of entertainment. Apple branched out into selling music videos, audiobooks, concert tickets, television shows (October 2005), iPod games and feature-length movies (September 2006), university lectures (May 2007), ringtones (September 2007), movie rentals (January 2008), and iPhone software (June 2008).

Thanks to the success of the Apple Store, Apple has conquered U.S. retail. It expanded the concept internationally, opening more than 30 stores in the UK, Japan, Canada, Italy, and Australia. Domestically, Apple opened several mini stores that were about half the size of a regular store, carrying only the most popular items. The new, smaller store concept allowed the company to go into smaller markets that might not support a larger retail presence.

For more on the individual products Apple released, see Chapter 6, "Technology Timeline."

Chapter Two

Founders and Key Players

STEVE JOBS

Innovation distinguishes between a leader and a follower.

—Steve Jobs

Very little can be said about Apple Inc. without mentioning its enigmatic leader and co-founder. Several words are frequently used to describe Steve Jobs, including visionary, iconic, charismatic, quirky, individualistic, different, and evangelic bad boy.

Jobs's story is truly one of rags to riches. Born an orphan, he pioneered the personal computer when he was 21, made his first million by age 23, had a net worth of $10 million by 24, and by age 25 was worth more than $100 million. Today Apple's co-founder is worth approximately $5.7 billion. Not bad for someone who takes home a token salary of $1 per year from his job at Apple.[1]

Jobs is the perfect front man. He's a charismatic leader who motivates the people around him to do their best, if not better. He has a unique vision that's inspired by excellence, beauty, and brilliant design. Jobs is a textbook visionary. He has an uncanny vision of the future and the ability to translate dreams into products—and profits. He has a unique combination of high-level thinking and down-in-the-trenches practicality that can be both inspiring and exhausting. He's known for his tireless work ethic as much as his insufferable tirades. Jobs has no patience for mediocrity.

He can't entirely take credit for designing Apple's early success, though. That distinction belongs to Mike Markkula, who provided Apple with critical early funding. Nor is Jobs the creator or engineer behind the company's machines. That job was handled by Steve Wozniak, then by a team of excellent contributors drawn to Cupertino by Apple's compelling products and intangible sense of hipness.

Steven Paul Jobs was born on February 24, 1955, in San Francisco, California, and grew up surrounded by apricot farms, which eventually came to be known as "Silicon Valley." According to Jobs's commencement address at Stanford University in June 2005,[2] his biological mother, an unmarried grad student, gave him up for adoption at birth with demands that his new parents be college graduates. After a lawyer and his wife backed out, he was eventually adopted by Paul and Clara Jobs of Mountain View, California. Neither had a college degree.

According to Jobs:

> My parents, who were on a waiting list, got a call in the middle of the night asking: "We have an unexpected baby boy; do you want him?" They said: "Of course." My biological mother later found out that my mother had never graduated from college and that my father had never graduated from high school. She refused to sign the final adoption papers. She only relented a few months later when my parents promised that I would someday go to college.[3]

His biological parents studied at the University of Wisconsin in Madison and went to California to surreptitiously have the baby. Not even the family knew. They later married and had a daughter, novelist Mona Simpson.

The Jobs family soon found out that young Steve was a handful as a child—he was bright and somewhat hyperkinetic. He had a tendency to wake up at four in the morning, prompting his parents to buy him a rocking horse and a record player to keep him occupied in the early morning hours. His parents had to bring him to the hospital on several occasions during his childhood. Once to have his stomach pumped after he swallowed a bottle of ant poison, and another time after suffering burns on his hands after inserting a bobby pin into an electrical outlet.

One's physical environment has an undeniable influence on one's upbringing and values and Steve was no exception. The Jobs family home in Mountain View, California, was located in what would become the heart of the Silicon Valley, and it wasn't far from the epicenter of the beatnik rebellion and hub of hippie culture in San Francisco, all of which rubbed off on Steve.

Silicon Valley Is Born

In 1956 the Nobel Peace Prize for Physics was awarded to the inventors of the transistor, which made the large, hot, vacuum tube obsolete. Transistors relied on the property of silicon to conduct electrical current in one direction, and as they got more complex, they were dubbed "semiconductors." One of the Nobel Laureates, William Shockley, set up his semiconductor company in an area north of San Jose along the peninsula, which became known as

"Silicon Valley." In the 1950s, the brightest electrical engineers from around the country flocked to the area to pursue their passion.

San Francisco's North Beach community, just 40 miles to the north of the Jobs residence, became the hub of the beatnik rebellion against postwar conformity. The movement developed around beat poets like Allen Ginsberg and author Jack Kerouac who experimented with drugs and alternative lifestyles. Beatniks laid the foundation for what would become the hippie era and the "Summer of Love" 10 years later.

After the Russians launched their first unmanned satellite, Sputnik I, in October 1957, America's sense of technological superiority was bruised and the resulting competitiveness with Russia drove a technology revolution in the United States. The federal government began offering grants for science and educational curriculums and schools rededicated themselves to the sciences. The Silicon Valley was the beneficiary of much of the country's newfound attention to technology.

Steve's adoptive father was a certified car buff. Paul Jobs loved to restore cars and kept an immaculate work area. His garage was spotless, his overalls pressed, and his toolbox perfectly organized. The senior Jobs meticulously documented his car restorations in a scrapbook and hung a framed picture of his latest project proudly on the living room wall.

Paul was an excellent negotiator and a shrewd businessman. He had a cunning knack of getting the lowest prices for car parts at the junkyard and had a keen ability to sell his fixer-uppers for top dollar. Although Steve enjoyed the negotiation and the business side of his dad's hobby, he didn't gravitate to the nuts and bolts aspect of it. Paul Jobs tried to get young Steve interested in helping him work on cars. "I figured I could get him nailed down with a little mechanical ability," he recalled, "but he really wasn't interested in getting his hands dirty. He never really cared much for mechanical things." Then he made a prescient statement about his son, "Steve was more interested in wondering about the people who owned the cars."[4]

Starting at age 10, Steve became fascinated by technology and the seemingly limitless possibilities of electronic gadgets. His neighborhood was a beehive of entrepreneurial electronic and computer engineers from companies like Hewlett-Packard that were more comfortable with a soldering iron than a baseball bat. Steve befriended a neighbor that worked at HP named Larry Lange. Lange brought home a carbon microphone one day and showed it to Steve in his garage. Steve's interest was piqued and he came back each day to hang out in Lange's garage and ask the HP engineer countless questions.

Hewlett-Packard was founded in a Palo Alto garage not far from Lange's house when Bill Hewlett and David Packard toiled over their workbench to build control devices for animation cameras. Their first customer was Walt Disney, and they went on to build a company that had an engineering philosophy of doing things right, regardless of cost. They also believed in keeping their employees happy by allowing them to work flexible hours in beautiful campuses that inspired creativity. HP fostered a loyalty in its employees that was widely respected.

Lange encouraged the energetic Jobs to join the Hewlett-Packard Explorer Club, a group for aspiring engineers that met on Tuesday evenings in the company cafeteria. Company engineers would come to demonstrate the company's latest products. Steve was fascinated by the club and the technology at HP and approached it with intensity. Company employees, recognizing his high level of interest, would give him special tours of different labs and it was at HP where Steve saw his first computer.

Somewhat of a loner, Steve was bored by school and was an underachiever. He didn't deal well with authority and refused to do things that he thought were a waste of time. In the fourth grade, a teacher had to bribe him into learning. One teacher offered him cash to finish a workbook, which rekindled a passion in him to learn.[5] Motivated, Steve learned more in that year than any other. His teachers, recognizing his talent, recommended he skip two years of school and go directly to junior high. His parents objected but later agreed to allow him to skip one year.

Steve's next stop was Crittenden Middle School in Mountain View where he started in fifth grade. The combination of the switch to a new school and being lumped into the general population didn't sit well with Steve. He belonged in an advanced or gifted class, but there was no such thing in his school district and Steve was miserable. Crittenden was a rough school with kids from the poorest neighborhoods; it was a melting pot of ethnicities and the police were often called in to break up fights. Steve's brilliance was overshadowed by chaos and commotion. In 1967 Steve told his parents that he refused to return to Crittenden for the seventh grade and sensing his frustration, the family moved to Los Altos, a few miles south.

Cupertino, Los Altos, and Sunnyvale were all part of the same school district, which was head and shoulders above Mountain View's. Steve still had trouble making friends, though, because he skipped a grade, he was younger than everyone in his class. But he was now in a gifted program, which his previous schools didn't have. Steve was bright, but quiet and withdrawn. He didn't quite fit in because he didn't like team sports like the other kids. Bill Fernandez, also an outsider at Cupertino Junior High, befriended Steve because the two could relate. Like many people in Silicon Valley, Fernandez had a garage stocked with electronics and Steve loved to stop by on his way home from school to tinker.

Fernandez introduced Jobs to the eldest son of the family living across the street from him, a family that Jobs knew from the Mountain View

Dolphins Swim Club, the Wozniaks. Bucking the trend, the Fernandezes didn't work in the electronics industry, so Bill got his education in the subject from his neighbor, Jerry Wozniak. Although Jerry's son Steve was five years older than Bill, the two would share their passion for electronics and had built a number of science fair projects together.

Steve Wozniak, or "Woz" as he was known, had a reputation that preceded him. He had a well-earned reputation as a brilliant designer of electronics, having won electronic fair contests for his early computer designs. Woz was more than an electronics geek, though; he had a tremendous sense of humor and was known for his pranks and playful sensibilities. He conjured up elaborate practical jokes and his combination of intellect and humor drew Jobs to him. However, Woz was almost five years Jobs's senior, and there was a bit of a generation gap between the two.

Woz, at 18, had designed a computer on paper, was well read, and spent weekends in the Stanford Linear Accelerator library brushing up on his skills. Jobs and Fernandez, on the other hand, at 13, were still kids that liked to tinker a little but seemed juvenile around the more mature Woz. Although they badly wanted to hang out with the neighborhood electronics genius, it took a few years for them to click.

Jobs continued to attend meetings of the Hewlett-Packard Explorer Club and decided to build a frequency counter. One day when in need of some parts for his project, he called Bill Hewlett, co-founder of Hewlett-Packard, by looking him up in the Palo Alto white pages. After about a 20-minute chat, Steve had his parts, and Hewlett was so impressed by the 15-year-old's bravado, he offered him a summer job assembling frequency counters at HP. Steve never did finish his own counter, but that didn't matter because he was in heaven working at HP.

Jobs entered Homestead High School in Cupertino in 1968. At the advice of Woz, Jobs and Fernandez enrolled in John McCollum's Electronics 1 class and earned the badge of "Wireheads," popular slang for electronics club members. The class was beneficial for Jobs, who only had a basic understanding of electronics. McCollum's class mixed theory with an emphasis on practical applications and he was a stickler for detail and obedience. While Woz thrived in the class four years prior, McCollum's teaching style and rigid class structure didn't fit with Jobs's personality and he quickly lost interest. McCollum recalled Jobs as competent but "somewhat of a loner. He always had a different way of looking at things."[6]

In his sophomore year, Jobs got weekend work at Haltek, an electronics shop in Mountain View with a block-long warehouse crammed with obsolete electronic components. It was not unlike the junkyards that his dad used to forage for auto parts. Haltek was a paradise for wireheads, because although obsolete or rejected, most of the parts they carried were perfectly functional and many were brand-new. The place was a major source for parts for every tinkerer and electronics junkie in the area and Jobs picked up a valuable skill in pricing parts.

When Woz went on to study at Berkeley in 1971, Jobs would visit him several times a week. He liked hanging out with slightly older crowd (like Woz) and was tiring of the wirehead crowd at school. At the same time, he wasn't quite a hippy either; he was too intellectual to get wasted all the time. He still enjoyed the hippy ethos, though, and, like most students at the time, read Shakespeare, Dylan Thomas, and Herman Melville.[7]

When Jobs was a senior at Homestead, he began taking freshman English classes at Stanford and further drifted from electronics to English. Woz's mother gave him an article from the October 1971 issue of *Esquire* called "Secrets of the Little Blue Box" and he shared it with Jobs. The article detailed the exploits of phone "phreaks" that had engineered a way to make free phone calls on the AT&T long distance phone network. The pair was enthralled with the article and identified with the shadowy figures in it. Motivated, they built their own digital "Blue Box" under the aliases Berkeley Blue (Woz) and Oaf Tobark (Jobs).

Wozniak and Jobs got to meet the famous phone phreaker Cap'n Crunch, who got his name when he discovered that a plastic whistle found in certain Cap'n Crunch cereal boxes emitted a perfect 2600Hz tone that could be used to bypass the phone company billing system and make free

Steve Jobs (left) scrutinizes a "blue box" that Steve Wozniak (right) built after reading about it in an issue of Esquire magazine. 1975. Margaret Wozniak.

long distance calls. After selling Blue Boxes in the dorms to make money, the pair soon called off the venture after someone explained the possible legal consequences. It was a fun way to learn about technology and how things worked, but neither wanted to go to jail for their hobby. Woz brought out a boyish curiosity and mischievous side of Jobs, and together they found clever and creative ways to have fun through pranks.

After graduating from Homestead High, Jobs didn't want to attend Stanford or Berkeley because they were too close to home. He wanted to go farther away and escape from the grips of his parents. He decided on a private liberal arts school in Portland, Oregon, called Reed College. His parents didn't approve because it was expensive and far away. As with most things, they eventually relented and Jobs got his way. After attending Reed for only one semester, Jobs dropped out in December 1972. But instead of going back home, he hung around Reed, living in abandoned dorm rooms for a year while he took up the study of philosophy and foreign cultures.

Jobs met Dan Kottke at Reed, a wild-haired freak at the time, like him. Kottke saw that Jobs was an outsider and could relate with him. The two immediately bonded. Jobs lived in Kottke's room for a while, and they read books on Eastern mysticism and discovered Buddhism together.

After returning to his parent's house in California in 1974 the reality of earning a living and minding his finances hit him. Although Jobs still maintained strong spiritual beliefs and often traveled to his friend's farm, he needed a job. His passion for technology led Jobs to Atari, the leading manufacturer of video games at the time. While working nights at Atari, Jobs met Ronald Wayne, a technician who used to fix slot machines in Las Vegas, and the two bonded.

When he had saved enough money, Jobs and his partner in spiritual discovery, Kottke, traveled to India in the search of enlightenment. After experiencing the extreme poverty and illness of India, the pair returned home unsatisfied and unfulfilled and returned to their jobs at Atari in the fall of 1974. After returning to Atari, Jobs renewed his friendship with Wozniak, who was working at HP's calculator division, and the duo attended meetings of the Homebrew Computer Club. During this phase Jobs rediscovered Zen Buddhism, which seemed to provide him some answers.

In 1975, Jobs was 20 and working at Atari, living at his parent's house, and making regular trips to the Los Altos Zen Center and the All-One farm in Oregon with his hippie friends from Reed. Jobs was also showing a growing interest in Woz's new computer design.

Woz was starting to become a respected member of the Homebrew Computer Club, whose popularity was rapidly increasing. Its members consisted mostly of hobbyists and engineers who came to show off their latest achievements and share tips and information about computer kits, programming, and computer design. Jobs's skill in computer design was limited, but he keenly realized that Woz's current project was an amazing feat of engineering. Jobs became increasingly involved and after a few months, he convinced Woz that they should join forces to build and sell his computer to other hobbyists.

While Woz really just wanted to build a computer for himself (and for bragging rights at Homebrew), Jobs understood that there were hundreds of hobbyists that were desperate to buy such a machine so that they could use it for programming. Jobs co-founded Apple Computer Inc. in 1976 when he was 21 years old with Steve Wozniak, 26, and together they pioneered the personal computer and made a permanent and indelible mark on the computer industry.

"Basically, Steve Wozniak and I invented the Apple because we wanted a personal computer. Not only couldn't we afford the computers that were on the market, those computers were impractical for us to use. We needed a Volkswagen."[8]

For more on Steve Jobs's history at Apple Computer, see Chapter 1, "Origins and History."

As described earlier, Jobs founded Apple with Woz and Mike Markkula and lasted until he lost an internal power struggle with new Apple CEO John Sculley in 1985. The Apple board took Sculley's side in the argument and demoted Jobs who later resigned. He returned to Apple in 1997.

Besides starting NeXT, Jobs also purchased the visual effects house Pixar during his hiatus from Apple. In addition to his duties at Apple, Jobs remains the CEO of Pixar Animation Studios, which has become the leading animated movie studio. Pixar won 20 Academy Awards and has taken in more than $3 billion in box-office receipts. Pixar has earned the distinction of creating some of the most critically acclaimed animated movies of all time, including *Toy Story, A Bug's Life, Toy Story 2, Monsters, Inc., Finding Nemo, The Incredibles, Cars,* and *Ratatouille.* In 2006, Pixar merged with the Walt Disney Company and gave Jobs a seat on the Disney board of directors, where he is the largest single shareholder.

Jobs is a long-time Buddhist and vegetarian[9] and lives in Palo Alto, California, with his wife, Laurene Powell, and three children. He also has a daughter, Lisa, from a previous relationship.

Accolades

Jobs's accomplishments in the technology industry have earned him numerous awards and accolades.

1985: The National Medal of Technology from President Ronald Reagan.

1987: The Jefferson Award for Public Service.

2004: One of *Inc.* magazine's America's Most Fascinating Entrepreneurs.[10]

2007: *Fortune* magazine's Most Powerful Businessman.[11]

2007: California Governor Arnold Schwarzenegger and First Lady Maria Shriver inducted Jobs into the California Hall of Fame, located at the California Museum for History, Women and the Arts.[12]

STEVE WOZNIAK

Stephen Gary Wozniak was born August 11, 1950, in San José, California, and is better known by the shortened version of his surname, *Woz*. Often described as amiable, affable, soft-hearted, and sometimes even naïve, Woz is perfectly happy in his role as an all-around good egg. Wozniak is the son of an engineer at Lockheed and a prolific tinkerer. From an early age he was interested in electronics. Woz is a lifelong computer engineer, tinkerer, prankster, and technology buff.

Woz's passion for electronics began in the fourth grade when his dad helped him with some science fair projects. With an early disposition for electronics, Woz earned his Ham radio license in the sixth grade. By the time he entered college, Woz was already building computers. He attended Homewood High School in Cupertino where he showed a lot of interest in an electronics course taught by John McCollum. In 1968 he took electrical engineering courses at the University of Colorado at Boulder. Then, in 1969 he left Boulder to take courses at DeAnza College in Cupertino.

His most notable accomplishments are his creation of the first "personal" computers in the 1970s—the Apple I and II. He designed them partially for the intellectual challenge and partially to impress his friends at the Homebrew Computer Club, a group of electronics enthusiasts based in Palo Alto, California.

Says Cringely in *Accidental Empires*, "Steve Wozniak deserved to be considered Apple's number 1 employee. From a technical standpoint, Woz literally was Apple Computer."[13]

Woz had a vision how his first computer would work as early as 1977. His design of the Apple II became the genesis of the personal computer revolution and even Woz would probably admit that he underestimated the power of his design. Each time we reach into our pocket for our tiny handheld computers and smartphones, we owe a debt of gratitude to Woz. Without Woz's keen interest in computers, and his genius for board design, the world would probably be a different place today. He's largely responsible for the world of information that we now have at our fingertips.

In his 2006 autobiography, *iWoz*, he writes that he became friends with Steve Jobs, four and a half years his junior, in 1970 when Jobs had a summer job at the same business where Wozniak was working on a mainframe computer.

For more on more on how Jobs and Woz met, see the "Steve Jobs" biography.

Steve Wozniak with a framed Apple I wearing his "Apple" sunglasses. Margaret Wozniak.

Woz enrolled in the University of California, Berkeley in 1971, but withdrew by 1975 to co-found Apple Computer Inc. He would later return to Berkeley (under the alias Rocky Raccoon Clark) to finish his Bachelor of Science degree in Electrical Engineering and Computer Sciences (EECS), which he received on May 17, 1986.

Woz co-founded Apple on April 1, 1976, and took the title of Vice President of Research and Development at Apple. The two Steves couldn't be more different. While Jobs was a marketing whiz and a good front man, Woz designed the hardware and the software for the Apple II. While he didn't work directly on the Macintosh project, his engineering prowess, integrity, and sense of humor are legendary and considered to be inspirational to many of the Macintosh team.

Woz left Apple in 1981 after crashing his plane into a 12-foot embankment in February shortly after taking off from Santa Cruz Sky Park. An investigation by the National Transportation Safety Bureau (NTSB) showed that Woz wasn't rated for the airplane he was piloting and didn't have the necessary "high performance" certification on his license. After the accident, he suffered amnesia and had no recollection of the accident. He also did not remember his hospital stays or the things he did after he was released: he followed his previous routine (except for flying), but could not recall what had happened.[14]

Woz returned to Apple in 1983, but he was very specific that he wanted only to be an engineer and that he didn't want to be in management. He left his full-time position at Apple on February 6, 1987, but still remains an employee and a shareholder. He stays on the rolls at Apple Inc., saying "I have never left the company. I keep a tiny residual salary to this day because that's where my loyalty should be forever. I want to be an employee on the company database."[15] He also still maintains communication with Steve Jobs.

Steve Wozniak arrives at Macworld Expo 2008 on his Segway. Jason D. O'Grady.

Known as somewhat of a nomad, Woz has started several business ventures over the years, including Cloud Nine in 1985, where he created the first universal remote control. One of his other endeavors is the creatively named Wheels of Zeus (W.O.Z.), which has a mission to create digital technology "to help people find things." His nomadic tendencies carry over to his personal life, he's been in and out of several colleges and loves to travel in his spare time.

After his departure from Apple, Woz continued to donate financial and support resources for technical curriculum at local schools, reaffirming his philosophy of educating our youth. "Making significant investments of both his time and resources in education, Wozniak 'adopted' the Los Gatos School District, providing students and teachers with hands-on teaching and donations of state-of-the-art technology equipment. Wozniak founded the Electronic Frontier Foundation, and was the founding sponsor of the Tech Museum, Silicon Valley Ballet and Children's Discovery Museum of San Jose."[16]

Wozniak lives in Los Gatos, California, with his wife and family.

Woz and His Segway

One of Woz's favorite toys is his Segway, a unique two-wheeled, electric vehicle invented by Dean Kamen in December 2001. It's his vehicle of choice when he attends Macworld Expo in San Francisco, and he even founded a Polo Segway team. Woz usually travels everywhere with his Segway; he built a special trailer to carry it on the back of his car. Woz owns a bunch of Segways and is getting licensed to be a Segway trainer.

In a SegwayToday.Net podcast[a] Woz gives insight into how he integrates the Segway Personal Transporter into his everyday life. "Whether he's exploring an unfamiliar town, gliding into Los Gatos for a bite to eat, or enjoying a game of Segway Polo, 'Woz' explains in detail why he's always got his trusty Segway under his feet."

[a] Segway Today Podcast, http://www.segwaytoday.net/SegwayToday/Podcast/Entries/2007/8/27_Segway_Today_episode_3.html.

MIKE MARKKULA

A. C. "Mike" Markkula was one of the linchpins of the early Apple because he provided essential business expertise and, more important, he co-signed for a critical $250,000 bank loan during the formation of Apple in 1977. Markkula was given a one-third share of Apple in return for securing the financing.

Markkula, an electrical engineer, also had marketing skills. He started at Fairchild Semiconductor, a Silicon Valley chipmaker famous for spawning several large and successful companies like Intel Corporation and Advanced Micro Devices (AMD). Markkula later worked at Intel, where he made an excellent return on his stock options after the company's IPO.

Markkula recruited Michael "Scotty" Scott to be Apple's first CEO because both Steve Jobs and Steve Wozniak weren't sufficiently experienced for the job. Markkula replaced Scott in 1981 to become Apple's second CEO. Steve Wozniak credits Markkula as a major reason for Apple's success. Markkula was succeeded by John Sculley as CEO of Apple in 1983.

KEY CONTRIBUTORS

> What's the difference between Apple and the Cub Scouts? The Cub Scouts have adult supervision.
>
> —Guy Kawasaki, quoted in *Apple*, 1998

While the founders are inextricably associated with the success of Apple, the company was famous for its team philosophy in which many people contributed to the overall success of a project. With the exception of top management, Apple was very horizontal in its hierarchy. Software and hardware engineers worked together with interface designers, marketing, and documentation personnel to build a complete product. The following are some of Apple's key contributors over the years.

Jef Raskin

Jef Raskin was a professor of computer science and music at the University of California at San Diego who was hired in January 1978 as Apple employee #31. Raskin was originally hired to write the Apple Basic user manual with Brian Howard. Apple liked the Basic manual so much that it hired Raskin and Howard to be founders of its internal publications group.[17]

Raskin recommended that Jobs and Markkula acquire VisiCalc and when they declined, Raskin took a leave of absence from Apple to write the tutorial section of the VisiCalc manual. After returning to Apple, Raskin started the Macintosh team at the beginning of 1979. He settled on the name *Macintosh* as a tribute to the many varieties of apples found in New York state. As soon as Steve Jobs saw the Mac, he immediately adopted it as his own. Raskin led the Mac team until he left after a personality conflict with Jobs in January 1981, ultimately leaving Apple in February 1982.

Bill Atkinson

Bill Atkinson studied under Jef Raskin at the University of California at San Diego and started at Apple in 1978. Atkinson wrote the LisaGraf primatives software (which Raskin renamed *QuickDraw*) that allowed the Lisa and Mac to draw graphics on screen. He also wrote one of the original Macintosh applications that was included with every machine shipped— MacPaint. One of his final contributions to the Macintosh was writing HyperCard in 1987, a simple, yet powerful programming environment that, despite being discontinued in 1998, is still in use today.

Burrell Smith

Burrell Smith got his start at Apple in 1979 as a service technician. Bill Atkinson, while working on the Lisa team, noticed that Smith was doing good work in the Apple II maintenance department and introduced Smith to Raskin. After Smith built a Mac prototype from a gutted Apple II and a television, Raskin hired him as the second member of the Macintosh team.

Smith designed five different Mac digital boards during the course of the project and also designed the digital board for the LaserWriter and a low-cost version of the Apple II that eventually became the Apple IIe. He left Apple in February 1985 to co-found Radius in 1986.

Chris Espinosa

Perhaps one of Apple's youngest employees, Chris Espinosa started at Apple at age 14 in 1976. Officially he was Apple employee number eight. He began writing BASIC programs in Steve Jobs's garage and has worked at Apple his whole life with the exception of a short hiatus to attend the University of California at Berkeley. Jobs convinced Espinosa to drop out of Berkeley in 1981 to work for Apple's publications department. Although Espinosa didn't participate in the Apple IPO, Steve Wozniak offered up to 2,000 pre-IPO shares and an advantageous price to certain employees (like Espinosa) he thought were undervalued. The plan became known as the "WozPlan." Espinosa worked at a variety of positions at Apple over the years, including as an AppleScript engineer and in developer support.

Joanna Hoffman

Joannna Hoffman started at Apple in 1980 in the Mac marketing department when it was still in the embryonic stages. She went on to draft the *Macintosh Interface Guidelines* and later moved on to lead the international Macintosh marketing team. After leaving Apple, Hoffman eventually became vice president of marketing of General Magic, a company cofounded by Apple alums Bill Atkinson and Andy Hertzfeld.

Jerrold C. "Jerry" Manock

Jerry Manock graduated from Stanford University and was handpicked by Jef Raskin to be on the original Macintosh design team. Manock worked as an industrial designer at Apple from 1977 to 1984. He is most famous for designing the Apple II, III, and Macintosh enclosures. Manock is considered by many to be the father of Apple's Industrial Design Group. Manock is president and principal designer of Manock Comprehensive Design Inc. in Burlington, Vermont.

Susan Kare

Susan Kare started at Apple in January 1983 as a graphic designer. She's best known for designing most of the Mac icons and fonts and much of Apple's original marketing materials. Kare left Apple in the fall of 1985 and followed Steve Jobs to NeXT. According to the Museum of Modern Art in New York, Susan Kare is "a pioneering and influential computer iconographer. Since 1983, Kare has designed thousands of icons for the world's leading software companies."[18] After leaving NeXT, Kare designed the buttons, icons and many of the screen images for Windows 3.0, founded a digital design practice in San Francisco, and is currently creative director of the Internet appliance company Chumby.

Andy Hertzfeld

Andy Hertzfeld started at Apple in August 1979 on the Apple II project, then moved over to the Mac team in February 1981. Hertzfeld was considered a software wizard and was the primary developer of the Macintosh system software. He developed the User Interface toolbox and the Mac's innovative desk accessories. After leaving Apple in 1986, Hertzfeld cofounded Mac monitor maker Radius, then he moved on to General Magic in 1990 and Eazel in 1999. He also founded the Folklore Web site, which is packed with information about Apple's early days (http://folklore.org/).

Daniel Kottke

Born in Bronxville, New York, Dan Kottke bears the distinction of being the first official employee of Apple. Kottke was responsible for assembling and testing the original Apple I with Steve Wozniak in Steve Jobs's garage in 1976. Kottke was close friends with Jobs when they attended Reed College in Oregon, and the pair backpacked across India together.

Kottke was responsible for testing the original Apple II logic boards, and he helped construct the prototypes for the Apple III and the Macintosh. As one of the original members of the Mac team, Kottke's signature permanently adorns the inside of the case of the original Mac 128k.

Brian Howard

Brian Howard started at Apple in January 1978 and was a close friend of Mac team leader Jef Raskin. Howard began writing documentation for the Macintosh, then graduated to become Burrell Smith's assistant. He's most famous for co-designing some of the most beloved Macs created, including the popular Mac IIci.

Steve Capps

Steve Capps learned about the Graphical User Interface (GUI) at Xerox in Rochester, New York, and started at Apple in September 1981 on the Lisa team. Capps moved over to the Macintosh team in January 1983, working on the Finder with Bruce Horn and writing text editing routines that became part of the Mac's ROMs. Capps left Apple in 1985 but came back in 1987 and developed the first Newton Message Pad prototype for Apple CEO John Sculley.

Bruce Horn

Bruce Horn was a veteran of the Xerox Palo Alto Research Center (PARC), developer of the first Graphical User Interface (GUI). He started at PARC at age 14 and joined Apple in January 1982 as a developer of the Macintosh system software. Horn was responsible for the Resource Manager, Dialing Manager, and the Finder. He left Apple in 1984 and received his Ph.D. in Computer Science from Carnegie Mellon in 1999.

Chapter Three

Historical Context

> There are occasionally short windows in time when incredibly important things get invented that shape the live of humans for hundreds of years. These events are impossible to anticipate, and the inventors, the participants, are often working not for reasons of money, but for personal satisfaction of making something great.
>
> —Steve Wozniak, Revolutionary, from the foreword
> to *Revolution in the Valley*, 2004

Apple will be remembered as the creator of the personal computer and much more. Once relegated to a niche, hobbyist computer manufacturer, Apple has matured into a media powerhouse with its long tentacles in every aspect of the business. Apple plays a major role in the consumption (iPod and Mac) and distribution (iTunes Store) of music, once thought to be the exclusive domain of giant record labels. Having expanded into television and movies, Apple shows no sign of slowing down.

The company's endeavors into portable media players have allowed it to take risks and successfully expand the business into set-top boxes and mobile phones, also previously thought to be outside the scope of a so-called traditional computer manufacturer. Apple Inc. is anything but traditional, though. Apple has expanded its expertise across multiple disciplines and into ones where virtually no one could have predicted it would go.

If Apple continues cutting a swath of innovation through Silicon Valley, it's difficult to predict what market it will conquer next. One thing's for sure, though—no one can write Apple's epitaph just yet.

APPLE INC.

Apple, as a company, made a huge mark on history. Growing from two employees to a staff of more than 20,000 across the globe, Apple had worldwide sales of more than $24 billion and earned $3.5 billion in profit in fiscal 2007. Apple has no debt and more than $15 billion in cash.

But what makes Apple's feat even more impressive is that it should, by all accounts, have gone bankrupt sometime in 1995 or 1996. It was hemorrhaging money and market share and lacked leadership. Apple took a turn for the worse in the early 1990s when quality slipped and it flooded the market with a confusing array of Macintosh models. The problem was exacerbated by licensing the Apple ROMs to third-party cloners that were supposed to build market share but instead stole sales from Apple.

Apple was on its deathbed in 1997 when Steve Jobs returned, after Apple purchased NeXT. Jobs came back and quickly turned the company around by eliminating unprofitable products, tearing up the agreements with the cloners, and whittling down Apple's product offerings to two markets (professional and consumer) with only two models in each (a desktop and a notebook). Jobs surrounded himself with brilliance and hired only the best and brightest to take the company to a new level. Since then, Apple's has been a storybook tale of one of the greatest business turnarounds in the history of business, for which it will always be remembered.

Some of Apple's recent financial milestones include:

- Apple entered the *Fortune* 500 at number 414 and in 2008 ranked at number 103 on the list.
- Apple is number 8 on *Fortune*'s list of the 20 most profitable tech companies, passing longtime rival Dell, who is number 10.[1]
- Ranked as the "Top Brand Worldwide," Apple was first in almost all the positive questions, including "What brand can you not live without?" and "What brand, if sent back 100 years, would have the biggest impact on the course of history?"[2]
- Apple leads *Fortune*'s Most Admired Companies List, ahead of Google (#4) and Microsoft (#16). Apple also topped the Global Top 20 list, which included companies from other countries.[3]
- Apple is the top retailer in the United States in terms of sales per square foot.[4]

CORPORATE CULTURE

Apple's corporate culture will be remembered as bucking the trend of the formal, stoic, businessman in a blue suit with a briefcase. Apple changed the traditional organizational hierarchy from tall to very flat. Apple allowed casual dress when other large companies had an official business dress code that resembled parochial school uniforms. Steve Jobs has been known to walk around the Apple campus barefoot in cutoff shorts and a black shirt. According to Scott Lewis at answers.com, "By the time of the famous '1984' TV ad, this trait had become a key way the company attempts to differentiate itself from its competitors."[5]

It wasn't until many years later that many businesses adopted a "casual Friday" dress code that tried to emulate the dress that companies like Apple had pioneered—for one day of the week. Many companies have since abolished casual Friday and returned back to a policy requiring formal business attire.

COMPUTERS

There's no denying the impact that Apple created with its computers. The Apple I and II were the first real "personal" computers and established new markets for computers in the home and at school, previously the realm of large corporations, scientists, and academia. The personal computer spread like wildfire and was eventually distributed by hundreds of manufacturers across the globe. The PC became such an integral part of the home that many today would find it difficult to live without one.

The U.S. Census Bureau's Current Population Survey[6] says that only 8.2% of U.S. homes had a computer in 1984. That number has climbed to more than 60% in 2003, thanks in large part to the work of Apple, which played a huge role in popularizing the personal computer and making it what it is today. Apple's mark on computer technology will be with us for a long time.

1984	8.2%	7.00M households
1989	15%	13.7M households
1993	22.8%	22.6M households
1997	36.6%	37.4M households
2000	51.0%	53.7M households
2001	56.3%	61.4M households
2003	61.8%	70.0M households

MEDIA PLAYERS

When Apple released the first iPod in 2001, it was met with a lukewarm reception, mostly due to the high price tag: $400 was considered by many to be too expensive for a consumer-oriented music player. Although it was the first time you could put your entire music collection in your pocket, other larger, hard-drive–based music players were already on the market. In retrospect, since Apple has sold more than 150 million iPods in less than seven years, it's pretty obvious that it found the recipe for digital music and MP3 players—the company can't seem to make them fast enough.

The iPod's stratospheric growth can only be compared to the Sony Walkman. The Walkman sold 50 million units in its first 10 years and took 16 years to sell 150 million units. Apple's iPod sold 150 million units in just over six years, more than twice the growth of the Walkman.[7] Sony has sold more than 350 million units worldwide since it created the Walkman in 1979, so it still maintains a unit lead over the iPod, but it also had a 22-year head start.[8]

Sony's Walkman sold 13.5 million units per year and the iPod is currently averaging more than 24 million units per year and shows no sign of reaching its peak. By comparison, the venerable fax machine peaked at 3.6 million units sold per year in 1997and slowed down to 1.5 million per year in 2004.[9] The iPod's share of the MP3 player market as of January 2008 was 72% (of unit sales) and 84% (in dollars).[10]

The iPod has already made its mark on history and will undoubtedly be remembered as one of the most commercially successful electronics devices in history. If it continues at its current pace, iPod could surpass the Walkman's 350 million sales in its first 10 years—something that took Sony 25 years to do.

For more on iPod unit sales, see Chapter 10, "Finances."

TELEVISION, MOVIES, SET-TOP BOXES

When you think of Apple, you don't usually think of television, or even your living room, but Apple is working hard to change that. Apple released the Macintosh TV in October 1993, which was its first attempt at computer-television integration. It shared the appearance of the Mac LC 500 series, but in black, but it never took off. In 1995 Apple's Pippin was another attempt at developing a multimedia platform. Pippin was designed to be an interactive, multimedia CD appliance first and a gaming platform second. Pippin suffered the same fate as the Mac TV after failing to get any traction in the market.

After several failed attempts at a TV-connected Mac, Apple dove into the living room with both feet in 2007 with the announcement of the Apple TV, a new $299 set-top appliance with a 40GB hard drive. Apple TV was designed to play iTunes content (music, television shows, movies, etc.) from any computer (Mac or Windows) connected to the local network. It could be connected to any Enhanced Definition (ED) or High Definition (HD) television but not to a Standard Definition (SD) set still popular in millions of living rooms. The Apple TV could be connected to any wide-screen TV with either HDMI or component video, supported both analog and digital audio via RCA and optical S/PDIF outputs, and supported resolutions from 480p to 720p.

Apple TV was Apple's first serious attempt at conquering the living room, and even it turned out to be somewhat of a dud. In 2008, the company announced a significant software update for the AppleTV called *Take 2* that featured a new interface and was able to download TV shows and other digital content directly to the device.

At the All Things D conference on May 30, 2007, Steve Jobs called Apple TV a hobby, saying, "The reason I call it a hobby is a lot of people have tried and failed to make it a business. It's a business that's hundreds of thousands of units per year but it hasn't crested to be millions of units per year, but I think if we improve things we can crack that."

With 95% of households already getting television content from either cable or satellite providers,[11] the home television market is going to be tough for Apple to penetrate. The historical context of the Apple set-top box still remains to be seen, but given Apple's storied success with the iPod, iPhone, and iTunes, it's dangerous to underestimate the company.

The iPod created an entirely new platform to enjoy videos, television programs, and movies. Once thought to have too small a screen to watch

The device that changed the music world—The original iPod, circa 2001. Image © John Greenleigh, www.flipside studios.com.

video of any length, the iPod changed that perception completely in 2005 with its fifth-generation version with a larger, 2.5-inch screen. People quickly adapted to putting video on their iPods and watching it on the go. The ability to watch video caught on so quickly that Apple changed the design of the iPod nano in 2007 to include a wider 2-inch color screen. Apple had created an entirely new category of television!

Prior to iTunes, the concept of selling individual television shows seemed impossible. After all, who would pay for something that they could watch for free on their television at home? But Apple did just that, expanding its iTunes Store to many other categories of entertainment. After its initial success selling digital music, Apple branched out into selling television shows (October 2005), feature-length movies (September 2006), and even movie rentals (January 2008).

The iPod and iTunes took the concept of *time-shifting,* popularized by Digital Video Recorders (DVRs), to the next level. Instead of just being able to watch a television program at a different time (time-shifting), consumers could now watch it away from home—a concept called *place-shifting.* The iPod forever decentralized the enjoyment of television and movies.

In January 2007, when Apple announced iPhone, and the iPod touch in September, it further expanded the concept of place-shifting television and movies, thanks to the new devices' larger, 3.5-inch screens. People who previously resisted watching video content on the iPod because of its small screen were becoming more receptive to watching it on the iPhone and iPod touch. Adding to the video Apple, the iPhone and iPod touch can be rotated to watch television and movies in a wide-screen format similar to the theater and High Definition (HD) screens.

Apple has earned a place in the history of television and movies for changing the world's perception about how and where video content can be consumed and how it is purchased.

Apple's first real set-top box—The Apple TV. Image ©
John Greenleigh, www.flipsidestudios.com.

MOBILE PHONES

According to the CTIA wireless association, an amazing 250 million Americans own mobile phones, or 82.4% of the U.S. population.[12] When Steve Jobs announced iPhone in January 2007, he set a goal of selling 10 million handsets by the end of 2008. With more than one billion mobile phones sold per year, selling 10 million would only give Apple a 1% market share. "Exactly what we're trying to do, 1% market share in 2008, 10 million units and we'll go from there," Jobs said. To keep that in perspective, industry leader Nokia sold 435 million mobile phones in 2007 and would sell more than Apple's annual iPhone sales target in a little more than 8 *days.*

The mobile phone market is massive. In 2007, worldwide mobile phone shipments crossed 1.15 billion units, a 16% overall growth over 2006. Five manufacturers account for 80% of mobile phones sold.[13]

Following is the 2007 mobile phone handset market share:

1. Nokia 38%
2. Motorola 14%
3. Samsung 13%
4. Sony Ericsson 9%
5. LG Electronics 7%
6. Other 19%

Apple is a minor player in the worldwide mobile phone market, and it's a massive market to enter, but Apple's just getting started and taking things slow. Steve Jobs is happy to eke out a 1% market share and grow from there. Apple may not make a dent in the historical context of mobile phones in unit sales, but in terms of excitement and buzz, you'd be hard pressed to find another item in the history of consumer electronics that was talked about more than Apple's iPhone.

SUBCULTURE

Are they customers or fans? Apple has one of the most fiercely loyal, dedicated, and faithful customer bases in the world. Apple fans border on rabid and are well known for their fanatical dedication to the platform. The Mac is more than a computer, and Apple is more than a company to them. Apple is more of a philosophy than a computer brand. Apple has inspired a community of like-minded individuals, who share their passion for the things that they do *with* their computers—art, science, and entertainment—as well as their passion *for* the computers themselves.

Apple's annual Macworld Expo conference kicks off with a keynote presentation by Steve Jobs that's more similar to a rock concert than a technology presentation. Tickets are coveted and difficult to get. They're only given in advance to people that purchase the most expensive all-inclusive conference passes, and even the media list is closely scrutinized. Apple doesn't offer media credentials to many controversial, smaller independent journalists (often called bloggers) and has denied access to those that published rumors about unannounced Apple products.

What Is a Blog?

A *blog* (short for we*b* + *log*) is a Web site written and edited by an enthusiast on a particular topic. Blogs, usually serial publications with the newest entry displayed at the top of the page, don't usually publish at a set interval but tend to publish randomly (at the whim of the writer), ranging from daily to monthly. Since the term *blog* was popularized in the late 1990s, the concept has been embraced by small and large corporations, nonprofits, and news-gathering organizations. Many organizations maintain a less formal, employee-driven blog as an adjunct to their official Web sites.

A *blogger* is a person who writes blogs. The word was initially used in the name of a Web site, launched in 1999 from Pyra Labs, called Blogger.com. This Web site provides the tools for creating blogs.

There's a small portion of seats in the keynote hall reserved for people with any type of conference badge and people line up in the street to claim those seats, beginning the night before in order to ensure that they get a seat. After the VIPs and invited guests are seated, when the doors finally open, there's usually a rush to the seats that borders on a stampede. Attendees want to get as close to their messiah as possible. Once seated, savvy keynote veterans check the bottom of their seats because at Macworld keynote in July 2000 Jobs gave away a newly announced Apple optical mouse by taping a coupon under every chair in the hall.

The only other business event that compares to a Macworld Expo keynote address is the annual pilgrimage of 15,000 faithful each year to Omaha, Nebraska, to attend the annual shareholder meeting of Berkshire Hathaway, which has been called "Woodstock for Capitalists."[14]

Read more about Macworld Expo in Chapter 7, "Macworld Expo."

Apple's fans are an enthusiastic bunch and take their love of the computers and Apple to an entirely new level. They're known to wait in line for hours or days for a new product or store opening. They've camped out to wait for new Mac OS releases in the early years at Midnight Madness sales. They've waited in line to be the first to attend a new Apple retail store opening (but to give them credit, the free T-shirts are highly prized). They also lined up, some as early as 24 hours before, to be the first to purchase Apple's iPhone when it was released in June 2007.

Apple fans have a reputation for never parting with a retired Mac. Working Macs always get handed down to family or friends, for which the giver automatically becomes obligated to provide free, unlimited, lifetime, technical support via some weird, unwritten rule. Less useful or hardware-challenged Macs are stored on shelves, in basements, attics, or garages. Some people have extensive Mac museums that they proudly maintain. Bragging rights are bestowed on curators of working Macs that are especially old or rare.

Mac heads discovered that old all-in-one Macs make great fish tanks. According to Leander Kahney's *Cult of Mac,* Jay Leno, Timothy Leary, Abbie Hoffman, and Steve Jobs reportedly have Mac aquariums.[15] According to legend, veteran Mac columnist Andy Inhatko started the trend in 1992 in a Q&A column when he recommended that the best way to upgrade a 512K Mac was to turn it into an aquarium. You've got to be careful what you say to a Mac fan.

The Apple logo is a very popular brand and loyalists find creative ways to display it. T-shirts are the most common, and there is a veritable plethora of T-shirts (both official and unofficial) that pay homage to Apple. Walking around Macworld Expo is probably the best way to see them. Like Macs themselves, kudos and high fives are awards to those that own vintage or particularly witty Apple T-shirts. Haircuts are also a popular way to profess your love for Apple. Leander Kahney's *Cult of Mac* and *Cult of iPod* both feature stunning examples of Apple coifs on their covers. Tattoos are the most permanent way to show your true devotion, and Mac fans find unique designs and places for their Apple ink, which are copiously documented online.

Chapter Four

Strategies and Innovations

Apple has earned a strong reputation for beauty, simplicity, and quality over the years, all part of its mission. From award-winning design to meticulously crafted hardware, Apple focuses on the entire user experience and is rewarded with strong sales and fierce loyalty as a result.

Apple is famously quiet and secretive about its future plans, especially when it comes to new products. Staff members are instructed to respond with one simple question when queried about anything unreleased, "Apple doesn't comment on unannounced product." It's a familiar refrain to members of the media covering Apple—so common, in fact, that many journalists will print it without even bothering to call Apple for comment.

Surprisingly, Apple enjoys much commercial success with little, if any, focus group testing, barely any beta testing, and a public relations department that's wound tighter than a drum. The element of surprise is Apple's primary strategy. Apple keeps mum because it builds suspense and because there's big money at stake. A new Apple product announcement generates millions of dollars in free publicity on the Internet and in the mainstream media, and the bigger the surprise, the great the amount of free coverage.

It's all part of Apple's carefully planned strategy to win attention, customers, and ultimately, money. There are a number of other strategies that Apple employs, and each has helped it create essential "disruptions" that changed business forever.

STRATEGIES

Apple's strategy is a simple: mediocrity is the enemy of excellence.

Apple successes aren't just luck or good fortune. While those certainly play a part, Apple has spent the last decade perfecting an intricate strategy that yields a seamless mix of hardware, software, and services. Apple products achieve a goal of being easy-to-use and powerful. They're unobtrusive and inviting and encourage users to be creative without getting in the way.

Apple's underlying philosophy is to design products that are easy-to-use and beautifully designed. Simplicity is the mantra. For years Apple's calling card has been that it "just works." In addition, most of Apple's products are intuitively designed so that you don't need to read a user manual to figure them out. If you ask most Mac users if they read manuals, you'll hear a resounding "no." Many Mac users claim to have *never* read an Apple manual.

Unfortunately, the simplicity part got away from Apple in the early 1990s. Without Steve Jobs's eagle eye watching over the coop, Apple released too many confusing and similar products in an attempt to battle the IBM PC, and it scared customers away. When Jobs came back in 1997, his strategy was to simply clean house. He accomplished this by:

1. Eliminating all unprofitable products. Jobs immediately killed the clones, which were cannibalizing Apple sales, and the Newton, which was a $500 million money pit.
2. Simplifying the Mac models. Apple went from dozens of computer models to four. Jobs distilled all Macs down to just four models that neatly fit into his two-by-two "product matrix."
3. Beefing up existing product lines and making them the best they could be. Jobs would upgrade or "speed-bump" best-selling products every 9 to 12 months with compelling new features that users wanted.
4. Only entering established markets that had profit potential. Apple would sit on the sidelines and let other companies pour R&D money into new markets and products, then study what they did wrong and release its own version with all the good parts and none of the bad.

Other Apple strategies that contribute to the bottom line include:

1. *Beautiful design.* Attractive products sell more than unattractive ones. Apple goes to great lengths to make its products visually appealing. Steve Jobs personally recruited visionary industrial designer Jonathan Ive for his beautiful, yet simple designs. Apple's iMac, iPod, and iPhone are universally recognized for their beautiful design and enjoy amazing sales as a result. Apple takes design to a new level and every part of the experience is carefully designed, including the box, the packaging, and the accessories and cables. Before a user ever opens the box, every part of the experience is carefully choreographed in Cupertino.
2. *User interface.* In addition to its beautiful hardware design, Apple exercises tight control over its software look and feel.

Apple publishes user-interface guidelines that software developers must follow, and the result is a consistent and predictable experience for users. A good user interface is transparent and doesn't get in the way. Apple wrote the book on excellent user interfaces.

3. *Low-entry points.* After years of selling products that were expensive, Apple began offering inexpensive products that got people in the door, like the $49 iPod shuffle and the $499 Mac mini, then enticing them to upgrade later on. Apple did similar things with the iMac with great results.

4. *Complete solutions.* All new Macs ship with iLife, a powerful and full-featured software suite. Right out of the box, a Mac user can be productive without buying any additional software. Apple software is designed to be interoperable and compatible so that it works with other Apple software. Also, Apple makes the hardware and the software, so if you have a problem, there's only one company to ask and no finger pointing by vendors trying to pass your problems off onto someone else.

5. *Proprietary formats.* Many commercial music tracks purchased on iTunes are encrypted with FairPlay DRM, which enables them to be played only on Apple products. Once customers have an investment in music from Apple, it's not in their best interest to switch to another platform, lest they want to lose access to their purchased tracks. This type of consumer lock-in creates repeat customers.

6. *Support.* Apple consistently gets high customer satisfaction rating for technical support, recently winning top honors in *Consumer Reports* annual survey by double digits over its closest rival.[1] Part of this is because Apple is responsible for the entire experience, from the hardware to the software to the service. This allows it to maintain tight control over quality and ensure that everything will work together.

7. *Branding.* From Apple's famous "1984" television commercial, to "Think Different," to "I'm a Mac," Apple has a great marketing sense. Its campaigns are insightful, funny, and interesting. People like Apple's ads so much that they analyze them, buy the posters, and post their television commercials on their Web sites for others to watch. What could be better than people watching your commercials repeatedly, without having to buy airtime? Apple is the envy of every corporation when it comes to free publicity.

8. *Buzz.* Apple's employees and public relations department are notoriously tight-lipped, which created a cottage industry of independent journalists that follow the company's every move looking for any hint about new products. The term *blogger* was

practically invented for the hordes of enthusiasts that write about Apple's every whim. Apple enjoys millions of dollars per year in free publicity from the buzz generated by its followers.

Another winning Apple strategy, Apple's retail stores, is also an innovation. They are covered in Chapter 1, "Origins and History," and in the next section.

INNOVATIONS

Apple is an innovation specialist. From the Apple I and II to the mouse, GUI, and LaserWriter, Apple has a pedigree of developing new technologies and adapting existing technologies for the masses. Let's explore some of Apple's biggest innovations.

The LaserWriter—1985

In late 1985 Apple released the Macintosh Office, featuring the Laser-Writer and the AppleTalk networking technology in an attempt to make the Mac more attractive to small businesses. Pamela Pfiffner tells this story best in *The Birth of Desktop Publishing* from 2004:[2]

> In the summer of 1984, Jobs called Seybold. "Steve wanted to see me urgently," he recalls. "He said they had a deal with Adobe, they were signing a deal with Linotype, they had real fonts. I went to Cupertino and walked into this tiny room, and there stood Jobs and [Adobe cofounder John] Warnock with a Mac and a LaserWriter. He showed me what they were up to. I turned to Steve and said, 'You've just turned publishing on its head. This is the watershed event.' When I turned to John, he had this look on his face. He was just so happy. I could tell he was thinking, 'This made the company. This is my validation.' It was a magic moment."
>
> The LaserWriter debuted to great fanfare at Apple's annual stockholder meeting on January 23, 1985. The LaserWriter cost $6,995—steep by today's standards, yet astoundingly cheap compared with the IBM and Xerox laser printers of the day, which cost three to ten times that. Plus, the LaserWriter had Adobe's special ingredient: PostScript. Almost immediately, analysts commented on the LaserWriter's output, praising its "near-typeset quality."

Apple's LaserWriter combined with Adobe's PostScript was a bona fide revolution for the printing and publishing world. When you add Al-dus's PageMaker software to the mix, end users finally had real publishing tools available to them on an end-user budget. For the first time, a professional publishing workflow could be assembled for much less than $20,000 and could fit on top of a desk. The LaserWriter ushered in an era of Desktop Publishing (DTP) that suddenly made millions of people into home print shops.

While Guttenberg would have undoubtedly been proud, the DTP revolution also created legions of bad typography and design. The appeal of an unlimited palette of fonts and styles was irresistible to many aspiring layout artists, with some using almost all of them on a single page. Regardless, the three *As* (Apple, Aldus, and Adobe) changed the publishing world forever and the benefits from their contributions to the field are being reaped by everyone who prints a page today.

PowerBook 100—1991

In 1991 Apple released its first serious notebook computer, the Power-Book 100. It weighed only 5.1 pounds and sold for $2,500 and was essentially the same as the Mac Portable except that it weighed about 10 pounds less. The PB100 was designed by Sony and shipped with 2MB RAM (expandable to 8MB) and a 20–40MB hard drive. A floppy drive was only available as an external option.

Two other PowerBooks were launched simultaneously with the PB100. The PowerBook 140 and the 170 were based on PowerBook 100 but with a simpler design, and both were designed entirely by Apple. The PowerBook 100 wasn't extremely innovative by itself, but it opened the door for an entire line of PowerBooks that came in all shapes and sizes. PowerBooks went on to become the notebook of choice for writers, artists, and businesspeople of all types. The spirit of the PowerBook lives on in Apple's MacBook series of Intel notebooks.

Hey, it wasn't the Mac Portable!

QuickTime—1991

QuickTime was the beginning of video playback on computers and has become a standard feature on computers, Personal Digital Assistants (PDAs), and smart phones. Apple released QuickTime 1.0 in December 1991 for System Software 6. Bruce Leak, its lead developer, first showed the technology at Apple's Worldwide Developer Conference in 1991. Microsoft's Video for Windows followed shortly after in November 1992.

The First PDA—1993

The Newton MessagePad, announced in August 1993, was a completely new product for Apple and represented a brave step into the unfamiliar territory of PDAs. The name for the MessagePad is an allusion to Isaac Newton's famous apple, which is also part of the first Apple

The Sony-designed PowerBook 100. Image © John Greenleigh, www.flipside studios.com.

corporate logo. Although Apple's official name for the device was *MessagePad* (*Newton* was actually the name for the operating system it used), people began referring to the device and its software as the *Newton*.

Diminutive, handheld computers are somewhat taken for granted today—most of their functions are built into many mobile phones—but at the time, this was a bold move for Apple. It took a lateral step outside its traditional comfort area, desktop and notebook computers, and attempted to shrink their computer technology into something that would fit into the palm of your hand.

It wasn't a complete stretch, though. Apple had a pedigree of building user-friendly computers, so it was logical that it would eventually build a handheld computer. The problem is that small computers bring big challenges in the areas of miniaturization and battery life, areas where Apple didn't have any experience.

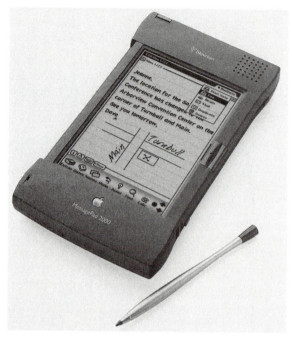

The dawning of the PDA: Apple's Newton Message-Pad 2000. Image © John Greenleigh, www.flipside studios.com.

The market for PDAs was in its infancy in 1993, and although the Newton wasn't a commercial success, it paved the way for a flood of handheld devices that followed, including the Palm Pilot and Pocket PC. The Newton MessagePad came with a software bundle that included an address book, calendar, notepad, and the ability to fax and e-mail when connected to a standard telephone line. The most innovative feature, however, was its pen-based interface and handwriting recognition software.

The driving force behind the Newton MessagePad was Apple CEO John Sculley. Read more about John Sculley in Chapter 8, "Apple Leadership."

The Newton MessagePad featured an innovative handwriting recognition system that adapted to the user and could be trained to understand an individual's handwriting style. The handwriting recognition, while its most technologically advanced feature, was also its most maligned. It was difficult to learn (especially for beginners) and would often suggest hilarious, but incorrect, phrases as the user wrote. The Newton's misrecognitions became the butt of many jokes in the national media. Not exactly the kind of attention that Apple was hoping for.

Newton shipped with a 20 MHz ARM 610 processor and retailed for $699. Its successor, the MessagePad 100, was released in March 1994. The Newton received a badly needed ROM upgrade with many bug fixes in October 1993, but it wasn't enough to keep the project alive. Apple discontinued the Newton in 1997 when Steve Jobs returned, much to the objection of fans worldwide.

Newton Still Popular Today

Apple's Newton MessagePad was definitely ahead of its time. Long before the advent of the Palm Pilot, Newton introduced the world to several advanced technologies, including the touch-screen display, handwriting recognition, the PCMCIA (a.k.a. PC Card) slot, and the stylus. While they sound pedestrian today, these were ultramodern features in 1993.

Despite having been discontinued in 1998, the Newton Message-Pad is still in use today by enthusiasts. When a technology has been discontinued for more than a decade, it's usually long forgotten. Not so with the Newton MessagePad. The handheld computer released by Apple in 1993 invented the PDA category and is the great-grandfather of the iPhone, but it's far from forgotten. People still actively keep them running, and some use them on a daily basis. There are numerous working Newtons for sale on auction sites like eBay, but most people tend to hold onto them.

Newton was so popular that an active enthusiast community still gathers to discuss the device of yore and to trade tips on upgrading and keeping the machines running. There are currently more than 20 active Newton user groups. Paul Filmer maintains a list of their meetings, which he hosts on a—what else?—Newton OS Web Server. There are also hundreds of actively maintained shrines, newsgroups, mailing lists, and technical support information on the Internet.[a]

[a] "The Newton Community on the Internet," http://www.chuma.org/newton/faq/newton-faq-community.html, accessed June 2, 2008.

The Trackpad—1994

Introduced in May 1994, the PowerBook 520 was the world's first notebook to ship with a *trackpad*—Apple's term for a touchpad surface used to position a cursor on the screen. Beginning in 1994, the trackpad replaced the popular trackball found on all previous PowerBooks. Since then, the trackpad has become a staple on all PowerBooks and MacBooks and has even been adopted by many Windows notebooks and some keyboards.

While Apple didn't invent the touchpad (early Apollo desktop computers were one of the first to use them), it deserves credit for being the first to implement it in a notebook computer. This was a stroke of brilliance because the low, flat devices allowed Apple's notebooks to become thinner and not have to waste valuable space (and weight) with a large spherical ball that was previously used to control the cursor on the screen.

Apple's modern notebooks feature updated trackpads that can detect more than one finger at a time, enabling a whole new range of features, including the ability to scroll without using a button and a double-finger tap that brings up a contextual menu. Apple's trackpad technology trickled down to other products over the years and is now found in the Apple iPod in the form of its touch-sensitive *click wheel.*

The World's Fastest Notebook Computer—1997

The combination of the new PowerPC 750 (or G3) processor from Motorola/IBM and 512KB of cache made the PowerBook G3 the fastest notebook in the world at the time. In benchmark testing, the PBG3 performed near the Power Mac 9600/300, which was unheard of for a notebook. Apple promoted this new speed demon heavily in its marketing materials.

The Apple (Online) Store—1997

Apple opened its Web-based retail store (at http://store.apple.com) in November 1997 with the help of NeXT's WebObjects technology. The Apple online store allowed customers to purchase most of Apple's hardware and software and gave people from even the remotest areas of the country access to Apple goods from the comfort of their home. Ironically, WebObjects was also being used by Dell for its online store at the time. When Apple purchased NeXT, Dell didn't want to be associated with the same technology that a competitor was using. According to legend, Microsoft dispatched teams of engineers to migrate Dell off WebObjects and onto Microsoft technology at its own expense because it wanted to show off the Dell e-commerce site as part of its portfolio.

iMac: Dumping the Floppy—1998

After returning to an Apple Computer that was mismanaged and in dire financial straights, Steve Jobs took the reigns and quickly got the company back on track again. Shortly after his return in 1997, he made one of the largest bets in his career and developed an entirely new computer. This new Mac would not only change the complexion of Apple, but also the entire computer industry as a whole.

On August 15, 1998, Apple introduced the iMac, and by the end of the month, it had 150,000 pre-orders for the new machine. The new and colorful $1,300 Mac was a totally redesigned machine "for the rest of us." Designed with the everyday user in mind, it was simple to set up. iMac allowed users to get onto the Internet within minutes of opening the box. The all-in-one design included a built-in monitor and even a handle—a throwback to the "toaster" design of the original 128k through Classic Macs. The Macintosh design team responsible for iMac was led by Jonathan Ive, a design wunderkind from the UK handpicked by Steve Jobs.

For more on Jonathan Ive, please refer to Chapter 8, "Apple Leadership."

Instead of coming in a traditional beige or platinum enclosure, iMac was built from Bondi blue (a reference to the color of the water at Sydney's Bondi Beach) and translucent grey plastics, allowing users to see inside their computer for the first time. This was nothing short of a design coup, and it caught every other computer maker flat-footed. Initially, some mocked iMac's colorful plastics, but after it posted impressive sales numbers, Windows PC manufacturers frantically revamped their computers to have more colorful designs in hopes of emulating Apple's success. For the first time ever, PCs were trying to emulate the Mac's design. When the iMac was introduced in five colors in 1999, peripheral makers and competitors again scrambled to match Apple's color scheme. It seemed that, with every advance made by the iMac, competitors were at least a step behind.

For more on Apple's competitors, please refer to Chapter 9, "Competition."

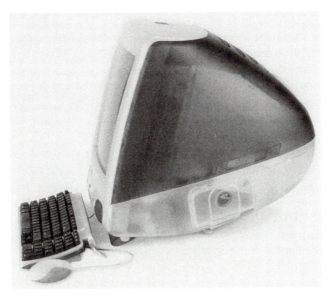

The machine that saved Apple—Say hello to the iMac. Image © John Greenleigh, www.flipsidestudios.com.

From a design perspective, iMac was nothing short of a revolution, but inside it was only evolutionary. For the most part, the hardware was pedestrian; iMac came with a fast G3 processor (introduced the year before) and normal amounts of RAM and hard drive. Apple made a major bet with the hardware and did something unthinkable—it dropped the floppy drive from the new computer. The iMac was the first machine in more than 15 years not to ship with a floppy drive. Apple was betting that the antiquated floppy's days were numbered and figured that most software came on CD-ROMs anyway, so it effectively hastened the floppy's demise. The removal of the floppy drive was controversial at the time but was later adopted by every major PC manufacturer.

FireWire—1999

FireWire (also known as IEEE 1394 and Sony's i.Link) was developed between the late 1980s and 1995 by Apple, Digital Equipment Corporation (DEC), IBM, INMOS/SGS Thomson, Sony, and Texas Instruments as a replacement for the aging Small Computer Systems Interface (SCSI). FireWire was designed as a high-speed interface for audio and video peripherals and is commonly used for connecting external hard drives and DV (digital video) cameras. It is preferred over USB because it has a greater effective speed and power distribution capabilities. FireWire features high sustained data transfer rates that are required by users moving a large volume of data.

The blue and white Power Mac G3 was the first pro Mac to get FireWire (January 1999), and the iMac DV was the first consumer Mac to get FireWire in April 1999. In 2001, the standard iMac got FireWire, finally bringing in the entire Mac family. The Power Mac G4 and the PowerBook G4 17-inch introduced in January 2003 were the first Macs to include the faster, FireWire 800 port. FireWire 400 is capable of data transfer at up to 400 Mbps, while FireWire 800 can transfer data between devices at up to 800 Mbps.

AirPort Wireless Networking—1999

AirPort is Apple's brand name for wireless networking technology based on the IEEE 802.11b standard. Easily the most anticipated aspect of Apple's new iBook consumer notebook computer was its newfangled AirPort slot. That slot accepted a $99 card (about the size of a PC Card) that enabled the new notebook to be connected to a network and the Internet wirelessly using industry standard protocols. Up to 10 iBooks could connect to a wireless access point (which Apple called a *base station*). The companion base station could be connected to an existing Ethernet network or dial-up Internet connection and share that connection to all the wireless clients.

AirPort was announced on July 21, 1999, with the iBook at Macworld Expo New York. Steve Jobs held up the iBook as he surfed the Web, and the audience realized there were no wires connecting it and erupted into thunderous applause. Initially, AirPort was offered as a $99 expansion card for the iBook with a companion base station that acted as the central access point that the AirPort clients connected to.

The original AirPort cards and base stations were based on the 802.11b standard and allowed transfer rates up to 11 Mbps. AirPort quickly gained in popularity and was routinely used to share Internet connections between multiple computers in a home, office, or classroom. Needless to say, the technology took off and is in use in many homes, offices, and classrooms as well as any place frequented by travelers (airports, hotels) and students (coffee shops, bookstores, and libraries).

AirPort Extreme

AirPort Extreme was announced at Macworld Expo in San Francisco in 2003. The next generation wireless networking technology (now called Wi-Fi) was based on the new IEEE 802.11g standard and was capable of speeds up to 54Mbps. AirPort Extreme supports the 802.11a, b, g, and draft-n protocols, making it compatible with previous generation 802.11b devices. The Power Mac G4 was the first Mac to include support for AirPort Extreme.

AirPort Extreme Base Station

The AirPort Extreme Base Station comes with three Local Area Network (LAN) ports and, unlike the previous base stations that looked like a melted Hershey Kiss, featured a more flat and square form factor. In addition to the faster speed and new design, the AirPort Extreme had an AirPort Disk feature that allowed a USB hard drive to be connected to the base station that would be available wirelessly to anyone (with the right credentials) who connected to it. On August 7, 2007, Apple added Gigabit Ethernet to the AirPort Extreme, bringing it in line with most other Apple products.

Time Capsule

Time Capsule was introduced at Macworld Expo on January 15, 2008, and is essentially an AirPort Extreme Base Station with a 500GB or 1TB hard drive in it. The device is a wireless Network Attached Storage (NAS) that can be used as a backup device with Apple's Time Machine backup software (introduced in Mac OS X 10.5 Leopard).

The Apple Retail Store—2001

Apple's launch of a line of retail stores was met with great skepticism. Gateway Country Stores had cropped up in suburban areas across the United States but were faltering, and retail, in general, was a gamble. In April 2004, Gateway announced the closure of all its stores.

Apple reinvented the retail store from the ground up. Jobs started by hiring the best in retail, including Mickey Drexler, a veteran of The Gap, and Ron Johnson, merchandising chief at Target and a specialist in afford-able design. Apple rented a warehouse to build a prototype store. The first prototype store was designed around product categories, which was not how people shopped. So Apple rearranged it so that it was based more around interests rather than simply products.

After some internal testing, 16 of 18 people said that their best ser-vice experience was at a hotel. The Genius Bar was born from attempts to emulate the helpful and practical advice dispensed by the concierge desk at a hotel.

The first Apple Stores opened in May 2001, in Tyson's Corner, Vir-ginia, and in Glendale, California. Apple opened its 200th store a little more than six years later in Gilbert, Arizona. The Fifth Avenue location in New York City alone attracts more than 50,000 customers per week.

iTunes—January 2001

iTunes was launched at Macworld Expo 2001 in San Francisco as a way to play back MP3 and digital music files stored on a Mac. More important, it provided an easy way to organize large libraries of digital music. In October, iTunes became the conduit for moving music to and from the iPod digital media player. iTunes is constantly being improved and today is closely linked to Apple iTunes store, launched April 28, 2003. The software and store combination is capable of managing (and later, purchasing) music, podcasts, audiobooks, iPod games, music videos, tele-vision shows, feature-length films, ringtones, movie rentals, and iPhone software.

iTunes began life as a media player called SoundJam MP written by Jeff Robbin and Bill Kincaid[3] and released by Casady & Greene in 1999. SoundJam was acquired by Apple in 2000 and was released as iTunes 1.0 at Macworld Expo on January 9, 2001. Although there were other MP3 players available for Windows (notably WinAmp) and other Mac pro-grams in development (like Panic's Audion[4]), SoundJam MP was first out of the gate and it forever changed the way we consume music, and later, videos and television.

iTunes innovated because it allowed users to easily organize large music collections via a series of fields, called metadata or ID3 tags. Meta-data embedded in each music file provided the perfect structure to orga-nize, find, mix, and play back music, and iTunes made this easy. iTunes allowed users to create an unlimited number of playlists, and each could contain the music organized by genre, artist, or just about anything. It also features a powerful search capability that could locate tracks quickly, even in large libraries.

Shuffle

One of iTunes' most powerful features was borrowed from the CD player: shuffle play. Shuffle or random music playback took on an entirely new meaning with the advent of digital music, especially with large libraries. Instead of shuffling maybe 16 tracks on a CD, iTunes could shuffle hundreds or thousands of songs. All of a sudden artists and genres were being randomized and played back in ways never before dreamed of. Probably the greatest part of the shuffle feature was the ability to discover music that was either forgotten or never heard. Apple capitalized on shuffle play and later released iPods without screens that were designed to play back music in shuffle mode.

Windows Support

The only thing that was holding iPod back from exploding was its exclusivity to the Macintosh platform. After iPod sales began to accelerate, demand for the product by Windows users also increased. Apple was deluged by requests for a Windows version of iTunes but is believed to have deferred as long as possible in an attempt to encourage people to switch platforms. Apple maintains that developing the Windows version was complicated and took longer than anticipated.

On October 16, 2003, Apple released iTunes 4.1 with support for the first time for Microsoft's Windows, and the floodgates flew open. It didn't happen immediately, but within a year, iPod sales more than doubled, then grew exponentially from there. iPod sales skyrocketed as the device was now available to the roughly 90% of computer users that use Windows PCs.

Releasing iTunes for Windows might have been one of the smartest decisions that Apple ever made. Not only did it open up a market of literally billions of potential iPod customers, but the little music player became a sort of Trojan horse. Windows users bought the unassuming device and brought it into their homes, and after becoming enamored with the iPod, Windows PC users became curious and more interested in Apple. After all, if it made a music player this good, maybe its computers were worth a look.

iPod—October 2001

Without question, the most significant product of 2001, and maybe the decade, was a little white handheld device that could play MP3 audio files through a pair of headphones, called iPod. Announced October 23, 2001, the white plastic and chrome device had a unique wheel interface that you turned to navigate a simple series of hierarchical menus to select the song, album, or artist that you wanted to listen to. "To have your whole CD library with you at all times is a quantum leap when it comes to music," said Steve Jobs. "You can fit your whole music library in your pocket."[5]

In mid-October 2001, Apple sent invitations to the media to attend an event at its corporate headquarters in Cupertino, which promised "the unveiling of a breakthrough digital device." Short on details, the invite also mentioned the date and time, October 23, 2001, at 10:00 A.M., but it was a little teaser at the end that sent the Apple faithful into a frenzy. The end of the invite simply said, "Hint: it's not a Mac."

The mainstream media, Mac bloggers, and the rumor mill went into overdrive in an attempt to decrypt Apple's secret message. Many guessed (successfully) that it would be a portable music player because iTunes and MP3 files had become especially popular. And on October 23 about 200 members of the press, invited guests, and VIPs attended the Jobs presentation at Apple. Jobs has a reputation as a good presenter, and for good reason. He has the ability to capture the attention of his audience and build the suspense to the inevitable crescendo of the main announcement that he makes.

He began his presentation by reiterating his digital hub strategy, which he debuted at Macworld Expo in January 2001. The concept was that the Mac would "become the digital hub of our emerging digital lifestyle, adding tremendous value to our other digital devices."[6] Jobs noted that Apple made software that worked with a lot of different digital devices, but as of then, no device had been made to work specifically with its software.

"The field we chose is music," Jobs said. "Why music? Well, we love music, and it's always good to do something you love." Jobs went on to explain that music is part of everyone's life. "It's a large target market," he said. "It knows no boundaries. And there is no market leader. No one had really found the recipe yet for digital music. And not only will we find the recipe; we think Apple is a great brand for this."[7]

After a brief discussion of the competitive landscape, mentioning no names, Jobs revealed his white, hard-drive–based music player, named iPod, saying, "I think this blows them away." Jobs went on to extol the virtues of his latest creation like a proud father beaming over his son's straight-A report card.

The iPod was innovative for four key reasons:

1. *Size.* Its tiny footprint and thin profile made it ultra-portable and easily "pocketable."
2. *Capacity.* Its spacious (for the time) 5GB hard drive could hold 1,000 songs, which was more than most people could listen to.
3. *Speed.* The iPod's exclusive FireWire port made music transfer from your computer to the device fast; a CD can be downloaded to the iPod in 5 to 10 seconds.
4. *Ease of use.* The iPod interface is simple and intuitive; most people can pick one up and master the basics of navigation and playback within a few minutes.

In retrospect, after Apple sold 100 million iPods in the first six years, it's pretty obvious that it found the recipe for digital music, and it can't seem to make the stuff fast enough. But at the time, not everyone was convinced. Initial reaction to the iPod was divided: there were the expected cheers for its "impressive" compact design, but negativism prevailed. The consensus was tepid and bordered on angry at times, mostly due to the high price tag: $400 was considered by many to be too much to charge for a music player. *MacSlash* said in its review, "The iPod sells for an absolutely hideously outrageous $399 and will be available to the two people that buy them on November 10."[8]

Why was Apple releasing a product that played music? Shouldn't it have been designing a new computer? Not many people would have wagered that the little music player would not only reinvent Apple, but also consumer electronics, mobile phones, music, and almost the entire entertainment industry too. But it did, and it shows no sign of letting up.

For more on how iPod impacted popular culture, see Chapter 5, "Impact on Society."

Technical Specs

The original iPod was Apple's first foray into digital music. The unit was about the size of a deck of cards and came equipped with a 5GB hard drive, headphone jack, and a FireWire port—the first and only music player at the time with this feature. FireWire was an important feature as it greatly increased the speed at which you could move large amounts of music to and from the device. Other Windows-based music players had USB 1.1 connections, which transferred data at a maximum rate of 1 MB per second, which was painfully slow.

The 5GB iPod was capable of holding 1,000 songs in MP3 format ripped at a bit rate of 160kbps. The iPod supported MP3, WAV, and AIFF formats and had a 20-minute buffer that was marketed as "skip protection" but is also a way to conserve battery life, as the hard drive could spin down after it loaded 20 minutes of music into the buffer.

Hard Drive versus Flash

Although other hard-drive–based music players existed, Apple's was different because it used a 1.8-inch hard drive mechanism, making it much smaller and more portable than the competition. In fact, iPod was able to compete with flash-based MP3, which had a fraction of the capacity. The most popular flash-based player at the time, the Diamond Rio PMP300, held 32MB of music or roughly 12 songs and sold for $250 (which works out to about $21 per song). The iPod 5GB, on the other hand, held 1,000 songs and sold for $400 or 40 cents a song.

Competition

iPod wasn't the first digital music player on the market, but it was the first one that got it right. The first digital music player was the Compaq Personal Jukebox (or PJB) released in October 1999 with a 6.5GB hard drive and a nonbacklit screen. Its biggest problem was its size. Because it was based on a 2.5-inch (notebook) hard drive, it was substantially larger than the iPod, measuring 5.9 × 3.15 × 1.0 inches and weighing 10.7 ounces. The iPod, on the other hand, measured 4.02 × 2.43 × 0.78 inches, weighing just 6.5 ounces.

Archos Technology from France made the Jukebox 6000, which also preceded the iPod and was relatively popular. In addition to playing MP3 audio files, it could also record audio directly to MP3 from a line-in source with the provided cables. It shipped with a 6GB, 2.5-inch hard drive and suffered from the same size and portability problems as the PJB.

Creative's Nomad Jukebox was another of the first crop of portable music players. It had already been through several revisions before the iPod was announced and was selling a 20GB player that had four times the capacity of the iPod and also sold for $399.

The Perfect Storm

The timing of the iPod's arrival couldn't have been better. It was announced just after a literal tidal wave of free music had been downloaded from file-sharing networks such as Napster and Audio Galaxy. Napster thrived from July 1999 through July 2001 with a peak of more than 26 million users, mostly college students, and ushered in a generation of people that thought that music was free. As a result of free file-sharing software, free music, and cheap hard drives, people amassed huge libraries of digital music. For the most part, that music was relegated to your hard drive, and you had to be in front of your computer to enjoy it. The iPod changed all that. Now you could literally carry your music library in your pocket.

The Switch to USB

The first iPod to support Microsoft's Windows operating system was the second-generation model released on July 17, 2002. It required a FireWire connection, which was uncommon on PCs, and MusicMatch software, which was inferior to iTunes, effectively stifling sales. Apple turned a major corner on October 16, 2003, when it released iTunes 4.1, which supported Windows. Suddenly, the software was available to a massive, new market that was largely untapped.

A similar turnaround took place when Apple added USB support to the third-generation iPod on April 28, 2003. Now most Windows users could connect the iPod to their machine without having to buy a separate FireWire card. It took about a year after Windows was fully supported, but iPod sales took off.

Apple supported both FireWire and USB via a proprietary; 30-pin dock connector through the third- and fourth-generation iPods, then did the unthinkable. It dropped support for FireWire syncing (you could still charge an iPod with FireWire) on the fifth-generation iPod on October 26, 2004, in favor of USB 2.0. Many were surprised that Apple removed FireWire, a technology it invented, from the iPod, but the move speaks volumes about the amount of clout Windows users bring to the table. It was probably too expensive for Apple to continue to support both types of connections when USB 2.0 was just as fast and all Macs came with USB ports.

The switch to USB had a dramatic effect on sales. Prior to the switch from FireWire, Apple had sold 1 million iPods. But within the next six months, Apple had sold another million iPods, and nearly 3 million more were sold within a year. In the next 18 months, 9 million more were sold.

The Halo Effect

The iPod gave many Windows PC users their first exposure to an Apple product, and many eventually switched to the Mac platform as a result of their experience with the iPod. This is known as *the halo effect* because the iPod casts a large halo around it, making other Apple products shine brighter than they normally would.

The unique troika of hardware (iPod), software (iTunes), and service (iTunes Store) puts Apple in the position of being able to control the complete user experience from beginning to end. It also allows Apple to profit from all aspects of the system. On one hand, it allows the company to maintain a high level of quality because it can guarantee interoperability among all three components; on the other, it can be viewed as monopolistic because Apple has control of all aspects of the system and such a dominant share of the market that it can control prices, standards, and choices available to the consumer.

iPod must be doing something right; as of this writing, it commands a 70% share of the market (in units) and 84% market share in volume of sales.[9]

For more on the cultural impact of the iPod, see Chapter 5, "Impact on Society."

Death of the CRT Monitor—2002

Apple began its transition to flat-panel monitors in 2000 when it replaced all its CRT-based monitors with new, flat-panel designs. The new iMacs were the culmination of Apple's strategy. When he announced the new iMac in his keynote address at Macworld Expo in 2002, Steve Jobs told attendees "the CRT is officially dead."

Like dropping the floppy disc in 1998, a move later adopted by all PC manufacturers, Apple was the first of the majors to drop CRTs in favor of flat-panel monitors. Apple claimed the move was mostly for environmental reasons (they don't have arsenic in the glass), but flat-panel monitors cost less to ship, have better aesthetics, and higher profit margins. Other PC manufacturers quickly jumped on the flat-screen monitor bandwagon, and old-style CRT monitors are quickly fading from the technology landscape.

World's First 17-inch Notebook and Backlit Keyboard—January 2003

At Macworld Expo 2003 in San Francisco, Apple announced the new PowerBook G4 with a massive 1440 × 900, 16:10 aspect ratio, 17-inch screen, making it the world's first 17-inch notebook.[10] The PowerBook G4 17-inch was the most full-featured Apple notebook computer ever and includes several Apple firsts in addition to the huge screen.

The PBG4 17-inch also included the world's first fiber-optic backlit keyboard and ambient light sensors that can automatically adjust screen brightness and keyboard backlighting. In dark rooms the PowerBook G4 17-inch can be set to automatically illuminate the backlit keyboard and lower the brightness of the screen. The backlit keyboard is a boon for non-touch typists that use their PowerBook in dark places, like on an evening flight, in a dark coffee shop, or even at home on the couch. When the room gets brighter, the ambient light sensor can also brighten the screen and turn off the keyboard backlighting.

This integrated keyboard and screen lighting system represented a first and was so well received that it eventually trickled down to every machine in the MacBook lineup.

iTunes Store—April 2003

The iTunes Music Store (later shortened to just "iTunes Store" when Apple branched out of just music) is an online digital media store that Apple launched on April 28, 2003, in conjunction with iTunes version 4. It can be accessed from a computer and from portable media players such as the iPhone and iPod touch over a wireless Internet connection.

The iTunes Store offers digital music downloads for sale for 99 cents each and full albums for $9.99 each. Music purchased from the store is protected by Apple's FairPlay Digital Rights Management (DRM) software and can be played on up to five computers simultaneously and an unlimited number of iPods. A playlist containing a protected audio track can be burned to CD up to 7 times (down from 10 times).

Apple contended that the FairPlay DRM encryption scheme was necessary to protect artists, but most believe that DRM was required by the record labels to get them to agree to put their artists' content for sale on the iTunes Store.

Steve Jobs on DRM

On February 6, 2007, Steve Jobs, CEO of Apple Inc., published an open letter titled "Thoughts on Music"[a] on the Apple Web site. It urged record labels to offer their artists' music without the shackles of DRM. Jobs said that Apple doesn't like to use DRM on the iTunes Store but is forced to by the record labels. Jobs also points out that DRM isn't perfect and that it's easily defeatable. He also said that DRM only hurts people using music legally and that its restrictions encourage users to obtain unrestricted music illegally. Finally, Jobs noted that most music sold today does not come with DRM (referring to CDs). Jobs's missive was met with praise by the consumers who dislike DRM and was criticized by labels.

[a] Steve Jobs, "Thoughts on Music," Apple.com, February 6, 2007, http://www.apple.com/hotnews/thoughtsonmusic/.

The iTunes Store was the first true alternative to downloading music illegally from file-sharing networks, offering more than 200,000 songs for sale from all five of the major record labels, including BMG, EMI, Sony Music Entertainment, Universal, and Warner. The iTunes Store allowed users to listen to free 30-second previews of any song, which can then be purchased with a click. At launch, the iTunes Store even offered several free music videos, which was a hint of things to come in the future.

Apple's newest foray into music was a bona fide revolution, giving consumers the options to purchase a single digital track instead of having to buy an entire album. Consumers embraced the concept with open arms, but record labels were threatened because it challenged their decades-old business model of selling $16 to $20 CDs, which was very profitable.

The iTunes Store was a bold move for Apple, considering that people had become accustomed to downloading music freely with file-sharing software. Apple invested a lot of money and resources developing the iTunes Store and subsequently proved the viability of online music sales.

Several high-profile artists resisted selling their music on iTunes, including AC/DC, the Beatles, Radiohead, Led Zeppelin, Metallica, Frank Zappa, Garth Brooks, Kid Rock, and the Red Hot Chili Peppers. Many have since conceded and agreed to sell some or all of their music through the iTunes Store. Bob Dylan jumped online with both feet, and in addition to selling music, used iTunes to presell concert tickets. There are still some major holdouts, like the Beatles and AC/DC. Some bands, such as AC/DC, have released music on other, more flexible sites, but not iTunes.

Originally, the iTunes Store was restricted to customers living in the United States. In 2004, Apple launched the iTunes Music Store in much of Europe, including Austria, Belgium, Finland, France, Germany, Greece, Italy, Luxembourg, the Netherlands, Portugal, Spain, and the United Kingdom. It was rolled out in Canada at the end of 2004, well after the European rollout. Global launches continue throughout the next several years, catapulting the iTunes Store to being the most widely used, legal music service in the world.

Apple continually expands the offerings, once mostly limited to music, in the iTunes Store to many other categories of entertainment, as noted in Chapter 1. Since arriving on the market, the iTunes Store has achieved some impressive milestones,[11] including:

- Selling 70 million songs in its first year.
- Selling one million music videos in its first 20 days.
- One billion songs downloaded in one year (2006).
- 88% market share of legal music downloads in the United States (2006).
- The most popular destination in the world to download movies (2007) with more than two million movies sold.
- Five billion songs sold to date (2008).
- Renting and selling more than 50,000 movies per day (2008).

Thanks to the iTunes Store, Apple is now the top music retailer in the United States,[12] online or offline. As of June 2008, the store has sold five billion songs,[13] accounting for more than 70% of worldwide online digital music sales.[14]

The World's Fastest Personal Computer—June 2003

Apple announced the Power Mac G5 on June 23, 2003, a fifth-generation PowerPC processor (dubbed the *G5*), wrapped in an industrial-looking aluminum enclosure. Apple and IBM worked closely to develop the 64-bit, PowerPC 970 processor, which was the first 64-bit consumer-level desktop computer ever sold and the world's fastest personal computer.[15]

The Power Mac G5 included several new features, including an 8X AGP slot, PCI-X slots, a Serial-ATA (SATA) bus, and up to 8GB of RAM. The front-side bus was ratcheted up to half of the processor speed—up to 1.0GHz—a sixfold improvement over the older Power Mac G4.

The Power Mac G5 was crowned the world's fastest personal computer according to SPEC CPU 2000 benchmarks that compared the performance of a series of professional software applications against a 3GHz Pentium 4 and a 3.06GHz Dual Xeon system.

Airport Express: 802.11g and AirTunes—June 2004

On June 7, 2004, Steve Jobs announced AirPort Express, which was the world's first portable 802.11g base station for Mac and PC users. The compact AirPort base station weighs just 6.7 ounces and supports Air-Tunes for $129.

The AirPort Express, just a little larger than a PowerBook or MacBook AC adapter, was snapped up by two groups of customers. The first was travelers who liked the convenience of having Wi-Fi wireless access but didn't like to bring along the larger, original AirPort base station. The second was people that liked to play their iTunes music through their home stereo speakers but don't like to have to plug into their computer each time.

The AirPort Express is an innovative product, because it's compact and packs four impressive features:

1. AirTunes allows iTunes music to be played to a remote set of speakers wirelessly. Instead of listening to your iTunes music through a pair of tiny notebook computer speakers, for example, you can jam out to your music on your home stereo—without plugging in a cable. Originally AirTunes only supported stream-ing music to one APX, as it was known, but later released an update that enabled streaming to multiple Expresses. You could have one in every room of your house, and they became very useful when entertaining. Apple probably could have sold an AirTunes Express–only device for $129.
2. The AirPort Express can also act as a stand-alone AirPort base station. Toss it into your bag when traveling, and if your hotel room only has Ethernet access (and a one-foot cable), plug in the AirPort Express for instant wireless access.
3. It can extend the reach of a current AirPort network. If your main AirPort base station is on one side of your house and the signal is weak on the other, you can plug in an AirPort Express to ex-tend the signal to reach farther. Using the Wireless Distribution System (WDS) feature, you can use up to five base stations as a unified network that shares one Internet connection.
4. The APX inherited the USB printing features of the larger Air-Port Extreme base station, making it great for connecting a USB printer to a wireless network without having to move it.

Apple pioneered wireless networking technology with easy-to-use and inexpensive offerings, and later, a truly portable solution that worked with 802.11b and 802.11g wireless devices.

In January 2007, Apple dropped the price of the AirPort Express from $129 to $99, and on March 17, 2008, it updated it to include 802.11n with greater speed and longer range than the model it replaced.

Intel Migration—June 2005

Apple's switch to Intel processors was more of a strategy than an innovation, but either way, it was one of Apple's most significant moves. For the first time, Apple would be using the same chips as its Windows-based competitors, eliminating delays in getting chips from smaller suppliers and putting it on a level playing field, chip for chip, with the competition.

At Apple's Worldwide Developer Conference (WWDC) in 2005, Steve Jobs announced that Apple was switching to Intel as its primary chip supplier, confirming rumors that Apple had been secretly testing versions of Mac OS X for Intel processors for at least five years. Jobs estimated the transition to Intel would last until the end of 2007.

The partnership with Intel allowed Apple to take advantage of all the latest Intel chip designs, be on par with Windows-based computers, and not have to rely on receiving processors in a timely manner from smaller chip fabricators like IBM and Motorola. Apple began producing Intel-based Macs in 2006 and completed the transition to Intel by the end of the year, a year ahead of schedule.

iPhone—January 2007

At Macworld Expo in January 2007, Apple announced one of its most significant products since the iPod and arguably since the Mac and the original Apple I: iPhone. During his keynote address, Steve Jobs told attendees that Apple was announcing three revolutionary products: a widescreen iPod with touch controls, a revolutionary mobile phone, and a breakthrough Internet communicator. Then, interrupting the cheers, he said that all three were actually one product: iPhone. The caption on his slide read: "Apple reinvents the phone."

The original iPhone was offered exclusively with AT&T and was limited to EDGE-based network access, rather than the faster 3G wireless networking standard. The lack of the 3G was a large omission for some users that already had the feature on their current mobile phone. The slow data access was (somewhat) offset by iPhone's integrated 802.11g Wi-Fi, which provided fast Internet access over the semi-ubiquitous technology.

iPhone couldn't run third-party applications out of the box, as Apple restricted iPhone to Web-based applications, but creative developers quickly circumvented Apple's roadblocks, and within a few months, third-party applications were available. Because AT&T was SIM-locked to the AT&T network, developers also found a way to circumvent that and "unlock" the iPhone to run on any network that supported GSM phones. iPhone quickly became one of the hottest unlocked phones on the international black market.

In its first quarter of sales, Apple Chief Operating Officer Tim Cook speculated that approximately 250,000 of the 1.4 million iPhones sold have been unlocked.[16] Apple CFO Peter Oppenheimer reported that Apple sold about four million iPhones during the last quarter of 2007, noting that the number of activated phones in the United States was far below Apple's sales figures.[17]

Apple TV—January 2007

At Macworld Expo 2007 in San Francisco, Apple announced the Apple TV, a new $299 40GB set-top appliance. Apple TV was designed to play iTunes content (music, television shows, movies, etc.) from any computer (Mac or Windows) connected to the local network. It could be connected to any Enhanced Definition (ED) or High Definition (HD) television but not to a Standard Definition (SD) set still popular in millions of living rooms. The Apple TV could be connected to any widescreen TV with either HDMI or component video, supported both analog and digital audio via RCA and optical S/PDIF outputs, and supported resolutions from 480p to 720p.

At Macworld Expo 2008, Apple announced a significant software update for the Apple TV called *Apple TV Take 2* and lowered the price of the hardware from $299 to $229. The update featured a new interface and was able to download TV shows and other digital content directly to the device.

The Take 2 is what the original Apple TV should have been. Rather than forcing the device to be tethered to an iTunes computer, the update gave Apple TV the ability finally to purchase and rent movies in High Definition (HD) and purchase television programs and music directly over the Internet—without a computer. The software update also allowed Apple TV to download podcasts, some in HD, and stream photos from .Mac and Flickr.

Apple moves into the living room with the Apple TV.
Image © John Greenleigh, www.flipsidestudios.com.

MacBook Air—2008

On January 15, 2008, Apple announced MacBook Air, the company's first-ever subnotebook and the world's thinnest notebook. MacBook Air measured 0.16 inches at its thinnest and 0.76 inches at its thickest point. It shipped with either a 1.6 or 1.8GHz Intel Core 2 Duo processor, 2GB RAM, 80GB 1.8-inch hard drive or optional 64GB Solid State Drive (SSD), 13.3-inch LED-backlit screen, 802.11n Wi-Fi technology, Bluetooth 2.1, a full-size (and backlit) keyboard, iSight camera, and large trackpad with support for multitouch gestures like pinch, rotate, and swipe—an Apple first.

The MacBook Air was a revolutionary product for Apple, both because of its tiny size and full-feature set, but also because it was an entirely new category of notebook, a subnotebook that Apple had never created before. The Air wasn't a consumer notebook because of its $1,800 starting price, and it wasn't a professional notebook by Apple's definition either, because it lacked many of the ports, notably FireWire, and the replaceable battery that pros demanded. It was in a category all to itself.

Chapter Five

Impact on Society

Apple is unique because not only did it pioneer in technology, but it also made a huge impact on society while doing so. Beginning with the success of the Apple II, which was quickly emulated by a host of larger PC manufacturers, to the radical design and transparent blue color of the original iMac, which filtered down to everything from irons to staplers, Apple has made its presence felt across products, genres, and generations. Apple's leading edge in design has seeped into almost every facet of modern life, all part of a carefully planned strategy to get you comfortable with using more, different, and better Apple stuff.

Apple has had a huge impact on society, particularly popular culture. Let's take a look at just one example.

IPOD AS A FASHION ACCESSORY

When the original iPod was launched in 2001, it was viewed as somewhat of a status symbol. The initial high price and larger capacity made it a premium item that was the *must have* gadget of athletes, celebrities, and rock stars. Although the iPods were mostly concealed in a pocket when in use, Apple executed a stroke of marketing brilliance by making the included ear buds white when everyone else's in the industry were black.

Apple had created a subtle but certain visual cue that someone had an iPod—even when the device itself was hidden from view. Apple's white iPod ear buds became as iconic as the iPod itself and came to identify its owner as a hip technophile. Unfortunately, the ear buds also told thieves that the wearer most likely had a multihundred-dollar gadget in his or her pocket or purse, and some areas of the world (notably New York City and London) experienced an increase in iCrimes related to the device. To combat the problem, some iPod owners found that the easiest thing to do was to switch to black headphones.

On January 6, 2004, at Macworld Expo in San Francisco, Apple announced the 4GB iPod mini, which was the size of a business card and came in five colors for $249. The iPod mini was Apple's first departure from the size and shape of the original iPod, which was about the size of a deck of cards.

The iPod mini was an immediate hit because its price was a lower barrier to entry and more affordable to students and parents. Its five color choices gave customers a choice other than white for the first time. The pink iPod mini was purchased in droves by girls, teens, and grown women alike and was frequently sold out (although available for a premium on online auction sites) during peak holiday seasons.

Just when iPod had started to saturate its key demographic, early adopters and teens, Apple convinced us of two things: (1) we needed to upgrade to a bigger, better model, and that (2) it was acceptable to own multiple iPods. Apple keeps a rigorous upgrade cycle for iPods, never letting the one you currently own get too old that it can't be easily sold or given to a family member or friend. And if your current model is just fine and functioning, well, wouldn't a model in a different color or a smaller size be the perfect complement to your other iPod? It may sound strange but this became the norm. People were beginning to purchase multiple copies of Apple's products. It was a marketing dream come true.

Announced at Macworld Expo 2005 in San Francisco, the iPod shuffle was Apple's first foray into the flash-based digital music player market. Apple dropped the display from the tiny iPod, stating that a screen that small wasn't practical. In a departure from its traditional marketing, Apple promoted the shuffle as more of a fashion accessory, like jewelry. The iPod shuffle's ability to clip onto clothing was heavily marketed as a fashion item, featuring print ads and posters that showed the shuffle attached to hip clothing—not as a music player.

Dropping *Computer* from the Name

At Macworld Expo 2007 in San Francisco, Steve Jobs announced that Apple Computer Inc. had officially dropped *Computer* from its corporate name, switching to just *Apple Inc.*, reflecting the company's metamorphosis into a consumer electronics company.

Changing its corporate name was the handwriting on the wall that big changes were afoot in Cupertino. Whether it was entirely expected or not is up for debate, but the reality is that by 2007, iPod represented half of Apple's sales and that Apple's reach had extended much further than just the computers. Apple had become a music provider and a consumer electronics company, seemingly overnight, and suddenly *Apple Computer* no longer fit.

Apple had begun influencing culture outside of the computer, and technology like iPod, iTunes, and iPhone had become pervasive in its own right, warranting a full-scale corporate shift.

Chapter Six

Technology Timeline

Now let's get down and dirty in the trenches. How did Apple change the world? Here, in detail, is how.

1976—APPLE I

On April Fool's Day (April 1) 1976, Jobs and Wozniak released the Apple I personal computer kit and simultaneously launched Apple Computer Inc. The Apple I came with video support, 8KB RAM, keyboard, and was contained on a single circuit board—but it had to be assembled. In order to keep prices low, Woz decided to use the $25 6502 processor from Rockwell and MOS Technologies and dynamic RAM.

The first Apple I was mounted on a piece of plywood when it was presented to great response at the Homebrew Computer Club in Palo Alto, California. The Byte Shop, a local computer dealer, immediate placed an order for 100 units at $666.66 each. A total of 200 units were sold in the duo's first 10 months of business.

1977—APPLE COMPUTER INC.

Apple Computer Inc. was incorporated and the company released the immensely popular Apple II. The public debut of the successor to the Apple I occurred at the first West Coast Computer Faire in San Francisco. The Apple II was offered at $1,298 and was also based on the 6502 processor, but it had color graphics (a first for a personal computer) and an audiocassette drive that could be used for storage. Originally shipping with 4KB of RAM, the Apple II was shortly upgraded to 48KB RAM and the cassette was replaced with a 5.25-inch floppy drive.

In 1977 a competing personal computer was released by Commodore called *PET* (for Personal Electronic Transactor). It was designed by Chuck Peddle and also ran on the 6502 processor, like the Apple II. The Commodore PET shipped with 4KB of RAM, monochrome graphics, and a cassette drive for only $795—half the price of the Apple II. In addition to costing less, the PET shipped with a version of Microsoft BASIC, which was later licensed to Apple and included as Apple BASIC.

Commodore, Radio Shack, and Apple

Steve Jobs and Steve Wozniak gave a demonstration of an Apple I prototype to some employees of Commodore. They were so impressed that they wanted to acquire Apple outright, but Jobs didn't want to sell. Wanting to enter the personal computer space, Commodore instead acquired MOS Technology and developed the PET—short for Personal Electronic Transactor.

The personal computer market was really beginning to pick up steam in 1977 when Radio Shack announced the Tandy TRS-80, which was built around the Zilog Z80 processor and shipped with 4KB RAM and 4KB ROM with BASIC. Like the Apple II and the PET, it used a cassette drive for storage. The TRS-80 was wildly popular, and the advent of the floppy disk drive kicked off a wave of software development for the new generation of personal computer because the floppy made software distribution easier.

1978—LISA PLANNING

In 1978, Apple began designing the computer that would succeed the Apple II and III personal computers. The new project was given the code name *Lisa*, which officially stood for Local Integrated Software Architecture. Unofficially, the name *Lisa* was believed to have been chosen after the name of Steve Jobs's daughter.

Jobs was completely engrossed by his project and took it on as a personal mission, adding many features and missing many deadlines. Jobs was eventually kicked off the Lisa project by Mike Markkula and despite the delays, the Lisa eventually shipped in January 1983.

1979—SPREADSHEETS AND WORD PROCESSORS

The year 1979 was a significant one in computer history because Dan Bricklin and Bob Frankston released a version of VisiCalc—the first computer spreadsheet program—for the Apple II. After BASIC and several games, VisiCalc brought computer software to an entirely new level, revolutionizing the financial industry. Previously, bankers and analysts did spreadsheets by hand, which left much room for error and required a recalculation of almost everything when a single number changed in a single cell. VisiCalc, for the first time, allowed users to change a value in a cell and the entire sheet would automatically recalculate.

Early Programming

I spent a lot of time on my parents' TRS-80 as a youth, but there wasn't a lot of software initially available, especially for a 10-year-old. I had to type the programs into the computer myself. Line by line. There were plenty of books available that had code for computer programs in them, but it was a painstaking and arduous task to type them in. I remember deciding to enter my own program into the TRS-80 one Saturday afternoon and flipping through a program book for something that piqued my interest. After looking for a while, I settled on a program called *One Arm Bandit* because it sounded fun to play with a slot machine on the computer. After typing the program character by character for several hours, I was ready to run it.

Not so fast, young Jedi! There were errors in my program. I had to go back through it and correct my code line by line to find the typos. After about an hour of debugging, I was really ready to run it. I was disappointed to discover that, after typing the Pull command, the TRS-80 simply displayed a single line that read "Cherry / Apple / Bell"—in text on the screen. Here I was expecting the glitz of spinning wheels like the slot machines I'd seen on television, only to be presented with a text-based slot machine. I was crushed. But not crushed enough to erase; I methodically saved it to cassette tape just in case I wanted to play it again. Which never happened.

"VisiCalc took 20 hours of work per week for some people and turned it out in 15 minutes and let them become much more creative," said Dan Bricklin.[1]

In the fall of 1979, VisiCalc for the Apple II was released and quickly became a best seller. In October, versions of VisiCalc were available for the Commodore PET, Tandy TRS-80, and Atari 800 and was selling briskly at $100 per copy.

VisiCalc was eventually sold to Lotus Development Corporation, where it was renamed Lotus 1-2-3 in 1983. Bricklin and Frankston never fully benefited from their ingenious software application because the Supreme Court didn't allow software to be patented until 1981.

The first word processor was WordStar by Micropro International, but it wasn't available for Apple computers. The first word processor for Apple was Apple Write I.

1983—LISA

The Lisa was called "The personal computer that works the way you do" in Apple marketing materials. Lisa was Steve Jobs's baby. He managed every aspect of the project and added feature after feature at the consequence of forever slipping deadlines. Apple president Mark Markkula ended up removing Jobs from the project, and Lisa eventually shipped in January 1983.

Like the Apple I and II, Lisa was packed with industry firsts, including:

- A mouse
- A Graphical User Interface (GUI)
- Drop-down menus
- Windows
- Multitasking
- A hierarchical file system
- Copy and paste
- Icons
- Folders

But those firsts came at a price—$9,999, to be exact.

By most accounts, Lisa was a failure, selling only 10,000 units. It reportedly cost Apple more than $150 million to develop Lisa ($100 million in software, $50 million in hardware), and it only brought in $100 million in sales for a net $50-million loss.

1984—LISA 2, MACINTOSH

In 1984 the original Lisa got a makeover with a single 3.5-inch floppy drive replacing the original's two 5.25-inch floppies, and the price was cut in half to $4,999. More important, however, Apple launched the original Macintosh in 1984 with 128KB RAM, a 400KB 3.5-inch floppy disk drive, and a What You See Is What You Get (WYSIWYG) monochrome monitor. Apple released a unique television commercial during the 1984 Super Bowl to announce the launch of the Mac featuring an Orwellian future world. The television commercial went on to win awards and is talked about to this day.

Apple's 1984 Commercial

Apple announced the Macintosh to the world with a television commercial ("1984") that was directed by Ridley Scott, an alumnus of such films as *Alien, Blade Runner,* and *Gladiator.* The commercial, written by Apple's advertising agency Chiat/Day, aired on January 22, 1984, during Super Bowl XVIII between the Washington Redskins and the Los Angeles Raiders. The ad featured a female character (played by Anya Major) wearing a white tank top, red shorts, and running shoes, running through an eerie, dark, futuristic world and throwing a sledgehammer at a huge TV image of Big Brother. The Big Brother character was giving orders to rows of people that looked like prisoners—a veiled reference to IBM. The commercial ended with a message read by Edward Grover: "On January 24, Apple Computer will introduce Macintosh. And you'll see why 1984 won't be like 1984."

In September 1984, Apple released the Macintosh 512KB, which was a significant upgrade. The "Fat Mac" got its nickname from the additional RAM under the hood (512KB vs. 128KB) and also supported an optional external 3.5-inch disk drive—a boon at the time because it didn't come with a hard drive. It was called the "Big Mac" by early adopters, but Apple could never use that term for fear of a trademark suit from McDonald's. Many considered the Mac 512 to be what the original Mac should have been.

1985—MAC XL, LASERWRITER

In 1985 the Lisa 2 was changed to the "Macintosh XL" and came with new MacWorks XL system software. The main feature of the new Lisa software was that it could run programs written for the Macintosh operating system. Steve Jobs predicted that Apple would sell two million Macs in 1985, but the company only reached 500,000. It didn't break the two million mark until 1988. It took seven years for the Macintosh to reach five million in sales.

Another landmark in 1985 was Jobs's resignation from Apple after a bitter battle with then CEO John Sculley. Jobs went on to found the aptly named "NeXT," which also designed computers.

In March 1985, Apple released the LaserWriter, a laser printer with serial and LocalTalk connections built on a Motorola 68000 processor capable of printing at 300 dots per inch (dpi) at eight pages per minute (ppm.) The LaserWriter included an Adobe PostScript interpreter, allowing it to

Graphical User Interface

PARC—a.k.a. Palo Alto Research Center (formerly Xerox PARC)—developed what is widely considered to be the first Graphical User Interface (GUI), consisting of various widgets that, when activated either by mouse click or a keystroke, performed a given task. Commands were executed by clicking on various items such as icons and buttons. Files and data were organized and manipulated using metaphors like windows, folders, and menus that were instantly familiar. Most important, the PARC GUI added a new device to complement the keyboard—the mouse.

print razor-sharp text and graphics, forever changing both the computer and printing industries.

The LaserWriter was one of the first laser printers that was affordable enough for the average consumer, and when combined with a Macintosh running Aldus' PageMaker software, enabled a level of Desktop Publishing (DTP) never before possible on the consumer level. Millions of Laser-Writers were sold over the years, and some credit the device with saving the Macintosh platform and Apple as a company.

Hands-on with Lisa

I remember using the original Lisa at a family friend's house in Lawndale, California. He was the manager of New Product Development at CCH Computax Inc. in Redondo Beach, and was evaluating the new Apple computer (Lisa) as a possible platform for his clients. Computax purchased three of them as an R&D project. They were leading edge at that point, and Computax had to stay ahead of its competitor, Fastax.

At the time, accountants did not have the ability to do any of their income tax work on computers in their office. Income tax processing was either all manual, or they filled out forms and sent them to the big service bureaus. Computax had deployed the ability to enter data remotely on an IBM PC and transmit the data to its processing center. The next thing it was doing was starting to offer the ability for accounting firms to print their own tax returns on "in office" laser printers from Xerox (HP LaserJets were not out yet). Calculations were still done on IBM mainframe computers. Computax pursued Apple as an alternative to the IBM PC, and possibly to hold the tax calculation engine.

The manager's son and I played with Lisa Paint for hours and found the fact that you could "paint" on the screen with a mouse nothing short of pure magic. He even had a printer attached so that we could see our creations on the printed page, which was also quite impressive. I remember creating "Do Not Enter" and "Toll Required" signs for our bedroom doors and thinking that it was the world's coolest thing. That and the checkerboard slip-on vans that I purchased at a local skate shop, that is.

What Happened to NeXT?

NeXT Software Inc. (previously NeXT Computer Inc.) was founded in 1985 by Steve Jobs after he resigned from Apple following a dispute with John Sculley. NeXT manufactured high-end computers that targeted the higher education and business markets. NeXT announced the first NeXT Computer in 1988, side by side with the NEXTSTEP operating system.

In April 1993, NeXT Inc. changed its name to NeXT Computer Inc. when the last original member resigned. Later in 1993, NeXT stopped selling hardware completely to focus on selling its OPEN-STEP operating system and the new Web application framework called WebObjects. On December 20, 1996, Apple purchased NeXT for $429 million and parts of the NeXT operating system were used as the foundation for Mac OS X, Apple's first truly modern operating system. Mac OS X was released in March 2001, sporting the new Aqua user interface.

Apple developed many successive models of the LaserWriter with improved speed, networking, and color. Other laser printer manufacturers also licensed Adobe's PostScript technology for inclusion into their own laser printers. Apple eventually discontinued the LaserWriter product line after the LaserWriter 8500 as part of a refocusing on core, profitable products when Steve Jobs returned to Apple in 1997.

1986—MAC PLUS

Announced in January 1986, the Mac Plus has the distinction of having the longest lifespan of any Mac model (1,719 days). And for good reason. The Mac Plus was the answer to the complaints that the original Mac wasn't expandable. It had double the ROM of the Mac 512KB (128KB vs. 64KB) and featured 1MB of RAM standard that was expandable to 4MB. The Plus was the first Mac to include a Small Computer System Interface (SCSI) port, which allowed an optional external SCSI hard drive to be attached—among other peripherals. It was the first Mac to ship in the platinum case, previous Macs were beige in color. The Mac Plus sold for $2,600 and was sold in educational settings as the Mac ED.

In April 1986, Apple released the Mac 512Ke, which was identical to the Mac 512, except it added an 800KB floppy drive (as opposed to the original 400KB floppy) and a 128KB ROM for $1,999.

1987—MAC II, SE

The first 32-bit Mac, the Mac II, was released in March 1987 and was huge departure from the previous all-in-one-form-factor. The Mac II was based on the new 68020 and included six NuBus slots, allowing expansion cards to be connected to the Mac for the first time. But what really set the Mac II apart was being the first Mac to support color graphics. An expansion card capable of displaying 16.7 million colors and a color monitor took the Mac to new heights. Color came at a price, though, the Mac II sold for $3,898 for the stripped box—video card and monitor cost extra. The deluxe configuration included 1MB of RAM, a single 800KB floppy drive and one 40MB internal SCSI hard disk drive and sold for $5,498.

The Mac SE was a new twist on the old all-in-one Mac design and was a significant improvement over the Mac Plus. The Mac SE (System

Expansion), like the Mac, was designed to address the Mac's lack of expansion. It came with an internal Processor Direct Slot (PDS) that accommodated third-party cards and an internal bay that could be used for either a second floppy drive or internal hard drive.

The Mac SE introduced the new Apple Desktop Bus (ADB) connector to the Macs. The ADB replaced the previous keyboard and mouse ports and supported up to 16 daisy-chained input devices at one time. The bare bones Mac SE configuration cost $2,898 and came with dual floppy drives.

1988—MAC IIX, SYSTEM 6

The Mac IIx was introduced in September 1988 and was similar to the Mac II, except that it came with a faster 68030 processor and 68882 FPU (both firsts) and sold for $7,769.

In April 1987, Apple released Macintosh System Software version 6.0 (a.k.a. System 6), which required a 68000 processor or later and at least 1MB of RAM. It featured an improved MultiFinder, which allowed for cooperative multitasking. An Apple-developed program called Macro-Maker was introduced with System 6.[2] The program let users record a set of computer instructions called *macros*. MacroMaker was designed to look and act like a tape recorder.[3]

System 6 shipped with an application called Font/DA Mover that allowed users to manage fonts and Desk Accessories (DAs). Font/DA Mover was also used to install fonts for use in software such as Apple's word processing application MacWrite. System 6 was included on all Macs shipping after April 1987, and a boxed version of the operating system could be purchased for $49.

1989—MAC SE/30, IICX, SE FDHD, IICI, PORTABLE

The year 1989 was a busy one for Apple, it released five Macs, including a watershed event—the release of the first portable Macintosh, if you can call it that.

In January 1989, Apple released the Mac SE/30 ($4,369), which was the guts of a Mac IIx stuffed into the much smaller Mac SE enclosure. An internal 40 or 80GB hard drive replaced the second floppy drive in the SE/30, making it a very popular Mac.

In March 1989, Apple released the Mac IIcx, which was essentially a IIx in a smaller case and with three fewer NuBus slots. The IIcx sold for $5,369.

In August 1989, Apple announced the Mac SE FDHD (Floppy Disk High Density), another version of the venerable Mac SE chassis. This time the SE was equipped with the newer, 1.4MB "high density" floppy drive and a 40GB internal hard drive standard. A version of the SE FDHD with a 20GB hard drive was sold in Europe as the Mac SE 1/20 for the same price.

In September Apple released the Mac IIci ($6,700), and it was one of Apple's most-loved Macs. The IIci was a faster version of the IIcx that had built-in support for a color monitor and 32-bit clean ROMs.

The Mac Portable was also announced in September 1989 and was Apple's first attempt at a portable Macintosh. Some people consider Apple's original all-in-one designs (the Mac 128KB, 512KB, Mac Plus, and SE) to be *portable* because they were compact and included a built-in handle. The Mac Portable was nicknamed the *Mac luggable* because of its large size (4 × 15 × 14 inches) and weight (15.8 pounds). The upside was that it had a lot of stuff in it for a portable computer, not many portables could support two Super Drives and a 3.5-inch half-height drive. The Mac Portable was a commercial flop because it was enormous, heavy, slow, and the active matrix screen wasn't (initially) backlit, making it useless in an unlit room at night. The $6,500 price tag helped cement the Mac Portable as one of Apple's biggest flops of all time.

1990—MAC IIFX, CLASSIC, IISI, LC

In October 1990, Apple announced a whopping six Macs: three desktop machines and three true portables.

The Mac IIfx was released in March 1990 and was the fastest Mac ever. The IIfx came in the same case as the Mac II and could support two Super Drives and an internal SCSI hard disk. It was declared "Wicked Fast" by the media and enjoyed a speed boost thanks to a couple of custom, Apple-designed Application Specific Integrated Circuits (ASICs). It sold for $9,870 and went as high as $12,000, depending on the configuration. The Mac IIfx also bears the distinction of being the most expensive Mac ever sold.

Apple focused on the low end of the market with its October 1990 introduction of three new Macs: the Classic, LC, and the IIsi.

Unfortunately, another firm (Modular Computer Systems Inc.), already owned the computer industry trademark rights to the word *Classic*. The company had been manufacturing the ModComp Classic since 1978. But that didn't stop Apple, it wanted to use the name and eventually negotiated a $1 million deal with ModComp to license the word for a period of five years. Apple last used the name on the Color Classic II (introduced October 1993) and didn't renew the agreement when it expired.

The Mac Classic ($1,500) shipped in a newly designed case with a larger 512KB bootable ROM, users could boot from ROM by holding down Command-Option-X-O at the beginning of the startup sequence. The Classic also included the 1.4MB "SuperDrive" floppy drive and was more or less a reissue of the Mac Plus. Many users complained that it was slow.

The Mac LC (which stood for "Low Cost") was released in October 1990 for $2,400 and featured a 16MHz 68020 in a new smaller case. The LC came with a microphone (a Mac first) and a Processor Direct Slot (PDS). The LC was discontinued in December 1992.

The Mac IIsi was introduced at $3,800 and featured a streamlined case used only for this model and a built-in microphone. It was originally designed for a 25MHz 68030 processor, but was dumbed down to 20MHz so that it wouldn't compete with the IIci.

1991—MAC PORTABLE, POWERBOOKS, AND QUADRAS

Hardware

The year 1991 was filled with hardware and software announcements from Apple. In February 1991, Apple released a backlit version of the Mac Portable, which, although a boon at the time, was considered a feature that should have been included in the original model announced in 1990.

The Mac Classic II was largely considered to be everything the original Classic should have been. It had a restyled case, 16MHz, 68030 processor, and a built-in microphone. The Classic II sold for $1,900 and was discontinued in September 1993. It was sold as the Performa 200 with a 2400/9600 baud fax/modem and extra software in September 1992. The Performa 200 was discontinued in April 1993.

The Quadra 700 was the first in a new family of Macs to ship in a tower case, which was really just a IIcx case turned on its side. The Quadra 700 cost a whopping $6,000 and included a 25MHz 68040 processor and was the first Mac to include an FPU (Floating Point Unit). The Quadra 900 ($7,200) was a more expandable version of the Quadra 700. It featured five NuBus slots and had room for three half-height internal bays over the Quadra 700's one.

After learning its lesson from the Mac Portable, Apple also in 1991 released the first truly portable Mac and gave the product line its own name—PowerBook. For help with the PowerBook design, Apple enlisted the aid of Sony.

The PowerBook 100 cost $2,500 and weighed only 5.1 pounds. Sony essentially miniaturized the Mac Portable when it designed the Power-Book 100, keeping the same processor (MC68000) and clock speed as its much larger and heavier cousin. It shipped with 2MB RAM (expandable to 8MB) and a 20–40MB hard drive. A floppy drive was only available as an external option. Even though it was relatively slow and had a fuzzy, passive-matrix screen and no floppy drive, the PowerBook 100 was well received—mostly because of the history of the Mac Portable.

Two other PowerBooks were launched simultaneously with the PB100. The PowerBook 140 and the 170 were designed entirely by Apple. The

Origin of the Term *PowerBook*

The venerable PowerBook has been with us since 1991, when Apple released the PowerBook 100 (with the help of Sony) and Xerox PARC veteran and longtime Apple Fellow Alan Kay, who coined the term. Apple trademarked PowerBook shortly thereafter, further solidifying the term in the modern technical vernacular.[a]

The PowerBook's introduction saw many innovative designs that soon became the standard for future notebook computer design. Innovations in design included ergonomic improvements like placing a wrist rest in front of the keyboard, which also allowed room for a trackball for navigation. A few years later, PowerBook introduced the first 256 color displays, trackpads, and the first built-in Ethernet networking port.

Apple launched its consumer notebook in 1999 and called it the *iBook* to differentiate it from its more expensive brother, the PowerBook.

[a] Jason O'Grady, "It's Been 15 Years: Time to Dump the Term 'PowerBook,'" O'Grady's PowerPage, June 29, 2005, http://www.powerpage.org/2005/07/its_been_15_yea.html.

PowerBook 140 was the mid-range of the three PowerBooks, featuring a 16MHz 68030 processor and an internal floppy drive—a feature missing from the popular PowerBook 100. The PB140 shipped with a passive-matrix screen for $2,000. It was discontinued in August 1992 when the PowerBook 145 replaced it.

The PowerBook 170 was the top-of-the-line model at $4,600 and featured a 25MHz Motorola 68030 processor with FPU, a 10-inch active matrix display (a first, and much brighter than passive matrix), a slot for an optional internal modem, and up to 8MB of RAM. The PowerBook 180 replaced it in 1992.

Software

On May 13, 1991, Apple released System 7 (code-named *Big Bang* and mostly referred to as Mac OS 7), which was the primary Macintosh operating system until Mac OS 8 was released in 1997. System 7 included such advanced features as cooperative multitasking, virtual memory, file sharing, QuickTime, QuickDraw 3D, and an improved user interface.

Other

IBM, Motorola, and Apple formed an alliance aimed at challenging the PC platform dominated by Intel hardware running Microsoft's

Windows operating system. The new platform was based on IBM's POWER1 CPU, which had a server chip (POWER1) and a desktop chip (PowerPC). IBM was to develop the chips and Motorola was to produce them. Apple's role was to port the Macintosh operating system to run on the new platform.

1992—PERFORMAS AND POWERBOOK DUO

The next year, 1992, continued the trend of more hardware releases from 1991 with four new desktop Macs and six new portables. On the desktop front, Apple released the LC II, Quadra 950, Performa 200/400/600, Iivi, and the IIvx. On the PowerBook front, Apple released the PowerBook 145, 160, 180 Duo 210, 230, and the DuoDock and MiniDock.

Released in March 1992, the Mac LC II came in the same pizza box case as the original LC but marked the last of the Mac II series. The case's form-factor lived on for many years. The LC II sold for $1,240, making it one of the most inexpensive Macs ever. Apple upgraded the processor to a 16MHz 68030 but kept the same 16-bit data path, when the 68030 was capable of 32-bit processing, making it only marginally faster. The LC II was discontinued in March 1993, when the LC III replaced it.

Apple's Shortest-lived Mac

The Mac IIvx was designed as a proof-of-concept project to test how Apple could include an internal CD-ROM drive in a Mac. Then John Sculley goofed and went off script at Macworld Expo in Tokyo, telling the audience that Apple would soon ship a Mac with a built-in CD-ROM drive—much to the surprise of his development team in Cupertino.

In their haste to deliver on Sculley's promise, the team had to build the IIvx with a lot of compromises in very little time. The included 32MHz processor was dumbed down due to its slow 16MHz bus and the serial port was half-baked, causing problems with many peripherals that connected to it. To make matters worse, a much more powerful Mac, the Centris 610, was released a scant four months later, relegating the IIvx to the trash heap.

Since then, people who buy an expensive Mac, which quickly becomes obsolete, are said to be "IIvx'ed." Interestingly, the IIvx was also the first Mac to have a metal case.[a]

[a] Brian Kendig, "Mac IIvx," Apple-History.com, October 28, 2001, http://www.apple-history.com/?page=gallery&model=IIvx&performa=off&sort=date&order=ASC.

The Quadra 950 (May 1992) was a speed-bump of the Quadra 900 jumping from 25 to a 33MHz 68040 processor and selling for $7,200.

The Mac IIvx had a 32MHz 68030 processor, 68882 FPU, and was designed for the mid-range market. Priced at $2,950, the IIvx was the first Mac to accommodate an internal CD-ROM drive. However, it was hobbled by a paltry 16MHz bus, which slowed it to the speed of a 25MHz IIci.

The Mac IIvi was the same as the IIvx, but with a slower 16MHz 68030 processor (instead of 32MHz), and no Floating Point Unit (FPU). It cost less than the pricier IIvx but was also discontinued after just four months on the market.

Apple's Performa Series

The Performa series was Apple's line of consumer Macs from 1992 through 1997. Performas were renamed Macs (Quadra, Centris, LC, and Power Mac) that were sold in computer stores. The series begun with the Performa 200 (a renamed Macintosh Classic II) in 1992. Almost every version of Mac LC was also sold as a Performa at some point or another, as was Power Macintosh 6100.

Performas came with a customized version of the Mac System software, denoted by a P in the version number (i.e., System 7.1P5). Performas were sold in bundles, which usually included a monitor, external modem, and third-party software. The software bundles were pre-installed and included titles like American Heritage Dictionary, America Online, At Ease, ClarisWorks, Datebook Pro, Mavis Beacon Teaches Typing, Quicken, Touchbase, and several games.

While Apple's desktop line was getting more complex, arguably cluttered, its portable computers were hitting their stride. After the Mac Portable debacle, Apple had been lauded for newer, smaller form-factors of the PowerBook 100, 140, and 170. Apple built upon its successes with more notebook computers based on the same design.

In August 1992, Apple released the PowerBook 145 that was a speed-bumped version of the PowerBook 140 that sold for $2,150. The Power-Book 160 had the distinction of being the first portable Mac that could drive an external monitor in 8-bit color. Introduced in October 1992, the 160 sold for $2,480.

In September 1992, the Mac LC II was bundled with several different hard drives and software, and re-released as the Performa 400, 405, 410, and 430.

In October 1992, the PowerBook 180 became the new top-of-the-line Mac portable, replacing the 170. The PowerBook 180 sported the same external monitor capacity as the less-expensive 160, but had a faster bus speed (33 vs. 25MHz) and had an FPU. The 180 sold for $4,110 and was discontinued in May 1994.

The PowerBook Duo ushered in a new era of portable computers for Apple. Apple was embarrassed by its first foray into portable computers with the Mac Portable but made up for it with the successes in the PowerBook 100 line. But Apple wanted more. It wanted to build a portable computer that was truly on par with its desktop computers—a true no-compromises portable.

Apple achieved this goal with the Macintosh Duo series. The Duo did away with the usual complement of ports found on portable computers in exchange for a universal docking connector (a 152-pin Processor Direct Slot), allowing it to be connected to a larger docking station when at home. This allowed the PowerBook Duo to drop weight and size over the previous PowerBook 100 series, to the delight of travelers everywhere.

The PowerBook Duo 210 and 230 weighed in at 4.2 pounds, which was less than the 160 and 180, which weighed 6.8 pounds. But their sleek form-factor didn't come without a penalty. In exchange for the extra weight savings and smaller footprint, the PowerBook Duo dropped the floppy drive and most of the ports found on the full-size PowerBooks.

The Duo 210 shipped with a 25MHz 68030 processor, passive-matrix screen, 4 to 32MB of RAM, and an internal hard drive. The Duo series was famous for its docking connector that could connect to a docking station with additional RAM, VRAM, and a hard drive. The Duo 210 sold for $2,250. The Duo 230 was the same as the 210 except that it shipped with a faster 33MHz 68030 processor and was priced at $2,610.

The DuoDock was an ingenious development from Apple—it looked like a desktop computer but it had a large flap at the front that allowed you to insert a closed PowerBook Duo computer. Once installed, the DuoDock turned a Duo into the full-scale desktop computer with all the ports and connectors you could expect. It even had an extra hard drive bay for more storage, and if you added more video RAM (VRAM), it could drive an external color monitor.

1993—CENTRIS, QUADRA, SERVERS, NEWTON

In 1991, Apple began a ramp of its hardware offerings that was hard to stop. In 1991, Apple released seven new computers; in 1992, that grew to 15 models; and in 1993, an unprecedented 39 models were released. Apple was like a train running off its tracks, releasing new computer models every two to three months, often only changing a single digit in its model number.

The harried pace of new hardware resulted in a glut of new Macs flooding the marketplace. While the initial amount of choices was impressive, it eventually led to customer confusion over which model to buy. When consumers are confused, they often don't buy, so the trend that began in 1991 wasn't a good one for the company.

In February 1993, Apple released seven new models: the Centris 610 and 650, Color Classic, LC III, Performa 250, PowerBook 165c, and Quadra 800.

The Centris 610 was the first mid-range Mac to ship with a Motorola 68040 processor, but it was a stripped-down version of the chip (68LC040) that lacked an FPU running at 20MHz. The Centris 610 was the first Mac to be housed in a low-profile case that was also called a "pizza box" because of its low, flat shape. The Centris 650 was a faster and more expandable version of the Centris 610 that came in the taller, narrower case of the Mac IIvx and was powered by a 25MHz 68040 processor. The Centris 650 sold for $2,700.

The Color Classic was the same as the Classic II but with a color screen, larger ROM, and a new case. The Color Classic was actually an LC II in a different form-factor; they shared many things, including a 16-bit data bus and a 10MB maximum RAM. The Color Classic differed in that it had a 68882 math coprocessor and a special *daughterboard* that could be removed for easy upgrading. The Color Classic sold for $1,390.

The Mac LC III sold for $750 and included a redesigned Processor Direct Slot (PDS) and was also sold as the Performa 450.The Quadra 800 was as powerful as the Quadra 950 from the year before but cost about half as much. It was powered by a 33MHz 68040 processor and sold for $4,700. The PowerBook 165c was the first color PowerBook ever and sold for $3,400.

In March 1993, Apple released its first "server" computers—the Apple Workgroup Server (AWS, sometimes abbreviated WGS). The Workgroup Server 80 was actually a Quadra 800 with some included server software. Likewise, the Workgroup Server 95 was just a rebadged Quadra 950, but

---

What Is A/UX?

A/UX (short for Apple Unix) was an operating system based on UNIX System V Release 2.2 and first released in 1988. It was adopted by Apple in 1993 with its Workgroup Server 95 and required a 68k-based Macintosh.

A/UX put a friendly user interface with Mac-like windows and menus on top of its complex UNIX underpinnings. A customized Finder was included that looked similar to System 7 but was designed to work with the UNIX kernel. A/UX also offered a command line interface to UNIX, something never before available on a Macintosh.

---

unlike the AWS 80, shipped with a special version of the Unix operating system called A/UX (a combination of *Apple* and *UniX*). The AWS 95 also featured a Digital Audio Tape (DAT) for backups and a Processor Direct Slot (PDS) card containing a fast SCSI connection and a 256KB level 2 CPU cache.

The LC 520, released in June 1993, was Apple's attempt to create a viable all-in-one computer design. At $2,000, it was a popular choice for a home computer. It was also released as the Performa 520. Also in June, Apple released the PowerBook 145B (which was exactly the same as the 145, but featured a lower price and two additional megabytes of RAM soldered to the motherboard) and the PowerBook 180c, which included the first active-matrix 256 color screen from Apple and sold for $4,160.

In July 1993, Apple introduced its first low-cost Audio/Video (AV) capable Macs, the Centris 660av ($2,300) and the Quadra 840av ($3,550). The 660av shipped in a Centris 610-style case with a 25MHz 68040 processor and a 55MHz AT&T 3210 Digital Signal Processor (DSP). It also came with s-video and composite video-in and out. The 660av was one of the first Macs to include a new type of serial port called a *Geoport* that could be used as a modem with the proper adapter.

The Quadra 840av was the first 68040 Mac to top 33MHz and the fastest Mac ever, utilizing a 40MHz 68040 processor. It came in a Quadra 800-style case and included AV features similar to the less expensive 660av. The difference was that the 840av came with a faster, 66MHz AT&T 3210 DSP.

Also in July 1993, Apple introduced the Workgroup Server 60 based on the Centris 610 motherboard. The AWS 60, as it was called, was speedbumped to 25MHz in October 1993.

In August 1993, Apple announced the PowerBook 165 that replaced the 160. The 165 was a grayscale version of 165c that lacked an FPU and sold for $1,500.

In October 1993, Apple announced more computers than in any previous year—19. Eight of them were Performas. The Color Classic II was released only in Japan and doubled the processor speed to 33MHz and increased the data path to 32-bit over the Color Classic. It also added stereo output and was released in the United States as the Performa 275.

The LC 475 was the first Motorola 68040-based LC and was officially sold as Quadra 605 and was also known as Performa 475 and 476. The LC III+ added a 33 MHz 68030 processor and was also sold as the Performa 460, 466, and 467.

The limited edition Mac TV was one of the few Macs that shipped in a black case. It was essentially a black LC 520 with a cable-ready TV tuner card and a CD-ROM drive. Only 10,000 Mac TVs were made, but its TV-tuner card has become a popular option on many LCs and Performas.

In 1993, Apple expanded its popular PowerBook Duo line with the Duo 250 ($2,500) and 270c ($3,100). The Duo 250 was the same as the Duo 230 except that it had a 4-bit active-matrix screen. The 270c included an active-matrix 640 × 480 pixel 256-color screen, and the improved battery could run for two hours on a charge. The 270c would also support 16-bit video if you changed the screen resolution to 640 × 400 under Options in the Monitors control panel.

The Quadra 605 was the most affordable Quadra ever at $900. It came with a 25MHz 68LC040 processor in a small, new case. The Quadra 610 ($2,520) and 650 ($2,700) were upgraded models of the Centrises of the same model number. The Quadra 650 replaced the Centris 610, adding a 25MHz 68040 processor while the price remained at $2,520. The Quadra 650 replaced the Centris 650, adding a faster 33MHz 68040 processor and sold for $2,700.

Other

In August 1993, Apple released its first completely new product in a long time—the Newton MessagePad. It was a completely new product line and was a risky move because Apple didn't have any experience in the area and other competitors in the market were already creating products that it would have to compete against.

The Newton Message Pad (or NMP) was a Personal Digital Assistant (PDA), which, while relatively commonplace today, represented advanced technology in 1993. The Newton MessagePad was a small handheld device with a touch screen and a number of built-in organizational applications such as an address book, calendar, notepad, and some unique communications programs that allowed the tiny device to fax and e-mail.

The original Newton ($699) came with a 20MHz ARM 610 processor and ran on AAA batteries. In October 1993, it received a ROM upgrade to version 1.10, which fixed a number of outstanding bugs.

1994—43 MACS AND NEWTON

Hardware

In 1994, Apple continued on its tear of hardware releases with 43 new computer models, besting the previous year's record of 39 in 1993. There was a problem, though, because Apple was diluting the pool of Mac choices that were on the market and further confusing customers. The company probably didn't realize it at the time, but looking back, the flurry of hardware released from 1993 through 1997 hurt Apple as a company.

Note: For the duration of this chapter, I'll focus on the significant hardware announcements and less on the speed-bump machines that simply added more CPU, hard drive, and/or RAM. Since the Performa line is just a rebadged Mac, I'll also skip it for the duration of the book—something Apple should have also done at the time.

The Mac LC series was gaining in popularity in 1994 because of its low cost, and Apple continued the line with its release of the LC 550 ($1,200) that replaced the LC 520 and was identical except that it had a 33MHz 68030 processor. The LC 575 ($1,700) added a 33MHz 68LC040 processor and was the first Mac to contain a specialized communication slot (which Apple shortened to "comm slot") that could accept a number of network and modem cards specially designed for it.

The Apple Communication Slot was an internal expansion data interface that was used to add communication expansion cards like network adapters and modems to Macs and Power Macs of the day. There was one major problem with it, though, when a card was installed, it disabled the modem serial port on the back of the computer.

In February 1994, Apple released the Quadra 610 DOS Compatible, which was basically a Quadra 610 with an additional 486SX processor (a modified Intel 486DX microprocessor with its floating-point unit disconnected) running at 25MHz on a Processor Direct Slot (PDS) card. This machine marked the first time Apple shipped a Mac with an Intel chip inside. Granted, it wasn't the primary CPU like the ones that Apple ships today, but it was an Intel chip nonetheless.

Apple introduced the "DOS compatible" Mac as an experiment and to see if there was sufficient demand. As it turned out, users that needed DOS capability in addition to the Mac quickly purchased the limited edition run of 25,000 units.

On the high end of the product line, Apple introduced a completely new line of Macs called "Power Macs." The name comes from an entirely new chip called the PowerPC, which was better and faster than the Motorola chips it replaced.

On March 14, 1994, Apple released its first Power Macintosh desktop computers (the 6100, 7100, and 8100), which were the first to ship with the new PowerPC processor from the AIM alliance (Apple, IBM, Motorola). PowerPC is a Reduced Instruction Set Computing (RISC) microprocessor architecture originally intended for personal computers.

The Power Macintosh 6100, 7100, and 8100 shipped in speeds from 60 to 110MHz. They replaced Apple's Quadra series of personal computers and were housed in similar enclosures. The Power Mac went on to become Apple's top-of-the-line hardware offering for 12 years with four major generations of PowerPC chips. In August 2006, the Power Mac was retired at Apple's Worldwide Developers Conference (WWDC) by Steve Jobs and Phil Schiller in anticipation of the new Mac daddy, the Mac Pro.

On the portable front, Apple introduced a new line of PowerBooks in May 1994. The PowerBook 520 ($2,270) and 540 ($3,160) were the first to ship with the Motorola 68040 processor—previous models had a 68030 chip. But miniaturization came at a price. Apple's notebook computers couldn't accept its latest and greatest CPUs like the PowerPC; the new chips were simply too large, too hot, and required too much power. Portable users were seemingly relegated to using the previous generation CPU while the desktop kids had all the fun.

The PowerBook 520 had a major notebook innovation—a trackpad replaced the trackball found in older PowerBooks. The 520 also came with a built-in microphone, stereo speakers, and a passive-matrix 4-bit grayscale screen.

See "The Trackpad—1994" in Chapter 4.

Meanwhile, the PowerBook Duo line of notebooks continued to gain steam and in May the company released two updated Duos. The Duo 280 ($2,600) added a 68040 processor and the Duo 280c ($3,750) added a 16-bit active-matrix color screen. Apple also released two new DuoDocks; the DuoDock Plus added an AAUI Ethernet port and doubled the VRAM to 1MB. The DuoDock II added a 68882 FPU.

In June 1994, Apple ended its successful Quadra line with the Quadra 630 ($1,200), which came in a new case design. The 630 was the first Mac to ship with an IDE hard drive (previous models were SCSI) and an optional CD-ROM drive. It was later released as the LC 630 and under nine different Performa model names, depending on the configuration.

In July 1994, Apple released its most inexpensive PowerBook ever, the PowerBook 150 ($1,300). Although inexpensive, the PB150 was replete with tradeoffs. Its low price came at the expense of a nice screen (the included passive-matrix screen was dim and blurry) and an Apple Desktop Bus (ADB) port for plugging in external mice and keyboards.

With all the hardware coming out of Cupertino in the mid-1990s, it was difficult to tell one model from the next. Apple did something smart on its Mac line to alleviate the problem, which was to put a slash into the model number between the first part (the case design) and the second part (the clock speed.) For example, the Power Macintosh 6100/60 was the low, flat case running at 60MHz. This gave consumers (and support personnel at Apple) a much easier way to distinguish between the models.

Says *Apple Confidential*, "Apple shipped over one million Power Macs and PowerPC upgrades by the end of 1994, three months before the company's one-year goal."[4]

Enter the Clones

In the summer of 1994, Apple began licensing the Mac operating system to third-party hardware manufacturers in an attempt to gain market share. The program involved licensing the Macintosh ROMs and system software to companies agreeing to pay a royalty for each clone Mac that they sold. From 1995 to mid-1997, you could purchase a PowerPC-based computer that ran the Mac OS from one of several manufacturers, including Power Computing, Motorola, Radius, APS Technologies, Daystar Digital, and UMAX.

Although clones ran the Macintosh operating system and Macintosh applications, that's where the similarities ended. The clone hardware wasn't anywhere near as aesthetically pleasing and more closely resembled the generic Windows PC towers of the day. Beige clone towers were off-putting for consumers that were used to Apple's traditional high level of attention to detail but were more economical than comparable Apple products and made sense for users that just stuck them under a desk and customers that had to justify their computer budgets against less expensive PCs.

When Steve Jobs returned to Apple in 1997, he backed out of contracts with the Mac OS licensees and hastily released Mac OS 8, as cloners' licenses were limited to using Apple System 7 software. Apple later purchased Power Computing's Mac clone business for $100 million, marking an end to the clone market.

Software

In June 1994, Apple released System 7.5, which, despite its incremental version number, was a major update to System 7. System 7.5 was code-named *Capone* as a reference to the gangster who put fear in Chicago (*Chicago* was the code name for Microsoft's Windows 95) as a subtle jab at Microsoft. System 7.5 had several new features, including Apple Guide, Stickies, WindowShade, Control Strip, Extensions Manager, PowerTalk, Launcher, a hierarchal Apple menu, systemwide drag and drop, a scriptable Finder, QuickDraw GX, and OpenDoc.

Other

In March 1994, Apple released the Newton MessagePad 100 and dropped the price from $699 to $499. The NMP, as it was known, included a new version of the Newton operating system with improved handwriting recognition and several bug fixes. The MessagePad 110 was released at the same time as the 100 for slightly more ($599) and included more RAM (1MB vs. 640KB).

For more on the Newton MessagePad, see Chapter 4, "Strategies and Innovations."

1995—54 NEW MACS

Hardware

In 1995, Apple continued its ambitious hardware release schedule with 54 new models, besting its previous high by more than 10. Apple released speed-bumps to the Power Mac 6100, 7100, and 8100 lines, then replaced them with a raft of new Power Mac models (5200, 6200, 7200, 7500, 8500, and 9500). More low cost (LCs) also came out, including the 580 and 630, and Workgroup Servers (6150, 8150, 9150).

More new PowerBooks hit the street, including the PB550c (a black model only released in Japan), the PB190 (the last 680X0 machine Apple ever built), and the 190c (a color version), but the news of the year was the introduction of the first PowerPC PowerBook, the PB5300.

The PowerBook 5300, introduced in August 1995, was highly anticipated because of the perceived performance jump over the previous 680X0 machines and was coveted by most Mac users. Ultimately, the 5300 failed to meet expectations and turned out to be a major disappointment for most customers.

It wasn't without its firsts, though. The PB5300 featured a sleep-swappable bay, allowing users to switch out modules while the machine was sleeping—as opposed to having to shut it down. Popular expansion bay modules included Zip, magneto-optical, and traditional hard drives. Another innovation was the internal expansion slot that allowed the installation of third-party expansion cards. An infrared port was added for wireless networking, and two PC card slots were included. As with previous PowerBooks, SCSI, serial, and ABD ports came standard.

A total of four PB5300 models were released. The PB5300/100 ($2,300) had a 100MHz processor, 8MB RAM, and a 500MB hard drive; the PB5300c/100 ($3,900) included an active-matrix color screen. A fully loaded PB5300ce/117, which had a higher resolution screen (800 × 600 vs. 640 × 480) with 32MB RAM and a 1.1GB hard drive, sold for a whopping $6,800. The more economical 5300cs, with a dimmer dual-scan color screen, sold for $2,900.

Apple had quality assurance problems with the PowerBook 5300-series and many of them were dead on arrival (DOA). Hardly the image you want to present to a customer that just spent upward of $7,000 on a computer. In addition, cracked cases were reported, and overheating batteries led to product recalls.

Many users complained about poor performance due to its lack of a Level 2 cache, and the lack of a CD-ROM drive was a sticking point for many. To make matters worse, two early, unreleased PowerBook 5300s caught fire when the Sony Lithium Ion batteries overheated. Apple recalled all PB5300s (only about 100 at the time) and replaced their batteries with Nickel Metal Hydride (NiMH) batteries that provided only about 70% of the run time of Lithium.

It was around this time in the mid-1990s that Apple had developed a reputation for shipping poor quality products—a reputation that took years to repair.

In January 1995, Apple released the Newton MessagePad 120, which sold for $599 and was largely the same as the 100, except that it could be purchased with either 1MB or 2MB of RAM. In November, Apple released

Newton OS 2.0, which had dramatically better handwriting recognition, improved backup capabilities, and a better user interface.

1996—STEMMING THE TIDE

Hardware

In 1996, the amount of computers released by Apple finally hit a plateau. Although Apple still released a large number of new computers (51), this marked the first time since the ramp up during the early 1990s that the number had declined year over year. It had only declined by three, but it was a decline nonetheless.

With the transition to PowerPC chips complete, Apple continued to churn out new Macs in the Power Mac (5200, 5400, 6300, 6400, 7200, 7600, 8200, 8500, 9500), Workgroup Server (7200, 8500), and PowerBook (1400) lines.

Innovation in the 1996 hardware included the first PowerPC tower with a CPU on a daughter card for easy upgrades (the Power Mac 9500) and the PowerBook 1400's internal CD-ROM drive, swappable bays, and unique "BookCovers" that allowed users to customize the look of the lid of the machine by sliding graphical inserts under a clear top panel.

The Network Server 500 and 700 were totally new products for Apple and the first Macintoshes in company history that didn't run the Macintosh OS. Instead they ran AIX (an IBM version of UNIX) in an attempt to enter the high-end server market. Ultimately, the Network Server didn't sell well—probably because AIX training or a network administrator were required to run them—and they were discontinued.

A Glut of Performas

The Performas were rebadged Macintoshes that were sold in computer stores, major electronics chains, and via television commercials, brochures, and paper ads from 1992 to 1997. Performas were sold configured with a monitor, modem, and a pre-installed software bundle that included programs like ClarisWorks, America Online, and some educational titles.

Although Performas were selling well, somewhere along the line Apple went off the tracks. In 1992, Apple released four Performa models and in 1996 it released 22. That in and of itself wouldn't be a problem if it weren't for the other 29 Apple computers released that year. Apple had released a total of 51 machines in 1996.

The problem was that there were too many computers that were similar to one another, and their vague numerical names didn't help the situation much either. After all, who could tell me the difference between a Performa 6116CD and a 6117CD? The consumer was just as confused, making it difficult for people selling Macs to easily explain the differences to consumers. The last thing that you want to do when selling a user-friendly computer is to confuse the customer.

Apple's 20th Anniversary

On April 1, 1996, Apple celebrated its 20th anniversary, and in June 1997, announced, appropriately enough, a Twentieth Anniversary Macintosh (or TAM for short) to mark the occasion.

Pippin

On December 13, 1994, Apple announced Pippin, a home multimedia system for gaming, learning, and surfing the Internet. (It shipped in Japan in 1995.) Pippin looked like a gaming console with a slide-out optical drive and connectors for two controllers that are common on many gaming consoles available today. Pippin was based on a 66MHz PowerPC 603 processor with a 4x CD-ROM drive, 14.4KB modem, and a video output port for connecting it to a television. Pippin ran a stripped-down version of the System 7.5.2 operating system and was designed primarily to play multimedia CD-ROMs, notably games, although it was also capable of networking via its built-in modem.

Apple didn't plan to market or distribute Pippin directly. Instead it wanted to license the technology to third parties. Bandai, the world's third-largest producer of toys, was looking at entering the console video game market, and chose the Pippin as its platform.

By the time Pippin was released (1995 in Japan, 1996 in the United States), the market was already crowded with major players in the console gaming market: Sega Saturn, Sony PlayStation, and soon Nintendo 64. Pippin had little software and was considered too expensive at $599 when compared to the competition—even though it was also a cheap computer system.

Software

On December 20, 1996, Apple purchased Steve Jobs's company, NeXT, and its NEXTSTEP operating system. NeXT beat out Be Inc.'s BeOS in its battle to be acquired by Apple.

NeXT versus Be Inc.

The Be Operating System (BeOS) was designed for AT&T hardware but was modified to run on Be's PowerPC-based processors. It was later modified to run on Apple hardware in hopes that Apple would purchase (or license) BeOS to be the next-generation Mac operating system.

Apple CEO Gil Amelio was keen on buying Be Inc., but ground to a halt when Be CEO Jean-Louis Gassée demanded $400 million. Apple's highest offer was $125 million. Apple's board eventually decided NEXTSTEP was a better fit and agreed to purchase NeXT in 1996 for $427 million.

Apple's acquisition of NeXT brought company co-founder Steve Jobs back into the fold after a much-publicized battle with then-CEO John Sculley in 1985. The UNIX-based NEXTSTEP operating system would go on to become the foundation of the Mac OS X operating system.

1997—THE RETURN OF JOBS

In June 1997, Apple CEO Gil Amelio announced a $740 million loss in the second quarter. On July 9, 1997, Amelio was removed as Apple CEO by its board of directors after company stock (AAPL on the NASDAQ) hit a 12-year low, and the company suffered massive financial losses on his watch.

The biggest news of 1997 was Steve Jobs's triumphant return to Apple after Apple purchased NeXT on December 20, 1996, for $427 million. Jobs officially became the interim CEO (or "iCEO") on September 16, 1997, and began a much-needed restructuring of the company's product line.

For more on Apple's upper management, see Chapter 8, "Apple Leadership."

A Deal with the Devil

In 1997, Apple did something few people would have predicted—it entered a partnership with Microsoft. Almost since the beginning of the Mac, there has been a friendly (and sometimes not) rivalry between Mac and Windows users. Macs have always been in the minority and that reflects in Mac users' underdog mentality. Many Mac users perceive Microsoft as the evil Big Brother that dominates computer technology. Mac users also tend to be quite vocal about their choice of the Mac platform and their sense of its superiority. So you can image the shock in the audience at Macworld Expo 1997 when Steve Jobs announced the partnership with Microsoft during his keynote address.

When Microsoft CEO Bill Gates appeared via satellite on the 50-foot-tall screen on the stage, a silence fell over the crowd. Several people in the audience thought that it was all an elaborate ruse. Then came the boos and hisses. Gates spoke only briefly, touching on Microsoft's software plans for the Mac and Apple's return to financial prosperity.

The deal involved a five-year commitment by Microsoft to continue to deliver its popular Office productivity package on the Macintosh platform as well as a $150-million investment in Apple. Jobs also announced that Internet Explorer, Microsoft's Web browser, would be included as the default browser on all Macintoshes shipped.

Sensing the audience's change in attitude and obvious disdain for Microsoft, Jobs said:

If we want to move forward and see Apple healthy and prospering again, we have to let go of a few things here. We have to let go of this notion that for Apple to win, Microsoft has to lose. We have to embrace a notion that for Apple to win, Apple has to do a really good job. And if others are going to help us that's great, because we need all the help we can get, and if we screw up and we don't do a good job, it's not somebody else's fault, it's our fault. So I think that is a very important perspective. If we want Microsoft Office on the Mac, we better treat the company that puts it out with a little bit of gratitude; we like their software.

So, the era of setting this up as a competition between Apple and Microsoft is over as far as I'm concerned. This is about getting Apple healthy, this is about Apple being able to make incredibly great contributions to the industry and to get healthy and prosper again.[5]

Hardware

Now in its second year of PowerPC chips, Apple continued to release new Mac models at a breakneck pace. A total of 44 new Macs were released, including mostly routine updates to the Power Mac (4400, 5500, 6500, 6600, 7200, 7300, 7600, 8600, 9600), PowerBook (1400, 2400, 3400), and Workgroup Server (7200, 8500) lines.

In April 1997, Motorola introduced the PowerPC 603e (sometimes called PowerPC 603ev), running at 300MHz and the first mainstream desktop processor to reach that benchmark. The new chip addressed performance issues in the PPC 603 it replaced and enhanced its Level 1 cache, improving performance. The faster clock speed was achieved by shrinking the fabrication process to 0.35 μm. In addition to being found in machines from Apple, the PowerPC 603 was also used by Be Inc. in the Be Box and in the ThinkPad 800 series notebook computers.

Power Macintosh

Another significant hardware milestone was reached in September 1997 when Motorola introduced the PowerPC 750 (a.k.a. G3) processor. The PPC750 was the first PowerPC processor with a high-speed, "backside" cache that could interact with the processor at much faster speeds than a standard L2 cache, which was bottlenecked at the motherboard.

In November, Apple released a new desktop and mini-tower Macs based around the new G3 chip—both called the Power Macintosh G3. The new desktop Macs were based on a motherboard design running at 66MHz. The desktop case was a new design that featured either a 233 or 266MHz chip, 16-bit audio in and out, and an internal Zip drive. The G3 mini-tower came in 266MHz and added s-video in and out and 4MB of VRAM (expandable to 6MB).

In November 10, 1997, Apple released the first PowerBook to use the PowerPC 750 (or G3) processor—the PowerBook G3/250. The PowerBook

G3 utilized the same case as the PowerBook 3400, but inside it had a 750 processor running at 250MHz with a 512KB backside cache. The combination of the new chip and high-speed cache made the PowerBook G3 the fastest notebook in the world. In benchmark testing the PBG3 performed near the Power Mac 9600/300, which was unheard of for a notebook. Apple promoted this new speed demon heavily in its marketing materials.

See other Apple milestones in Chapter 4, "Strategies and Innovations."

The Twentieth Anniversary Mac

In June 1997, Apple announced, appropriately enough, the Twentieth Anniversary Macintosh (or TAM) to mark the occasion. The system looked incredibly modern and had a tiny footprint thanks to a flat-screen monitor that was only found in notebooks at the time. The TAM also had a keyboard with a built-in trackpad. A custom sound system with external subwoofer manufactured for Apple by Bose and a unique bronze/brown color scheme completed the package.

While designed to look like a futuristic, concept computer, the TAM was built using parts from other shipping Macs. The 12-inch active-matrix screen, graphics card, and trackpad were borrowed from the PB 3400 while the TAM motherboard was borrowed from the Power Mac 5500. The TAM had a built-in TV/FM tuner and had cable TV connections and Picture In Picture (PIP) controls on the front of the display. The TAM was the first Mac to have an external power supply, eliminating many of the heat and space problems that other desktop computers had.

Only 12,000 TAMs were built, and they originally sold for $10,000. Included in the astronomical price was a concierge service with personalized delivery and setup, but that had to be scrapped when sales didn't pan out. Apple soon lowered the price, and TAMs could be purchased for as little as $1,999 in March 1998.

Newton and eMate

Apple continued updating its Newton MessagePad handheld computer, and in November 1997, released the NMP 2100 ($999), which increased the NMP 2000s RAM to 8MB with everything else being the same. Apple also released a new Newton in a notebook computer form-factor and called it the eMate 300.

The eMate 300 was introduced in March 1997 in an attempt to target the educational market. The eMate was essentially a repackaged Newton with a clamshell design and a keyboard—although a stylus could still be used. The design was unique in that it was the first use of translucent colored plastics later found in the Bondi blue iMac. A similar clamshell design was reused later in the original, first-generation iBooks, announced in July 1999.

The eMate 300 sold for $799 and came equipped with a 25MHz ARM 710a processor, 3MB RAM, a PCMCIA slot (later called "PC Card"), a Newton Inter Connect port, and Newton OS 2.1. It shipped with a similar backlit-grayscale screen to the NMP 2000 but in a landscape orientation.

Software

In January 1997, Apple released Mac OS 7.6, the last major update of Mac OS 7, which included an overhauled Extensions Manager, more PowerPC code for Power Macs, and more Internet tools.

Mac OS 8

On July 26, 1997, Apple released Mac OS 8, which was a major update to the operating system as indicated by the whole number change from 7 to 8. Minor releases were usually categorized in tenths (7.6) or hundredths (7.6.1), depending on the number of features that were added.

Mac OS 8 was the first major update to the Mac OS since System 7 was released six years prior. Mac OS 8 included many technologies that were destined for Apple's ill-fated Copland operating system. OS 8 was very commercially successful, selling more than 1.2 million copies in the first two weeks.[6]

Mac OS 8 included a new three-dimensional Platinum interface that was visually appealing and a native PowerPC multithreaded Finder. Apple also made major improvements to virtual memory, AppleScript, and shortened boot times. A new online Help system was added to supplement the existing Balloon Help and Apple Guide. The additional Help, accessed from the Info Center, was based on HTML and had the ability to link to pages on the Internet.

Other

When Apple announced the Power Macintosh G3 on November 10, 1997, it also made another significant announcement: the Apple Online Store. Both become instant hits. Apple's online store was built using NeXT's WebObjects Web application technology, which ironically also powered Dell's online store. When NeXT was purchased by Apple, Dell scrambled to rebuild its store using tools from Microsoft. Steve Jobs declared the new online store a success after receiving more than $12 million in orders in its first month of operation.

See other Apple milestones in Chapter 4, "Strategies and Innovations."

1998—APPLE'S RENAISSANCE

Hardware

The period between 1998 and 2001 is considered by many to be Apple's Renaissance because of the release of several new and innovative

Macs, including the iMac, iBook, and Power Mac G4 and also because it marked the company's return to profitability.

Read more about Apple finances in Chapter 10, "Finances."

In Steve Jobs's absence the company lost its focus, it was building too many products and not focusing on ones that were bringing in the most money. When Jobs returned, he killed the clones, dropped unprofitable products (like Newton), and winnowed Apple's product line down from dozens of SKUs to a simple quadrant of four major market segments. Along one axis were the segments, "consumer" and "professional," and along the other axis were the models, "portable" and "desktop."

The new simplicity made development and marketing much easier and also made it easier for customers to chose and purchase a Mac—which they did in droves.

PowerBook G3 Series

In May 1998, Apple introduced an updated PowerBook G3 in an all-new enclosure, which was an improvement over the previous PBG3's inherited 3400 enclosure. The new PowerBook G3 Series was given the extra moniker because it represented a new line of portable Macs, instead of just a single model. The PowerBook G3 Series was the first Configure-To-Order (CTO) portable, allowing buyers to configure virtually every aspect of the machine to fit their needs and budget, and prices ranged from $3,000 to $7,000 fully loaded.

Available options included a 233, 250, or 292MHz G3 processor and 12-inch passive-matrix, 13.3-inch or 14.1-inch Thin Film Transistor (TFT) active-matrix screen. Two RAM slots accepted industry-standard memory, like that used on the IBM ThinkPads. The PBG3 Series also included a redesigned keyboard with a new Function key that simulated the numeric keypad found on the full-size 105-key keyboard—without the extra space.

The new PBG3 Series came with two Card Bus compliant PC-card slots (formerly PCMCIA), a PowerBook first. The larger screen models (13.3- and 14.1-inch) also included an s-video out port. Another innovative first on the G3 Series was its two drive bays, which could accommodate an extra battery or a wide array of expansion modules, like floppy and Zip drives. The right drive bay was large enough to accommodate larger 5.25-inch mechanisms, including optical drives.

In September 1998, Apple made some critical changes to the PowerBook G3 line. Feature-wise the new Rev. 2 PowerBooks, as they became known, were merely incremental and somewhat expected: 233, 266, and 300MHz chips and a Level 2 cache. However, the more important change was the standardization on a single logic board and 14.1-inch screen for all PowerBooks. The new single design allowed Apple to streamline production and eliminate a major bottleneck that was plaguing the company all summer. Although mostly standardized, Apple kept a 12.1-inch model on the price list as a more economical alternative at $2,299.

Flat-screen Monitor

Although most Macs (other than the iMac) were still beige, Apple took another bold step in 1998, releasing its second flat-screen monitor. The first was released in 1984 for the Apple IIc and had no backlighting.

Apple released the 15-inch Apple Studio Display on March 17, 1998, with a resolution of 1024 × 768. It was the second Apple product to feature translucent plastics (the first was the eMate) and was announced two months before the iMac. Code-named *Manta,* the 15-inch panel was a hint of things to come with the iMac. The Apple Studio display came wrapped in a beautifully designed, transparent Azul blue bezel and adjustable stand. It came with DA-15, s-video, composite video, ADB, and audio connectors.

In January 1999, the color of the plastics was changed to a lighter blue with white accents to complement the new Power Mac G3s, and the connector was changed to VGA. The original Azul model is still considered a collector's item to many Mac fans.

iMac

After fielding a successful string of computers that utilized the PowerPC chips, Jobs took those chips and made a big bet on an entirely new Mac—one that fit squarely in the consumer desktop quadrant. On August 15, 1998, Apple introduced the iMac and by the end of the month, it had 150,000 pre-orders for the new machine. The iMac went on to become the fastest-selling computer in history.[7]

The $1,300 iMac was a totally redesigned, all-in-one computer "for the rest of us." Designed with the everyday user in mind, it was simple to set up and allowed users to get onto the Internet within minutes of opening the box. Apple touted this feature in new television commercials.

More revolutionary was its radical industrial design. Instead of the traditional beige and platinum boxes coming out of most computer manufacturers (including Apple), iMac was built from Bondi blue and translucent grey plastics, allowing users to see inside of their computer. Jobs had made the computer beautiful, separating it from everything else on the market, and turned the entire computer industry on its ear. Everything that came before it immediately looked dated at best, or mostly, just downright ugly.

For more on the iMac refer to Chapter 4, "Strategies and Innovations."

USB Keyboard and Mouse

Two other significant products were released with the iMac in 1998, the USB keyboard and mouse. The Apple USB Mouse (part number M4848) shipped in the iMac box and was included with all desktop Macs for the next two years. The "hockey puck" mouse got its name from its perfectly round shape. It was universally panned because the round shape and recessed mouse button made it difficult to tell which way was up without looking. Its small size gave some users hand cramps after extended use. Some called the round mouse one of Apple's worst mistakes.[8] The switch from Apple Desktop Bus (ADB) to the new, tiny round USB mouse was evolutionary, but many thought that the round design was form over function. So much so that a third-party company (Griffin Technology) released the iMate ADB to USB adapter that allowed iMac users to connect their old, familiar ADB mouse to the iMac. Another popular product was iCatch, a semitransparent shell that clipped onto the round mouse, making more elliptical in shape like the previous (ADB) mouse.

The original Apple USB keyboard (part number M2452) wasn't as universally criticized as its companion mouse. The iMac's USB keyboard became the new standard for all Macintosh models for the next two years. Like the iMac and USB mouse, its design was a radical departure from the keyboard it replaced. The square lines and solid colors of the past were replaced with Bondi blue translucent plastics and two notches along the top that supported connecting two other USB peripherals. The USB keyboard also came with a built-in stand and later came in a darker gray to complement the Power Mac line.

Death of the Newton

On February 27, 1998, Apple discontinued the Newton project due to the high losses. Apple reportedly spent more than $500 million on Newton, and it wasn't even close to turning a profit. One of Steve Jobs's goals when he returned to Apple was to bring the company back to profitability, and to achieve this goal, he eliminated products that weren't contributing to the bottom line—and Newton was one of them. Dropping Newton also fit with Jobs's mission of simplifying Apple's product line, which had grown wildly out of control in the early to mid-1990s.

Software

Mac OS 8.1, released on January 19, 1998, was the last version of the Mac OS to support 68KB processors. On October 17, 1998, Apple released Mac OS 8.5, which was the first Mac operating system designed to run exclusively on the PowerPC processor. Mac OS 8.5 greatly improved system performance because of the increased amount of PowerPC code.

New features in 8.5 included a search utility called Sherlock that searched both the Mac's hard drives and the Internet. Sherlock allows plug-ins to be installed that allowed users to search the contents of specific Web sites. Systemwide font anti-aliasing was also introduced, making type much easier to read on-screen, as were 32-bit icons. An application palette also appeared in Mac OS 8.5 as an answer to the Windows

95 taskbar. An application menu could be resized or torn off into a palette of buttons.

1999—COLORS OF THE RAINBOW

Rainbow-colored iMacs

In January 1999, Apple extended its iMac line and released revised models—in five new colors: Blueberry, Strawberry, Lime, Tangerine, and Grape. During his keynote address, Steve Jobs called the new colors "lickable" and consumers proceeded to eat them up. The new iMacs were simply a speed-bump of the original Bondi blue iMac minus the "mezzanine" slot and IRDA port. The Rev. C iMac, as it was known, sold for $1,199. For the first time, Apple offered the same machine in different colors. The problem with this strategy is that it caused inventory problems because resellers had to forecast their buyers' color preferences and subsequently keep much more than their normal amount of inventory in stock. Popular iMac colors, like purple, sold out quickly while there was a glut of less-popular colors, like Orange.

In April 1999, Apple released the Rev. D iMac, increasing the processor to 333MHz. A more significant change came in October when Apple introduced the iMac with a slot-loading optical drive, a first in a Mac. The slot-loading iMac was an extension of the success that Apple built with the Rev. D machine, adding a faster processor (350MHz), more RAM (64GB), better graphics (ATI Rage, 128MB), and an improved speaker system. Even with the improvements, the iMac SL was $200 less expensive than the previous model and at only $999 represented the cheapest Macintosh in many years.

The iMac DV (Digital Video) was the top-of-the-line machine in the iMac family. In addition to everything found in the iMac SL, the DV added a DVD-ROM drive, larger hard drive, two FireWire ports (a first on the consumer machine), and a VGA output for attaching a second monitor. In another first, the iMac DV was cooled by convection and didn't include an internal fan, making it the quietest Mac since the 512KB. The iMac DV came in five candy colors with 64GB RAM, and 10GB ATA hard drive for $1,299. A Special Edition (the iMac DV SE) was available in graphite, like the Power Mac G4, and came equipped with 128MB RAM and a 13GB hard drive for $1,499.

Blue and White Power Mac G3

Also in January, Apple released an entirely new desktop minitower enclosure that built on the design cues of the iMac. The new blue and white Power Mac G3 shared the same name as the previous tower, but that's about it. Designed in the same flavor as the iMac, the new B&W G3 featured a transparent blue-and-white enclosure that drew gasps from the audience at Macworld Expo when it was unveiled. The design was stunning, but it was more than just eye candy. The new case, code-named *El-Capitan,* featured an innovative, hinged door that swung open, making it easy to add cards and upgrade the memory. It was also the first Mac to support FireWire, and the first professional Mac to come with USB.

> For more on FireWire, see Chapter 4, "Strategies and Innovations."

The blue and white Power Mac G3 didn't come with standard serial ports, floppy drive, or SCSI—Apple went with Ultra ATA instead. The new Power Mac G3 started at $1,599 and went up to $5,000 fully loaded. In April 1999, it was speed-bumped to 450MHz.

PowerBook G3

In May 1999, Apple released a new PowerBook G3 with a bronze keyboard that was smaller and lighter than its predecessor. The new *Bronze* (as it became to be known) was a dramatic 20% thinner and nearly two pounds lighter and boasted significantly longer battery life than the previous model. However, some sacrifices had to be made to achieve the new form-factor. The largest sacrifice was a drop from two to one PC-card slot, which hardly made a difference to most users who gladly gave up the extra slot in exchange for the new model's lighter weight and svelte profile.

iBook

In a year of blockbuster product announcements, probably the largest was the announcement of an entirely new class of portable Mac, a consumer portable. Previously, Apple's notebook computer strategy targeted mostly the high end with machines that started at more than $2,000 and went as high as $7,000 fully configured. This price point left a lot of potential consumers (mostly students and teachers) out in the cold. Their budget simply could not afford to spend $3,000 on a notebook computer, and Apple was missing out on a major segment of the market.

Sensing this, Apple on July 21, 1999, introduced the iBook at the Macworld Expo in New York. Priced at $1,599, iBook cost almost $1,000 less than Apple's least-expensive professional PowerBook and was a boon for students and teachers. iBook targeted the same consumer market as the iMac and completed the simplified 2-by-2 product matrix (consumer, professional and desktop, portable) that Steve Jobs introduced a year earlier.

The iBook's specifications were similar to those of the iMac, offering the same essential lineup of ports, including USB and modem. In order to bring the price down, the design team dropped FireWire, PC slots, Infrared, and video-out and audio-in ports. FireWire became one of the defining distinctions between the consumer and professional portable lines.

The iBook included several firsts for Apple, including Accelerated Graphics Port (AGP)-based graphics, Unified Motherboard Architecture (UMA) that standardized components across motherboards, and a handle—something rarely found in a notebook computer.

Probably the most earth-shattering iBook feature was AirPort, a wireless networking standard that allowed it to surf the Internet and transfer files without connecting a single cable. AirPort wireless networking allowed up to 10 iBooks to access one wireless access point (which Apple called a *base station*). The companion base station could connect to an existing Ethernet network or dial-up Internet connection and share that connection to all the wireless clients. The iBook came with an AirPort antenna built into the monitor bezel and a PC-card sized slot. The $99 AirPort card had to be purchased separately, and it quickly became one of Apple's most popular options.

For more on AirPort, see Chapter 4, "Strategies and Innovations."

Announced in July, the iBook did not ship until late September, just in time for the back-to-school rush. And sell it did. By August, Apple took more than 140,000 pre-orders for iBooks.

Power Mac G4

On August 31, 1999, Steve Jobs introduced the first "desktop supercomputer," the Power Macintosh G4, at the Seybold conference in San Francisco. The Motorola MPC 7400 chip was a fourth-generation PowerPC chip, hence the *G4* moniker. Jobs called it a supercomputer because the G4 processor running at 500MHz was able to perform more than 1 billion instructions per second (a gigaflop). It was even classified as a weapon by the U.S. government, adding to the hype and mystique of the new machine.

The new G4 processor architecture allowed for multiprocessor configurations, and a Power Mac G4 running at 500MHz was up to three times faster than a Pentium III PC running at 600MHz. The G4 AGP also introduced a new professional color scheme that replaced the G3's blue and white with graphite (dark grey) and white. The new enclosure also featured a polished, almost mirror-like, finish where the previous G3 had more of a matte finish.

Much of the G4's performance came from a new set of instructions, which were executed by a new unit on the chip. Motorola referred to this new unit as the *AltiVec* unit, which Apple branded as the *Velocity Engine.* Regardless of what you called it, the new chip dramatically increased the speed of most processor-intensive tasks.

The Power Mac G4 shipped in two models. The Power Mac G4 with PCI graphics was based on the same motherboard as the blue and white G3 tower (minus the ADB port). The only difference was the addition of the Motorola MPC 7400, or G4, processor.

The Power Mac G4 with Accelerated Graphics Port (AGP) graphics (code-named *Sawtooth*) was based on the Unified Motherboard Architecture (UMA) that debuted in the iBook. The G4 AGP was built around an entirely new motherboard designed specifically for the G4 chip.

The Power Mac G4 (AGP) introduced a number of performance improvements, including AGP-based graphics, AirPort, faster memory, DVD-ROM or RAM, internal FireWire port, two separate USB buses, 2x (133MHz) AGP slot, and up to 1.5GB of RAM. The Power Mac G4 AGP started at $2,499 for the 450MHz model and $3,499 for the 500MHz configuration; both included internal Zip drives.

Supply chain problems plagued initial shipments of the Power Mac G4 that were blamed on Motorola. There was also a yield problem with the initial run of G4 chips that prevented them from achieving the 500MHz speed that Apple advertised. As a result, clock speeds were lowered in October to meet the new 450MHz ceiling that the chip was capable of. The 450MHz model was lowered to 400MHz, and the 500MHz model was lowered to 450MHz, although the price remained the same.

Mac OS 8.6

Mac OS 8.6 was released May 10, 1999, and was largely a maintenance release. Mac OS 8.6 added support for preemptive multitasking, but there was no process separation so the feature was mostly lost. Regardless, this free update for owners of Mac OS 8.5 and 8.5.1 was considered to be much faster and more stable than Mac OS 8.5. In fact, many considered 8.6 to be the most stable Classic OS ever released by Apple.

Mac OS 9

The most significant software release in 1999 was Mac OS 9. Released on October 23, 1999, Mac OS 9 (code-named *Sonata*) was the last version of the Classic Macintosh Operating System. OS 9 was marketed with 50 new features, including 128-bit encryption, automated software updates, support for multiple users, integrated support for Apple's iTools Internet applications (now known as .Mac), improved Open Transport networking, and Sherlock 2.

Sherlock 2 was a huge upgrade to Apple's search software (with a nod to Sherlock Holmes) and was considered the most important new feature in Mac OS 9. The new version improved over the original by adding support for searching numerous online resources. Sherlock 2 came installed with numerous channels and had a QuickTime-like metallic appearance.

2000—THE G4 CUBE

Apple starts off each year with a bang at its annual Macworld Expo conference and trade show in San Francisco, and 2000 was no exception.

Interim CEO Steve Jobs announced that he has accepted the job as the permanent CEO of Apple, dropping the *interim* from his title. Instead of focusing on major hardware announcements at Expo, the highlight of the 2000 show was a preview of the revolutionary new Mac OS X and its Aqua user interface. Apple announced new hardware, the Power Mac G4 cube at WWDC 2000.

For more on Macworld Expo, see the chapter Apple Conferences.

Hardware

Most of the hardware announced in 2000 was simply speed-bumps of existing Apple products that included faster processors, more memory, and larger hard drive. The iBook added FireWire, making the port standard on all Macs; the iMac got lower prices and new colors; the Power Mac G4 got Gigabit Ethernet (1000BaseT) and dual processors; the PowerBook got FireWire and the Unified Motherboard Architecture (UMA); and the Macintosh Server got AGP graphics and Gigabit Ethernet.

Apple started to turn more attention to its monitors in 2000 and began focusing on the transition to LCD, flat-panel designs. The previous Studio Display CRT monitors were replaced with the Studio Display LCDs in 15- and 17-inch sizes. The new monitors shipped with an innovative, hybrid Apple Display Connector (ADC), which carried data, USB, and power in a single cable. The new LCD monitors were thin and curvaceous and came wrapped in a beautiful clear acrylic bezel.

A couple of new accessories also hit the scene in 2000. The Apple Pro Keyboard and Mouse replaced their USB equivalents and, while still USB, feature dramatic new styling in glossy black and clear acrylics. Apple's new Pro Mouse featured an optical mechanism and made Apple the first company to ship an optical mouse with all its systems. The Apple Pro Mouse featured a unique mechanism that allowed three click force settings for the required pressure to click the mouse.

Power Mac G4 Cube

Probably the most exciting hardware announcement of 2000 was the Power Mac G4 Cube in July at Apple's Worldwide Developers Conference (WWDC). The Cube (as it came to be known) shipped in an entirely new form-factor that was like nothing Apple had ever produced before. The new computer, packing the powerful G4 chip, came in a tiny eight-inch cubed Lucite and grey box. Technically, it wasn't really a cube because it was slightly taller than eight inches, but that's for effect. The extra two inches or so give it the effect that the inner case, which is a cube, is suspended in the air.

The G4 Cube wasn't a Power Mac and it wasn't an iMac either, it was somehow both of them combined. Targeted at the business market, the Cube was positioned between the iMac and the Power Mac G4. It was designed for people that didn't have the budget for a Power Mac G4 and wanted more choice in monitors than the one that was built into the iMac.

In addition to being a thing of beauty, the G4 Cube was also an engineering marvel that packed a punch into a tiny footprint. While it didn't have the expandability of its larger brother, the Power Mac, the G4 Cube still managed to have three RAM slots, AirPort, two USB and two FireWire ports. Graphics were handled by a short 2x AGP card because the Cube didn't have room for a full-size AGP card. The Cube also featured a completely unconventional vertical, slot-loading DVD-ROM mechanism the ejected the discs up, like toast coming out of a toaster.

Apple Senior Vice President of Design, Jonathan Ive, won several international awards for the design of the Cube, and it was featured in many design magazines for breaking the mold of computer design. The Cube and its peripherals were shown in the Museum of Modern Art[9] and in the Digital Design Museum. Its ultra-contemporary design won it starring roles on several popular television shows, including "The Drew Carey Show," "Absolutely Fabulous," "The Real World: Chicago," "Curb Your Enthusiasm," and "24."

For more on Jonathan Ive, see Chapter 8, "Apple Leadership."

The base 450MHz model with 20GB hard drive, 64GB of RAM sold for $1,799 while the zippier 500MHz configuration with 30GB and 128MB sold for $2,199. Like the iMac DV, the Cube cooled itself via convection and thus didn't need a fan. As a result, it ran very quietly to the delight of owners that liked to display it on top of (as opposed to underneath) their desk.

Despite its good looks, the Cube had its detractors. It was criticized for lacking standard audio and input ports; instead of putting these standard ports on the case, Apple included an external USB amplifier with Harman Kardon speakers. While the amplifier had an audio output, the only way to get audio into the Cube was through a USB connection—a little ahead of its time.

Early runs of the Cube had "mold lines," "knit lines," "scratches," or "hairline cracks" around the screw holes on the top and near the drive slot on the front and top. The marks were quite controversial at the time and were called different things by different people. The marks turned out to be the result of the production process and were only cosmetic.

Positioning the Cube in the market was also a source of trouble for Apple. The Cube didn't fit into Steve Jobs's tidy two-by-two matrix. It was certainly on the desktop axis, but it was neither a consumer nor a professional machine. Price was an issue, at $1,799, it cost $200 more than a comparable Power Mac. The price premium took a toll on sales and relegated the Cube into the category of niche/art machines that were mostly purchased by high-end customers looking for more of a showpiece than a computer.

Mac OS X

The most significant Apple development in 2000 was Steve Jobs's public demonstration of Mac OS X (pronounced *Mac OS Ten*) at Macworld Expo in San Francisco. The new operating system strategy was a bold step into the future that was accelerated by Apple's acquisition of NeXT in 1996.

Copland

Copland was supposed to be Apple's next-generation operating system and the successor to Apple's Classic operating systems (up to and including Mac OS 9). System 7.5 was code-named *Mozart* and the next-generation OS got its name from composer Aaron Copland. The Classic Mac OS was growing increasingly unstable and suffering from crashes that would bring down the entire machine due to a lack of protected memory. Copland was designed to address these flaws with features like protected memory and multitasking. The Copland project began in 1994 and was abandoned in August 1996 in favor of buying NeXT's NEXTSTEP operating system, which eventually became Mac OS X.

OS X was a completely new type of operating system with a totally different architecture than anything Apple had shipped in the past. At its heart is BSD UNIX with complete access to system-level functions via the command line, a feature never before available to Mac users. Apple released the core of the operating system as free and open source software called Darwin.

Mac OS X included several features designed to make it more stable and crash-resistant. Protected memory and pre-emptive multitasking allow the operating system to run several applications in parallel, in their own memory. If one application crashes, it doesn't crash the other, or worse, crash the whole operating system. Apple included a new set

---

Taligent

Taligent came from a combination of the words *Talent* and *Intelligent*. It was the name of a modern object-oriented operating system project within Apple Computer during the 1990s that was being developed to replace the Classic Mac OS. Taligent was later spun-off into a joint venture with IBM as a defensive move to compete with Microsoft's Cairo and NeXT's NEXTSTEP operating systems. Taligent was dissolved in the late 1990s.

---

of programming tools for developers, most notably an Integrated Development Environment (IDE) called Xcode, which provided compilers that support several modern programming languages.

On January 6, 2000, Steve Jobs demonstrated Mac OS X's most visible feature during his keynote address at Macworld Expo in San Francisco, the Aqua user interface. Aqua was a definite crowd-pleaser; its rounded curves, anti-aliased edges, drop shadows, and transparency brought a new dimension to the OS that the Mac user had never seen before, and it was greeted with loud cheers of enthusiasm during Jobs's keynote address.

Because Mac OS X inherited Application Programming Interfaces (APIs) from NEXTSTEP (known as Cocoa), it wasn't backward compatible with previous versions of the Mac OS. Apple built a Classic Environment, the Carbon Application Programming Interface (API), to accommodate programs written for the older versions of the Mac OS. This allowed programs written with Carbon to run natively on both operating systems, easing the transition to OS X for both users and developers.

A public beta or "preview" version of OS X was released on September 13, 2000, in order to get feedback from users. The public beta was based on Developer Preview 4 (DP4) and sold for $29.95 with a T-shirt. It was very buggy and not recommended for production systems, but it gave the masses their first hands-on experience with the new operating system. In it the familiar Apple logo was moved to the middle of the menu bar, but after a public outcry, the Apple logo was moved back to its traditional location on the left side of the menu bar. The public beta expired and stopped working in Spring 2001.

Other

Apple.com was registered on February 19, 1987, making it the 64th-oldest registered.com domain name. In early 2000, the Apple's Web site was completely redesigned, featuring a new tabbed interface with tabs for Apple's online store; iReview, dedicated to reviews of online content; and iTools, which included free Internet services like Web space, iCards, free online greeting cards, QuickTime, and Support.

In 2000, Apple released the last version of its AppleWorks office software suite. AppleWorks 6 was ported to the Carbon API to work on Mac OS X and replaced the communications feature with a dedicated presentation application.

2001—THE ITUNES AND IPOD REVOLUTION

Hardware

Apple continued its trend of *speed-bumping* and improving its existing product line with faster processors, more memory, and larger hard drives. A new trend that Apple started to practice in 2001 was to release an updated model for the same price as the model it replaced. It was a win/win for Apple and its customers because the customer got something better and faster than the previous model for the same price as before and Apple didn't have to cut prices. It was like a price cut, only better for Apple.

The flipside of this strategy is that there was some speculation that Apple was practicing "planned obsolescence," or releasing products at intentionally lower speeds and capacities to "leave room" for the inevitable upgrade that was coming in 9 to 12 months.

New Desktop Designs

In 2001, the iMac got FireWire, finally bringing it to the entire Mac family; better graphics; and a dramatic change from the previous solid colors to outrageous patterns right out of the 1970s. Rather than being painted on, the new patterns were molded into the iMac case using a special technique that reportedly took Apple 18 months to perfect.

Apple replaced the rather pedestrian (in comparison) transparent Sage and Ruby color for Blue Dalmatian, which could best be described as a powder blue pattern with white polka dots or ovals and "Flower Power," which was a collage of pastel daisies on a white background. Reaction to the new iMac patterns seemed to be divided down party lines with Mac users generally in favor and traditional PC-types crying in agony. *PC World* magazine dubbed the Flower Power iMac one of the ugliest products in tech history.[10] In July 2001, Apple changed the iMacs back to more traditional graphite and snow color schemes.

On April 18, 2001, Apple announced that it has shipped its five millionth iMac, making it the most successful personal computer ever.

The PowerMac G4 got a built-in amplifier designed to power new USB speakers and the line did away with multiprocessor configurations so that Apple could ship sufficient quantities of machines. The most innovative part of the Power Mac line was a new, optional "SuperDrive," which could read and write DVDs and CDs; previous "Combo drives" could read and write CDs but only read DVDs. Apple shipped easy-to-use DVD authoring software, iDVD, alongside the new drives and sold a professional version called DVD Studio Pro. In July 2001, Apple slightly modified the Power Mac G4 enclosure (code-named *Quicksilver*) to be more streamlined and rounded but the color scheme was largely the same.

New Notebook Designs

The major hardware changes in 2001 were mostly to the notebook computers. Apple introduced an entirely new iBook design at a press event in May 2001 that brought the consumer notebook more in line with the design of the professional PowerBook. The new iBook was much smaller; its design more traditional and squared off. Apple traded the radical colors for pure white. The new iBook Dual USB included a faster G3 processor, 12-inch screen, two USB ports, more RAM, VGA output, and was the first Mac to include a Combo optical drive in the high-end model that could read and write CDs and read DVDs. In October 2001, the iBook got a speed-bump in CPU and bus speed; RAM and hard drives were also increased.

Simplicity and the Move to White

The year 2001 was the year that Apple dropped some of its more garish color schemes, like Flower Power iMac and the nearly fluorescent key lime green iBook for more traditional models in graphite (dark grey and white). It also dropped the radical, curvy design of the original iBook for a more conservative rectangular shape.

The PowerBook G4 also got a new design in January 2001 that was just as dramatic as the iBook's. The professional Apple notebook went from a dark gray plastic enclosure to a titanium case that was only one-inch thick when closed—0.7 inches thinner than the PowerBook G3 it replaced. The new, thinner design did away with the removable optical drive because

The PowerBook G4 Titanium. Image © John Greenleigh, www.flipsidestudios.com.

of space constraints, but consumers were more than willing to make the trade-off.

The new PowerBook Titanium also got a low-power G4 chip (the PPC 7410) and a wide-aspect 15.2-inch screen, running at 1152 × 768 resolution, which made the case wider but less deep. Prices for the new TiBook ranged from $2,599 to $3,499 and a speed-bump in October added Gigabit Ethernet, better graphics, L2 cache, and a $400 to $500 price drop.

iTunes

iTunes was introduced at Macworld Expo 2001 in San Francisco. The software was designed for playing and organizing digital music files and in October became the conduit for moving music to and from the iPod digital media player.

iTunes began life as a media player called SoundJam MP written by Jeff Robbin and Bill Kincaid[11] and released by Casady & Greene in 1999. SoundJam was acquired by Apple in 2000 and was given a new user interface and the ability to burn CDs. Apple removed the ability to record and dropped support for skins and released the resulting application as iTunes 1.0 at Macworld Expo on January 9, 2001.

Although there were other MP3 players available for Windows (notably WinAmp) and other Mac programs in development (like Audion[12]), SoundJam MP was first out of the gate and forever changed the way we consume music and later videos, television, and music.

For more on the iTunes, see Chapter 4, "Strategies and Innovations."

iPod

Without question, the most significant product release of 2001, and maybe the decade, was a little white handheld device that could play MP3 audio files through a pair of headphones. The white plastic and chrome device had a unique wheel interface that you turned to navigate a simple series of hierarchical menus to select the song, album, or artist that you wanted to listen to.

Why was Apple releasing a product that played music? Shouldn't it have been designing a new computer? Not many people would have wagered that the little music player would not only reinvent Apple, but also consumer electronics, mobile phones, music, and almost the entire entertainment industry too. But it did.

The original iPod was announced on October 23, 2001, and was Apple's first foray into digital music. The unit was about the size of a deck of cards and came equipped with a 5GB hard drive and a FireWire port—a first on a portable music player. The iPod was based on the Portal Player PP5002 system-on-a-chip, consisting of two embedded ARM7TDMI chips. It also had 32MB of RAM, which was mostly for "skip protection."

Although other hard drive–based music players existed, Apple's was different because it used a 1.8-inch hard drive mechanism, making it much smaller and more portable than the competition. In fact, iPod was able to compete with flash-based MP3 players that had a fraction of the capacity. The most popular flash-based player at the time, the Diamond Rio PMP300, held 32MB of music or roughly 12 songs and sold for $250 (about $21 per song). The iPod 5GB, on the other hand, held 1,000 songs and sold for $400 or 40 *cents* per song.

The Diamond Rio PMP300

The Rio PMP300 by Diamond Multimedia was actually the second portable consumer MP3 digital audio player shipping in 1998. The first MP3 player was the Eiger Labs MPMan F10, which was available during the summer of 1998.

In March 2002, Apple added a 10GB iPod to its lineup that was priced at $499. And in July 2002, Apple replaced the mechanical scroll wheel with a solid-state touch wheel, which was based on the trackpad technology found in its iBook and PowerBook notebook computers.

For more on the trackpad, see "The Trackpad—1994" in Chapter 4.

Apple's iPod numbers continue to impress: more than 15 hardware designs, 20 capacities, 20 colors, 70% market share (in units), 84% market share (in dollar volume), and more than 150 million iPods sold (as of this writing). iPod shows no signs of letting up.

For more on the iPod, see Chapter 4, "Strategies and Innovations."

Mac OS 9

Apple continued to revise Mac OS 9 in 2001 but it was only to fix bugs. The majority of Apple's operating system team had moved over to work on Mac OS X. Updates to Mac OS 9 included the following: 9.0.4 included fixes for USB and FireWire; 9.1 added CD burning support in the Finder and added a new Window menu in the Finder; 9.2 (July) increased performance noticeably but required at least a G3 processor; 9.2.1 (August); and 9.2.2 (December).

Mac OS X

After several years of development and a successful public beta period, Mac OS X was released on March 24, 2001. Mac OS X was a revolutionary upgrade where all previous operating system upgrades had been evolutionary. OS X combined the stability, reliability, and security of a UNIX operating system with the ease of use that Mac users were accustomed to. To top it all off, Apple included a beautifully designed, and completely overhauled, user interface called Aqua.

Aqua had many significant new features, including systemwide anti-aliasing of widgets; text graphics and windows; drop-shadows transparency in some windows and menus, which added depth; ColorSync color matching built into the core of the operating system; a Dock that was a launcher for applications and document shortcuts; OpenGL hardware accelerated drawing (later called Quartz Extreme); PDF support for both opening and saving documents; and a set of Human Interface Guidelines, which gave applications a consistent user interface and keyboard shortcuts.

Mac OS X version 10.0 (code-named *Cheetah*) was publicly released on March 24, 2001, but was considered slow, buggy (kernel panics were frequent), and missing many features found in OS 9, like DVD playback. The release was a silent release and didn't have a big splash; instead Apple wanted to have a major release for Mac OS 10.1, which was more stable, at Macworld Expo in New York.

Mac OS X version 10.1 (code-named *Puma*) was publicly released on September 25, 2001, and was a free upgrade for owners of 10.0. Mac OS 10.1 included better performance and added features like DVD playback.

Apple's OS X Cats

Apple liked to code-name its Mac OS X releases after cats.

Mac OS X, version 10.0, was code-named *Cheetah,* 10.1 was *Puma,* 10.2 was *Jaguar,* 10.3 was *Panther,* 10.4 was *Tiger,* 10.5 was *Leopard,* and 10.6 was *Snow Leopard.* Apple has also registered trademark #78271630 for *Cougar* and #78271639 for *Lynx,* presumably for future versions of the OS.

Users discovered that Apple's free 10.1 upgrade CDs could be converted to full install CDs by removing a specific file. Apple later closed that loophole. Apple began selling a boxed version of Mac OS X in retail packaging to Mac OS 9 users for $129.

Retail

Apple developed a retail store chain in an effort to increase its market share. On May 19, 2001, Apple opened its first dedicated retail stores in Tyson's Corner, Virginia (near Washington, D.C.) and Glendale, California (near Los Angeles), offering hardware and software products for Macintosh, personal one-on-one support staffed by Apple "Geniuses," demonstrations, and training. All of Apple's hardware products are on display for customers to try. By the end of 2001, Apple opened another 27 stores across the United States.

For more on Apple's retail store chain, see Chapter 4, "Strategies and Innovations."

2002—XSERVE AND EMAC

Notebook Hardware

In 2002, Apple continued to build upon the success of its hardware line and released both speed-bumps (evolutionary increases in CPU, GPU, RAM, and hard drive) and entirely new hardware designs (iMac, eMac, and Xserve).

In the evolutionary category, Apple released speed-bumps of most of its hardware over the course of the year, usually around its major conferences, Macworld Expo and WWDC. Both the consumer and professional notebooks were enhanced. In January 2002, Apple released an iBook with a 14.1-inch screen, complementing the original 12-inch model and giving people needing a larger screen an alternative to the more expensive PowerBook. The 14-inch iBook came with 600MHz, 256MB RAM, 20GB hard drive, and a CD-R/DVD-ROM Combo drive for $1,799.

Apple also repriced the 12-inch iBook; the CD-ROM model moved to $1,199, the CD-RW model was dropped, the DVD-ROM model (available only as a Built to Order option) was now $1,299, and the Combo Drive model was dropped to $1,499. In addition, iBooks also got faster CPUs, more VRAM, and various changes in price and configuration.

The professional-level PowerBook G4 got a speed-bump as well in 2002 but also an architectural change. The new PBG4 announced in April got a DVI port (replacing the VGA out on the previous model), which could be adapted to both VGA and ADC, and an audio input port, which was eliminated in the original PowerBook G4. In addition, Apple added a higher-resolution screen (1280 × 854), faster CPUs, faster graphics, better optical drive, and larger hard drives. The PowerBook G4 (DVI) came in two configurations, 667MHz for $2,499 and 800MHz model for $3,199.

In November, the PBG4 made a large psychological jump to a 1GHz CPU and added a slot-loading SuperDrive that could read and write both CDs and DVDs—both firsts for Apple. The 1.0 GHz model, with 512MB of RAM, 60GB hard drive, SuperDrive, and built-in AirPort cost $2,999, making it one of the most inexpensive PowerBooks ever.

Desktop Hardware

Xserve

On May 6, 2002, Apple announced a new server called Xserve at the WWDC. This marked the first time the company announced a hardware product at the conference, which typically focuses on software.

Xserve was Apple's first machine specifically designed to be rack-mounted. Xserve is just 1U (1.75-inches) or one *rack unit* thick. One rack unit is commonly designated as *1U*. The size of a piece of rack-mounted equipment is usually described as a number in *U*. Most server racks have 42 U of height. Xserve was designed to consume as little vertical space as possible to reduce costs for customers paying to co-locate the machine at a hosting facility, which often charges by the rack unit.

Xserve represented a significant push into the server market after Apple failed to penetrate it with its Network Servers (in February 1996) and achieved only limited success with its Workgroup and Macintosh Server lines (which were the desktop Macs with a different software bundle).

Because it was engineered from the ground up to be a server, Xserve included several server-oriented innovations, including multicolored LEDs that showed hard drive access, processor load, and Ethernet status; and four unique front-loading drive bays that could be accessed while it was mounted in a server rack. The drive bays are hot pluggable with each running on its own UltraATA-100 bus. Xserve could originally be configured with up to 480GB of storage with four 120GB drives; today that number is much higher, limited only by drive capacity.

The original Xserve also included Double Data Rate (DDR) RAM, two full-length PCI card slots, and a PCI/4x AGP slot that was usually filled with graphics or Gigabit Ethernet cards. Xserve shipped with a second Gigabit Ethernet (multiple Ethernet ports were useful on servers), three FireWire ports, two USB ports, a serial port, and a tray-load 24x CD-ROM drive. Today's Xserves are still popular, shipping with faster system and memory buses and memory, multiple-core processors, and a hardware RAID option.

The original Xserve was available in two configurations, a 1.0GHz that sold for $2,999, and a high-end model with dual 1.0GHz processors that sold for $3,999. Both included Mac OS X Server 10.2 Jaguar.

Power Mac

After just receiving a slightly updated skin in July 2001, the Power Mac G4 was modified in August 2002 to include a 1GHz processor and a Level 3 cache (on the middle and high-end models and several new graphics card options). In August 2002, the Power Mac G4's enclosure was (again) slightly modified with mirrored doors over the optical drives. The motherboard was enhanced to include several features from the new Xserve rack-mount server. The bus speed was raised to 166MHz, a Double Data Rate (DDR) SDRAM memory bus was included, and dual processors and enhanced graphics cards were added across the line.

The "mirrored drive doors" (a.k.a. MDD) Power Mac G4 had the unfortunate distinction of being one of the loudest Power Macs ever and earned the nickname *G4 Windtunnel*. Apple later offered a fan and power supply replacement to address the problem. In July 2003, when Apple announced the Power Mac G5, the Power Mac G4 (MDD) was reissued as the last Mac OS 9 bootable Power Mac.

iMac

In 2002, the iMac continued to be a big seller for Apple—the machine that arrived in May 1998 was truly Apple's computer for the new millennium. Building on its previous successes, Apple announced the first totally redesigned iMac at Macworld Expo on January 7, 2002. The new design included a 15-inch flat-panel monitor attached to the articulating chrome arm reminiscent of the popular Luxo desk lamps. Not coincidentally, the flat-panel iMac looked a lot like the iconic "Luxo the Lamp" character from the first Pixar Animation Studios film and corporate logo—a company that Steve Jobs also heads.

The new flat-panel iMac was the first to ship with a G4 processor and the CD-RW/DVD-R SuperDrive. It also featured an elegant domed case that allowed users to position the new flat screen in multiple locations and move it easily, thanks to the new "desk lamp" design. Apple started the transition to flat-panel monitors in 2000, and the new iMacs were the culmination of Apple's strategy. When he announced the new iMac in his keynote address, Steve Jobs told attendees "the CRT is officially dead."

For more on flat-panel monitors, see Chapter 4, "Strategies and Innovations."

The flat-panel iMac shipped in three configurations, mostly differentiated by their optical drive, which Apple marketed as "Good," "Better," and "Best." The low-end model with a 700MHz G4 processor and CD-RW drive sold for $1,299, the middle or "Better" model came with the same processor and a Combo Drive for $1,499, and the top-of-the-line "Best" model had a 800MHz chip and SuperDrive for $1,799.

The middle and high-end model included Apple Pro Speakers and all iMac configurations included Apple's new white version of the Pro Keyboard and Mouse that it released with the G4 Cube in 2000. Introduced on July 17, 2002, the 17-inch iMac was identical to the 15-inch flat-panel iMac but with a larger, 1440 × 900 resolution monitor and was priced at $1,999.

For more on iMac, see Chapter 4, "Strategies and Innovations."

iPod

In March 2002, Apple speed-bumped the iPod to 10GB, doubling its capacity to accommodate larger music libraries for $499. In July 2002, Apple replaced the iPod's mechanical scroll wheel with a solid-state, touch-sensitive pad in the same shape. The new touch pad–based wheel borrowed Apple's popular trackpad technology introduced in the PowerBook.

Also in July 2002, Apple increased iPod's capacity to 20GB ($499) and lowered the prices of the 10GB ($399) and 5GB ($299) models. The 5GB model retained the original, moving scroll wheel.

eMac

In April 2002, Apple announced the eMac, which was short for "education Mac." eMac combined a 17-inch monitor and G4-based Mac in a design reminiscent of the first-generation, frost white iMac. eMac was designed to be less expensive (due to its CRT monitor) to compete with low-cost PCs in the competitive educational market. Originally sold only to schools, eMac was later mass-marketed to consumers to fill the gap between the discontinued $799 CRT iMac and the more expensive $1,499 flat-panel iMac. The public eMac came in two configurations, a 700MHz G4, which sold for $1,099, and an 800MHz G4 that sold for $1,499.

Apple Cinema HD Display

In March 2002, Apple replaced the 22-inch monitor with a slightly larger 23-inch Apple Cinema HD Display. The new 23-inch Cinema HD Display complemented its 17- and 22-inch (non-HD) models with a native resolution of 1920 × 1200 and supported full 1080p resolution, hence the *HD* moniker.

Software

At Macworld Expo 2002 in New York, the free service launched in 2000 as iTools was relaunched as a subscription-based service called *.Mac* with dedicated technical support and several new or upgraded tools to subscribers, including a personal Web hosting service (HomePage), an online disk storage service (iDisk), an e-mail service with @mac.com e-mail addresses, a personal back-up service (Backup) that allowed users to archive data to their iDisk, CD, or DVD, and an online greeting card service (iCards).

The move from free to paid was very controversial as many people thought that Apple would continue to provide these services for free. Apple said that the move was necessary to offset the massive costs associated with iDisk and e-mail storage space and increasing support needs. Apple also announced a digital photo management application called iPhoto that built on the success and ease of use of iTunes. iPhoto would later go on to become a key component of Apple's iLife software suite.

Mac OS 10.2

On August 23, 2002, Apple released Mac OS X version 10.2 *Jaguar,* which was the third major release of the Mac operating system and the first to use its code name as part of its branding. Apple included a Jaguar print desktop picture as part of the software and a large spotted *X* on the Jaguar-themed box. Because of an agreement with the car manufacturer Jaguar, Mac OS 10.2 was never officially referred to as *Jaguar* in the United Kingdom.

The newest version of the Apple operating system included more than 150 new features, according to Apple, including iChat, Address Book, Bluetooth support, Bonjour (formerly Rendezvous), Common UNIX Printing System (or CUPS), a revamped Finder, Mail, QuickTime 6, Quartz Extreme, Sherlock 3, Universal Access, Inkwell, support for Microsoft Windows networks, a journaled file system (which logs changes to a journal before committing them to the main file system), and overall speed increases.

The famous "Happy Mac" logo was dropped from Mac OS X 10.2 and replaced with a large grey Apple logo. Jaguar was sold for $129, or $199 for a "family pack," a new option from Apple that allowed the software to be installed on up to five computers in one household. OS X wasn't serialized or copy protected so the family pack option was offered on the honor system.

Retail

In 2002, Apple expanded its operations by opening 24 new stores for a total of 51, including flagship stores in New York's Soho district and in Los Angeles.

2003—IBOOK G4 AND ALUMINUM POWERBOOKS

Hardware

Apple continued its tradition of updating most of its hardware with speed-bumps every 9 to 12 months, with some exceptions, and new designs replacing old ones every two to four years.

iMac

In 2003, Apple enhanced the iMacG4 and simplified the product line down to two models—15- and 17-inch. The 17-inch included several new features to the motherboard, including internal Bluetooth, AirPort Extreme, and Double Data Rate (DDR) RAM. The 15-inch model sold for $1,299 and the 17-inch with SuperDrive sold for $1,799. In September, the 15-inch model was speed-bumped to bring it in line with the 17-inch model and a new model with a 20-inch screen was added in November.

Power Mac G4

The Power Mac G4 was speed-bumped in January 2003 with a FireWire 800 port, built-in Bluetooth, and support for the new AirPort Extreme wireless networking system. The new Power Mac G4 was the fastest and least expensive line of Power Macs Apple had ever introduced, with the 1.0GHz model selling for $1,499.

In 2003, the PowerMac G4 with mirror drive doors was re-released as the last OS 9 bootable Power Mac. This was necessary to accommodate Mac users that still needed OS 9 to run production applications that hadn't yet been ported to run natively in Mac OS X, like Quark XPress.

Power Mac G5

In June 2003, Apple announced the Power Mac G5, a fifth-generation PowerPC processor (dubbed the *G5*) wrapped in an industrial-looking aluminum enclosure. Apple and IBM worked closely to develop the 64-bit, PowerPC 970 processor, which was the first 64-bit consumer-level desktop computer ever sold and the world's fastest personal computer at the time.

The Power Mac G5 included several enhancements, including PCI-X slots, an 8x AGP slot, Serial-ATA (SATA) bus, and up to 8GB of RAM. The front-side bus speed was increased to half of the processor speed—up to 1GHz—a six-fold improvement over the Power Mac G4.

The PowerPC G5 was a much higher-power and higher-temperature chip than its predecessors, though. A lot of engineering resources went into the cooling system inside the Power Mac G5, which required nine computer-controlled fans. It came in three configurations: the 1.6GHz model sold for $1,999, the 1.8GHz sold for $2,399, and the dual 2.0GHz model sold for $2,999. In November, Apple dropped the price of the 1.6GHz model to $1,799 and replaced the single 1.8GHz model with a dual 1.8GHz model for $2,499.

Xserve

In February 2003, Apple speed-bumped the Xserve with a faster (1.33GHz) single or dual G4 processor, faster memory bus, and a slot-loading optical drive. Apple also introduced the Xserve RAID, a 3U (rack unit) storage system that could accommodate 14 hard drives, each on its own ATA-100 bus. At just over $4 per gigabyte, Apple's new RAID was a fraction of the cost of competing RAIDs from Dell, HP, or Sun. In March, Apple released the Xserve Cluster Node, which was designed to act as a cluster in a node of Xserves. It shipped without an optical drive or graphics card and only supported a single ATA hard drive.

iBook G3 and G4

In April 2003, the 12- and 14-inch iBook G3s were speed-bumped by 100MHz to 800 and 900MHz. In October, Apple released the iBook G4, completing the transition from G3 to G4 throughout the product line. The iBook G4 also inherited a slot-loading optical drive, better graphics, USB 2.0, AirPort Extreme, Bluetooth support, and faster system and memory buses.

PowerBook G4 Aluminum

On January 7, 2003, at Macworld Expo in San Francisco, new Power-Book G4s were announced that came packaged in a new, sleek 1-inch thick aluminum case. Two new screen sizes were offered (12- and 17-inch), expanding the professional notebook line to 12-, 15-, and 17-inch models.

The new PBG4 12-inch was similar to the iBook, except that it was housed in aluminum, smaller, and weighed just 4.6 pounds. The new PBG4 featured an updated motherboard design, which included Double Data Rate (DDR) RAM, internal Bluetooth, AirPort Extreme, NVIDIA graphics, and a mini-VGA port (borrowed from the iBook). In September, the Power-Book G4 12-inch was speed-bumped to include mini-DVI, and USB 2.0.

The new PBG4 17-inch shipped with a massive 1440 × 900, 16:10 aspect ratio screen—the largest screen of any notebook computer on the market and the world's first 17-inch notebook.[13] The PowerBook G4 17-inch was the most full-featured Apple notebook computer ever and included several firsts. It included the world's first fiber-optic backlit keyboard and ambient light sensors that can automatically control the brightness of the keyboard and the screen. It was also the first PowerBook to include FireWire 800, PC2700 Double Data Rate (DDR) RAM, and one of the first Macs to include internal Bluetooth and AirPort Extreme.

For more on the ambient light sensor, see Chapter 4, "Strategies and Innovations."

The titanium PowerBook G4 design, now two years old, was having trouble with paint flaking off and was generally starting to feel old, especially when compared to the spiffy, new aluminum PowerBooks. After the aluminum PowerBooks were announced in January, titanium Power-Book sales ground to a halt, as people anticipated the aluminum 15-inch, and nine months felt like an eternity. On September 16, 2003, at the Apple Expo in Paris, the day finally came. Apple announced one of the most-anticipated computers in years, the 15-inch aluminum PowerBook G4.

The PowerBook G4 15-inch aluminum was brought up to feature parity with its 17-inch sibling, including USB 2.0, AirPort Extreme, internal Bluetooth, FireWire 800, faster system and memory buses, and a faster optical drive.

iPod

At a special Apple Event on April 28, 2003, Apple announced an updated third-generation iPod that included a new all-touch interface. The new iPod had rounded edges and moved the four buttons that were previously located around the scroll wheel to the top of the scroll wheel. The new buttons were backlit and solid-state. The new iPod was thinner and lighter than previous models at only 0.73 inches deep and weighed just 0.39 pounds.

The previous iPod's FireWire port was replaced with a proprietary, 30-pin "dock connector" and cables for either FireWire or USB computers. The new dock connector enabled a whole new world of accessory options for the iPod and, while inconvenient for Mac users, made the iPod much more Windows PC-friendly.

Apple dropped support for the Windows MusicMatch software on October 16, 2003, in favor of the newly released iTunes 4.1 for Windows, a free download from Apple.com that was included with Windows-formatted iPods. Windows PC users no longer had any barriers to buying iPods, and sales soon skyrocketed.

Apple also added several software enhancements to the new iPods, including on-the-go playlists and voice notes, which weren't available on older models.

iTunes Music Store

At that same event, Steve Jobs announced a new iTunes 4 feature, an integrated music store, called the iTunes Music Store (later shortened to just "iTunes Store") where 200,000 songs are available for purchase for 99 cents each and full albums for $9.99 each. The store can be accessed from iTunes from a computer and from portable media players such as the iPhone and iPod touch over a wireless Internet connection.

The iTunes Store was the first true alternative to downloading music illegally from file-sharing networks, offering a large catalog of songs for sale from all five of the major record labels including, BMG, EMI, Sony Music Entertainment, Universal, and Warner.

Apple continually expands the offerings, once mostly limited to music, in the iTunes Store to many other categories of entertainment. Thanks to the iTunes Store, Apple is now the top music retailer in the United States,[14] online or offline. As of January 2008, the store has sold 4 billion songs, accounting for more than 70% of worldwide online digital music sales.

For more on iTunes Music Store, see Chapter 4, "Strategies and Innovations."

iSight Camera

At WWDC on June 23, 2003, Apple released iSight, a $149 Webcam especially designed for the use with iChat AV and iMovie. iSight was very elegantly designed and featured a maximum resolution of 640 × 480 pixels (24-bit) at 30 fps, built-in microphone, FireWire connection, and a series of mount kits for attaching it to the open lid of a PowerBook, iMac, or to any monitor.

Mac OS 10.3

Continuing the theme of marketing new operating systems by their cat code names, Mac OS X v10.3 *Panther* was released on October 24, 2003.

Panther required a G3, G4, or G5 processor and 128MB of RAM and wouldn't run on Apple's beige PowerMac G3s or on *Wallstreet* (Power-Book G3s). Apple included several new features in Panther, including a brushed-metal interface, real-time search engine, and customizable side-bar in the Finder, Fast User Switching, Exposé, TextEdit compatibility with Microsoft Word (.doc) documents, updated Xcode developer tools, enhanced Preview with PDF rendering, and updates to QuickTime.

Apple also included six totally new software applications in Panther: CoreAudio, Font Book, FileVault, iChat AV, X11, and a new Web browser, called Safari, that was developed to replace Internet Explorer when the contract between Apple and Microsoft ended.

Retail

In 2003, Apple expanded its retail operations by opening 22 new stores for a total of 73. New international Apple retail stores were opened in Japan, the United Kingdom, Canada, Italy, and Australia.

2004—MAC'S 20TH ANNIVERSARY

The year 2004 marks the 20th anniversary of the Macintosh and in memory of the event, Steve Jobs began his keynote speech by running the famous "1984" television commercial.

Hardware

Apple continued its tradition of updating most of its hardware with speed-bumps every 9 to 12 months, with some exceptions, and new de-signs replacing old every two to four years,

iMac

On August 31, 2004, at Apple Expo in Paris, Apple announced a completely redesigned iMac G5. The pivoting swivel arm and domed base from the Luxo iMac G4 was replaced with a sleek design that concealed the computer behind its flat-screen monitor. The iMac wasn't much larger than Apple's Cinema Display flat-screen monitors; with the case extending a few inches below the bottom of the monitor and only two inches deep, it could easily be mistaken for a monitor. Optical discs are fed, slot-loading into a slot on the right side of the bezel. The Apple design team led by Jonathan Ive had released another design masterpiece.

While not quite as dramatic as previous iMac designs, the new all-in-one Mac embodied one of Ive's principal design philosophies—minimalism. When combined with a wireless AirPort network and a Bluetooth wire-less keyboard and mouse, the iMac G5 had just one cable protruding from the rear for power, and even that was subtle. Reaction to the iMac G5 was mixed; although it was more powerful, critics clearly missed the design aesthetic of the articulating arm.

The iMac G5 also included a faster memory bus, better graphics, larger hard drives, and a new audio port that did double duty as an optical digital audio output. The iMac G5 was initially available with 1.6GHz or 1.8GHz, 17- or 20-inch monitor, with prices from $1,299 to $1,899.

eMac

In April 2004, Apple speed-bumped the eMac to a 1.25GHz G4 processor, USB 2.0, increased base RAM, faster memory, faster ATA bus, faster optical drive, and a faster graphics chip. The low-end model continued to sell for $799 and the high-end for $999.

Power Mac G5

On June 9, 2004, Apple quietly released revised PowerMac G5s in dual processor 2.5GHz configurations. Because of the volume of heat generated by IBM's PowerPC 950FX processor, the high-end Power Mac G5 featured a liquid cooling system. Faster graphics cards and optical drives were added to all models. In October, Apple released a new 1.8GHz configuration with slower front-side PCI buses based upon the iMac G5.

Xserve

On January 6, 2004, at Macworld Expo in San Francisco, Apple introduced the Xserve G5, the most powerful Xserve yet, delivering more than 30 gigaflops of processing power per system—about 60% more than the PowerPC G4-based Xserve. The Xserve G5 featured the same PowerPC G5, 64-bit processor used in Virginia Tech's cluster of Power Mac G5s, which was recognized at the time as being the world's third-fastest supercomputer.[15]

Apple also used the event to announce its new Xserve RAID storage system, a 3U high-availability, rack storage system that delivered multiple terabytes (TB) of storage capacity, via 14 hot-swappable Ultra-ATA harddrive bays. The most significant part of the new RAID was its aggressive price of just over $3 per gigabyte. With the new Xserve RAID, Apple announced support for Windows and Linux and industry support from 11 companies including Microsoft, VERITAS, Red Hat, Brocade, and QLogic.

eMac

On April 13, 2004, Apple released a speed-bumped eMac with a 1.25GHz G4 processor, faster system bus, faster ATA bus, faster memory, faster optical drives, faster graphics and, well, *faster* USB 2.0.

iBook

In April 2004, Apple speed-bumped the iBook G4 line, adding faster 1.0 and 1.2GHz processors, larger L2 cache, more on-board RAM, and a faster combo drive. In October 2004, Apple speed-bumped the iBook G4 again to include faster 1.2 and 1.33GHz processors, and the high-end model got a slot-loading SuperDrive and the low-end model got a price cut to $999.

PowerBook G4 Family

In April 2004, Apple speed-bumped the *PowerBook G4 family*—the name sometimes used for the unified aluminum PowerBook product line that was initially released on a staggered schedule. Now all three Power-Book G4 sizes (12-, 15-, and 17-inch) were updated at the same time. This round of revisions added faster graphics, faster optical drives, and AirPort Extreme standard.

iPod Mini

On January 6, 2004, at Macworld Expo in San Francisco, Apple announced the 4GB iPod mini, which was the size of a business card and came in five colors (silver, gold, pink, blue, or green) and sold for $249. The iPod mini was Apple's first departure from the size and shape of the original iPod, which was about the size of a deck of cards. In addition to the new form-factor, the iPod mini introduced a new "Click Wheel," which grafted the four hardware control buttons for play/pause, menu, skip forward, and skip backward onto the scroll wheel. This new input method would be carried through every iPod design until the iPod touch.

The iPod was miniaturized because Apple switched from its usual 1.8-inch hard drive to a smaller 0.8-inch hard drive. At its heart was a Hitachi (formerly IBM) MicroDrive Compact Flash (CF) card/hard drive that was typically used by professional digital photographers in high-end digital cameras. In fact, stand-alone 4GB MicroDrives were selling for around $500 at the time, and photographers were known to buy the iPod mini (at only $249) just to harvest the MicroDrive inside. The trade-off in size also meant a trade-off in capacity, and the iPod mini was limited to only 4GB of storage.

The iPod mini was an immediate hit because its price was a lower barrier to entry and more affordable to students and parents. Its five color choices gave customers a choice other than white for the first time. The pink iPod mini was purchased in droves by girls, teens, and grown women alike and was frequently sold out but available for a premium on online auction sites during peak holiday seasons.

For more on the iPod as a fashion statement, see Chapter 5, "Impact on Society."

Fourth-generation iPod

On July 19, 2004, Steve Jobs introduced the fourth-generation iPod that was thinner, lighter, and less expensive. The new iPod came in 20GB ($299) and 40GB ($399) capacities and featured the iPod mini's Click

Wheel. Improved battery life was achieved when Apple switched to the PortalPlayer PP5020 system-on-a-chip from the power-hungry PP5002 used in previous iPods.

iPod Photo and U2 Special Edition

On October 26, 2004, Apple announced the iPod photo, which was the first iPod with a color screen. It also featured new software that allowed it to synchronize and display photos from a computer. iPod photo held up to 25,000 digital photos alongside a music library and let users play back photo slideshows with music on the iPod itself. A new TV-out port added to the iPod dock allowed slideshows to be played on big-screen televisions and projectors.

Apple also released its first "special edition" iPod in 2004 to celebrate the band U2. The U2 iPod ($349) was mostly the same as the fourth-generation iPod released in July, except that it was black with a red click wheel (the colors of U2's *How to Dismantle an Atomic Bomb* album) and had the band's autographs engraved on the rear. It also included a gift certificate for $50 off the price of *The Complete U2*, a special Digital Box Set from iTunes, featuring more than 400 U2 tracks. *The Complete U2* was available on iTunes in October for $149.

AirPort Express

On June 7, 2004, at D: All Things D conference in San Diego, Steve Jobs announced AirPort Express, a supercompact AirPort base station with support for AirTunes that initially sold for $129. The AirPort Express, just a little larger than a PowerBook AC adapter, was snapped up by two groups of customers. The first was travelers who liked the convenience of having Wi-Fi wireless access but didn't like to pack the larger, original AirPort base station. The second was people that liked to play their iTunes music on their home stereo speakers but didn't like to have to plug into their computer each time. AirTunes required version iTunes 4.6.

For more on AirPort Express and AirTunes, see Chapter 4, "Strategies and Innovations."

Monitors

On June 28, 2004, Apple released completely redesigned Apple Cinema Display monitors clad in aluminum to match the Power Mac G5 tower. The new monitors are available in 20-, 23-, and 30-inch sizes and feature a DVI connection, making them compatible with Windows PCs. The new flagship in the series, a massive 30-inch model, boasts a native resolution of up to 2560 × 1600 but requires a special graphics card with a dual-link DVI port to drive it. The 30-inch monitor sold for a whopping $3,299 initially, plus $599 for the graphics card, much more than most people's entire computer setup. The price of the 30-inch Cinema Display was later reduced to $1,799 to be more competitive.

Software

A new consumer audio application called GarageBand was announced during Steve Jobs's keynote address at Macworld Expo in San Francisco on January 6, 2004; John Mayer assisted with its demonstration. Jobs also announced iLife '04 ($49), with new versions of iPhoto, iMovie, iDVD, and the new GarageBand application.

Retail

Apple opened 29 stores in 2004 for a total of 101, including flagship stores in San Francisco, London, and Osaka, Japan.

iTunes

On July 12, 2004, Apple announced that more than 100 million songs were downloaded from the iTunes Music Store, making it by far the most successful legal music download service.

For more on iTunes, see Chapter 4, "Strategies and Innovations."

2005—MAC MINI AND THE SWITCH TO INTEL

Hardware

Apple continued its tradition of updating most of its hardware with speed-bumps every 9 to 12 months with some exceptions and new designs replacing old every two to four years,

Mac Mini

On January 11, 2005, at Macworld Expo in San Francisco, Apple announced the most affordable and most compact Mac ever—the Mac mini. Starting at just $499 with a 1.25GHz PowerPC G4 processor, the Mac mini (with a nod to the iPod with the same name) had a very low barrier to entry to the Mac platform.

The Mac mini is quite small for a desktop computer, measuring only 6.5 inches wide, 6.5 inches long, and 2 inches tall. It weighs 2.9 pounds and comes with an external power supply that is almost half the size of the computer.

The Mac mini was an excellent low-cost machine, but also a perfect alternative for Windows users that wanted to switch to the Mac platform. The Mac mini came without a monitor or accessories and could easily be plugged in place of a PC it was replacing. Apple promoted the Mac mini as the perfect Mac for anyone looking to get started with Mac OS X and iLife '05, Apple's software suite for managing digital photo, music, editing movies, and creating music.

In July 2005, Apple doubled the standard RAM (to 512MB) across the Mac mini line and added a SuperDrive to the high-end model. In late September, Apple silently updated the Mac mini with faster 1.33 or 1.5GHz processors, faster SuperDrive, faster hard drives, Bluetooth 2.0+EDR, and better graphics.

iMac G5

In May 2005, Apple speed-bumped iMac G5, making AirPort Extreme, Bluetooth, and 512MB of RAM (the minimum required for Mac OS X 10.4 Tiger) standard on all models. In October 2005, Apple added an integrated iSight camera to the iMac G5, making it the first Mac with a built-in camera. In addition, Apple made the case lighter and slimmer and included a faster processor, graphics processor, bus, and memory.

The new iMac G5 revision also included a remote control and Apple's new Front Row software, which allowed the computer to function as a home media center. The iMac G5 also got a price drop to $1,299 (17-inch) and $1,699 (20-inch).

eMac

In April 2005, Apple speed-bumped the eMac with a 1.42GHz G4 processor, increasing the base RAM, adding a faster dual-layer SuperDrive on the high-end model, and including larger hard drives and faster graphics hips.

Power Mac G5

On April 27, 2005, the Power Mac G5 got a speed-bump in all the usual areas: processor, RAM, hard drive, and better graphics processor, which added support for driving Apple's new 30-inch Cinema HD Display.

On October 12, 2005, Apple bumped the Power Mac G5 to include dual-core PowerPC G5 processors, the last professional Mac desktop to use PowerPC processors. It also included faster bus and memory speeds, larger hard drives on the low- and middle-end models, better graphics cards, and PCI Express expansion slots. It was available in three configurations: the 2.0GHz model was $1,999, the 2.3GHz model was $2,499, and the 2 × 2.5 GHz model, with four processor cores, was $3,299.

Xserve

On January 4, 2005, Apple speed-bumped the Xserve to dual 2.3GHz PowerPC G5 processors with more than 35 gigaflops of processing power and up to 9.2GBps of bandwidth per processor and up to three 400GB drives for a total of 1.2TB of hot-plug storage. Xserve G5 configurations start at $2,999.

iBook G4

In July 2005, Apple speed-bumped the iBook G4, making AirPort Extreme, Bluetooth, and 512MB of RAM (the minimum required to run Mac OS X 10.4 Tiger) standard on all models. Apple also simplified the product line from three configurations to two.

PowerBook G4

On January 31, 2005, Apple speed-bumped the PowerBook G4 to 1.5 and 1.67GHz processors, adding faster hard drives and a faster 8x Super-Drive. On October 19, 2005, they were bumped with higher-resolution displays, up to one hour more battery life on the 15- and 17-inch models, and SuperDrives in all models. The 15- and 17-inch configurations got updated 8x SuperDrives with double-layer support (DVD+R DL/DVD±RW/CD-RW). Double-layer recordable discs are a derivative of DVD-R that can store up to 8.5GB of data.

iPod

In 2005, Apple unleashed a torrent of new iPods reminiscent of the ramp-up of new Mac releases from 1991–1995. The iPod was beginning a stage of rapid growth and Apple was determined to capitalize on it and maintain its market lead in both digital music hardware and software sales.

iPod Shuffle

At Macworld Expo in San Francisco on January 11, 2005, Apple did a complete about-face and announced its first flash-based iPod—the iPod shuffle. After publicly belittling flash-based players as "throw away" devices, due to their limited capacity, Apple was now ready to turn its sights on the low end of the music player market—the only music player market it had yet to conquer.

The shuffle looked unlike any other iPod before it. It was the first to do away with the expensive display, hence the name *shuffle*, which Apple marketed as a new way to listen to your music collection. It dispensed with the usual dock connector in exchange for a male USB connector (that allowed it to double as a flash drive), and dropped the click wheel for regular buttons.

The 512MB shuffle sold for $99 and a 1GB model sold for $149. In June 2005, the 1GB model was dropped to $129, and in February 2006, the prices were cut to $69 and $99.

For more on the iPod as a fashion statement, see Chapter 5, "Impact on Society."

iPod Mini

Released more than a year after the original iPod mini, the second-generation iPod mini was announced on February 22, 2005, with modest changes. The new mini came in a larger 6GB ($249) capacity while the original 4GB ($199) model was retained with a price drop. It came in four brighter colors (the less popular gold was dropped), had longer battery life, and the lettering on the click wheel was changed to match the body color.

iPod Color

While Apple was busy announcing the iPod shuffle and revving the mini, it didn't neglect the original iPod. On June 28, 2005, Apple merged the iPod and the iPod photo into one unified product line simply called the iPod. The new full-sized iPod was upgraded with a color screen and included all the functionality of the iPod photo. Due to its lack of physical changes, other than the color screen, people still called this iPod the fourth-generation model. Apple dropped the 30 and 40GB configurations and offered only a 20GB ($299) and 60GB ($399) option.

iPod Nano

On September 7, 2005, Apple did the unthinkable and dropped its most popular iPod line, the iPod mini, and replaced it with a totally new design. The brand-new iPod nano was available in black or white and used flash memory. It came in three capacities, 2 ($199) and 4GB ($249) capacities (with a 1GB to follow later) and had a small color screen for picture viewing.

The move from iPod mini to nano was risky because Apple was discontinuing a product that consumers loved and replacing it with something untested that cost more. Many believe that the move to a flash-based iPod was necessary because Apple couldn't get reliable quantities of the more expensive Compact Flash (CF) MicroDrives that were in the iPod mini.

The iTunes Phone

On September 7, 2005, Apple and Motorola released the ROKR E1, the first mobile phone to use iTunes. However, the announcement was buried in the iPod nano announcement and given less attention in the press conference than the nano. Jobs was reported to be unhappy with the ROKR and felt that it had too many compromises. ROKR could only hold up to 100 songs, which in the era of the iPod, was perceived as too little, and it wasn't designed by the Apple design team, regarded as one of the top technology designers in the world.

iPod Fifth Generation

And if that weren't enough iPods, on October 12, 2005, Apple released an entirely new fifth-generation iPod with a larger 2.5-inch, 320 × 240,

16-bit color screen that could display album artwork, photos, and play music videos, video Podcasts, movies, and television shows. The iPod video (as it was known) could play MPEG-4 and H.264 videos in resolutions up to 480 × 480 pixels on an external TV via an A/V cable accessory that plugs into the headphone mini jack. Videos purchased from the iTunes Store were limited to 320 × 240 resolution.

Mighty Mouse

After years of criticism for not having a multiple button mouse, Apple answered with the ultimate reply: a no-button mouse. While not completely buttonless, the Mighty Mouse has no *visible* buttons. The $49 Mighty Mouse actually comes with four independently programmable buttons: a left button, a right button, a clickable scroll ball, and side squeeze buttons hidden under its touch-sensitive top shell. An innovative Scroll Ball lets users scroll in any direction, even diagonally.

Mighty Mouse is the first multibutton mouse Apple has ever sold since beginning with the Lisa more than 22 years earlier. The single-button mouse has been a point of contention between Apple and its users for decades. Apple thought that one mouse button was adequate and simpler to use, but as Windows and other operating systems standardized on two-button mice, it became a criticism of Apple. When Apple added contextual pop-up menus, which reveal a list of options depending on what is clicked on, to OS 8 in July 1997, the single mouse criticism came to a head.

The problem was that invoking the new contextual menu feature required the user to hold down the Control key on the keyboard while clicking. This was perceived as slower than potentially clicking on a second mouse button. Later, Apple made contextual menus accessible by having users click and hold the mouse button, somewhat diffusing the debate.

The Mighty Mouse is still controversial today. Despite answering its critics with not two, but four, buttons, the Mighty Mouse's design caused complaints. The Mighty Mouse can sense both right and left clicks, but it's impossible to press both buttons simultaneously. Moreover, right clicks cannot be made while the user's finger is on the left touch sensor.[16] Another frequent complaint is that the Scroll Ball is too small or that it gets clogged too easily with dirt and isn't removable.

Apple uses the name Mighty Mouse under license from CBS Operations, owner of the 1940s cartoon character. In May 2008, Apple and CBS were named in a trademark infringement suit brought by Man & Machines over the use of the name *Mighty Mouse.* The company claims that it began selling waterproof and chemical-resistant computer mice under the Mighty Mouse brand name in 2004—a year before Apple announced its mouse under the same name.

On October 12, 2005, Apple began shipping Mighty Mouse as the default offering with every iMac, then on October 19, 2005, Apple included a Mighty Mouse with every PowerMac G5.

Mac OS 10.4—Tiger

Apple "unleashed" Mac OS 10.4 *Tiger,* the fifth major update to the desktop and server operating system, on April 29, 2005, with more than 200 new features. New features in Tiger included Automator, Core Image, Core Video, Dashboard, QuickTime 7, Safari 2, Smart Folders, Spotlight, and VoiceOver.

Mac OS X version 10.4 was available in separate PowerPC and Intel editions; there was no universal version of the operating system. Apple shipped the PowerPC version with PowerPC-based Macs and the Intel version with Intel Macs. The boxed retail version of Tiger sold in stores was the PowerPC version. Mac OS 10.4 Tiger also dropped support for older Macs that did not have a FireWire port and required a PowerPC G3, G4, or G5 with a minimum 333MHz processor.

The iPhone and Apple TV use a modified version of Tiger with different user interfaces and a custom set of applications.

Six weeks after its official release, Apple had delivered 2 million copies of Tiger, representing 16% of all Mac OS X users. Apple claimed that Tiger was the most successful Apple OS release in the company's history. At the Worldwide Developers Conference on June 11, 2007, Apple CEO Steve Jobs announced that out of the 22 million Mac OS X users, more than 67% were using Tiger.[17]

Intel Migration

In his keynote address at Apple's WWDC on June 6, 2005, Steve Jobs officially announced that after years of producing machines based on the PowerPC processor from Motorola and IBM, Apple would begin a companywide shift to Intel-based Macs beginning in 2006.[18] Jobs admitted to secretly building versions of Mac OS X for both PowerPC and Intel processors over the past five years.[19] Rumors had long circulated that Apple was testing a version of Mac OS X for Intel x86 processors because of its roots in NeXT's OPENSTEP, which was available for many platforms. Jobs publicly stated that the transition to Intel processors would not be completed until the end of 2007.

For more on the migration to Intel processors, see Chapter 4, "Strategies and Innovations."

Retail

Apple opened 34 stores in 2005 for a total of 135 and dramatically increased its international presence with one store in Canada, three in the United Kingdom, and four in Japan.

2006—INTEL TRANSITION COMPLETE

Hardware

The year 2006 was a major year for Apple hardware; it was the first year that Macs began shipping with Intel CPUs, after Apple had announced a switch to Intel six months prior at WWDC. The partnership with Intel allowed Apple to take advantage of all the latest Intel chip designs and be on par with Windows-based computers.

iMac Core Duo

On January 10, 2006, at Macworld Expo in San Francisco, Steve Jobs announced new iMacs and MacBook Pros running on the new Intel Core Duo processor. Intel's Core Duo processor had two processor cores on a single chip, making it up to twice as fast as its predecessor when running Intel-compiled code according to tests run by Apple using SPEC. The new iMac would be the first Macintosh to use an Intel CPU but retained the same white polycarbonate case design, features, and price as the iMac G5 it replaced.

The iMac Core Duo featured a faster bus, faster memory, better graphics, and a mini-DVI port, which allowed monitor spanning for the first time on a consumer Mac. It came in two configurations: the 17-inch 1.83GHz cost $1,299, and the 20-inch 2.0GHz cost $1,699.

In July 2006, Apple released a special $899 iMac Core Duo configuration for the education market as a replacement for the eMac. To keep costs down, the teacher's iMac didn't include on-board Bluetooth and shared a lot of the components of the Mac mini, including its less-expensive Intel GMA950 graphics chipset and a smaller 80GB hard drive.

On September 6, 2006, Apple speed-bumped the previous Intel iMacs to a Core 2 Duo chip with lower prices. Apple also added a new 24-inch configuration with a resolution of 1920 × 1200 (WUXGA), making it the first iMac to be able to display 1080 HD content in its full resolution. The new iMac, although in the same enclosure, could be removed from its stand and mounted on a wall (for example) because it shipped with a VESA Flat Display Mounting Interface. All the new Core 2 Duo iMacs included an integrated iSight camera and an 802.11n draft wireless card (except the 17-inch 1.83GHz model)—a first on the Mac.

MacBook Pro Core Duo

When it introduced the first Intel-based notebook computer, Apple also decided to change its name. The new *MacBook Pro* was a departure from the venerable PowerBook brand, which started in 1991, and reflected a change in corporate branding at Apple to include the word *Mac* in its product names. Although it had a new name, the MacBook Pro shipped in the same aluminum enclosure that debuted with the PowerBook G4 in

January 2003. The new notebook naming convention left customers to speculate that the iBook replacement would be called *MacBook,* and they were right. Initially customers found the term awkward but eventually adapted to it.

The MacBook Pro debuted on January 10, 2006, at Macworld Expo in San Francisco, replacing the PowerBook G4 as Apple's professional notebook computer. The new MacBook Pro 15-inch shipped with a 1.67 or 1.83GHz Intel Core Duo processor and featured Apple's new MagSafe magnetic power connector, which was designed to easily break away if the cord was accidentally tripped over while charging.

Reflecting an Apple trend toward cameras, the new MacBook Pro also included a built-in iSight video camera for video conferencing and the Apple Remote and Front Row media center software. The 17-inch MacBook Pro followed in April 24, 2006, with a 2.16GHz Intel Core Duo processor and all the new features found in the 15-inch model. Much to the dismay of commuters everywhere, the popular 12-inch PowerBook didn't make the transition to the MacBook Pro and was dropped completely.

MacBook Core Duo

The MacBook was the successor to the iBook, inheriting the Apple consumer notebook market. Announced on May 15, 2006, it also got a name change to reflect Apple's desire to use *Mac* in the name, but unlike the professional MacBook Pro, the MacBook was less expensive and came with a slower, built-in video, which paled in comparison to the MacBook Pro's dedicated video processor. The MacBook replaced the existing 12- and 14-inch iBooks, completing the transition of Apple's notebook computers to Intel processors.

The MacBook shipped in a totally redesigned polycarbonate case and was available in either white or black (for a $200 premium) built around a 13.3-inch "glossy" LCD panel. The MacBook included many of the enhancements from the MacBook Pro: a dual core Intel Core Duo processor, faster bus speed, faster and larger Serial-ATA (SATS) hard drive, integrated iSight camera, MagSafe power adaptor, and a bundled remote control with Apple's Front Row software.

MacBook also featured some new design elements not previously found on Apple's consumer notebooks: optical audio in/out, a DVI port capable of monitor-spanning, and gigabit Ethernet. Two features unique to the MacBook were a magnetic latching system with no moving parts, and a redesigned recessed keyboard.

Mac Mini

The Mac mini was speed-bumped to Intel processors in February 2006, the low-end got a 1.5 Core Solo processor ($599) and the high-end ($799) got a 1.66GHz Core Duo processor. In September, the Mac mini received a silent speed-bump, this time to include Intel Core 2 Duo processors in both models, 1.66GHz on the low-end and 1.83GHz on the high-end. Both got larger hard drives and 1GB of standard RAM. Prices and other specifications were unchanged.

Mac Pro

The last Mac to receive the Intel treatment was Apple's desktop tower. To reflect the switch from PowerPC chips to Intel and to continue the re-branding strategy started with the MacBook Pro, the new tower was called the *Mac Pro*. Again, like the MacBook Pro before it, initial reaction to the name change was tepid, but not entirely unexpected.

The Mac Pro was significant because it was the last machine to transition to Intel processors. At its announcement on August 7, 2006, at WWDC, Steve Jobs proclaimed, "Apple has successfully completed the transition to using Intel processors in just seven months—210 days to be exact."

Xserve

The Intel version of the Xserve was announced in August 2006 but didn't ship until November and was the first new Xserve in more than two years, replacing the Xserve G5. The new Xserve shipped with two dual-core Intel Xeon 5100 processors. Unlike previous Xserves, it shipped in a single configuration with a base price of $2,999. Configure-to-Order (CTO) options included an 8x double-layer SuperDrive, up to 2.2TB of storage via three hot-swappable bays, 32GB of RAM via eight slots, a Fibre Channel PCI Express, Dual-Channel Ultra 320 SCSI PCI-X cards, and an Xserve RAID card.

iPod

Apple had a lot on its plate in 2006; in addition to completing the transition to Intel processors, it also released a whopping six new iPods.

iPod Fifth Generation and U2 Special Edition

On June 6, 2006, Apple reintroduced the iPod U2 Special Edition at $329. The new version had the same features as the 30GB fifth-generation iPod, except that it had a black metal back. The new U2 iPod included an iTunes Store coupon that could be redeemed for a 30-minute U2 video. In September 2006, Apple dropped the price of the U2 Special Edition to $279 and upgraded the 60GB iPod to 80GB.

iPod Nano (Second Generation)

Announced in September 2006, the second-generation iPod nano was a throwback to the iPod mini it replaced. It was redesigned in an extruded aluminum tube and was available in five colors, like the iPod mini. Aside from the redesigned case and increased 8GB capacity, the second-generation iPod nano was similar to the previous iPod nano. It came in three models: 2GB ($149) was available in silver; 4GB ($199) was available in silver, blue, green, or pink; and a high-end 8GB ($249) model was available in black.

iPod Shuffle (Second Generation)

Also announced in September 2006, the second-generation iPod shuffle was even smaller than the original iPod shuffle. A 1GB configuration was sold in silver for $79. The new shuffle included an integrated clip and required a special, smaller dock to connect rather than Apple's usual 30-pin dock connector. The new iPod shuffle was heavily marketed as a fashion accessory, especially in later models.

Mighty Mouse

On July 25, 2006, Apple released a wireless Mighty Mouse with laser tracking (as opposed to optical in the wired version) that uses Bluetooth 2.0 for $69. The updated version held two AA batteries but only required one to operate. On August 7, 2007, Apple made a subtle change to the Mighty Mouse, changing the side buttons to white.

Mac OS 10.4.4 for Intel

On January 10, 2006, Apple released the Mac OS 10.4.4 update to Tiger to work with the first Intel-based Macs. This special build of Tiger was designed to run on Intel and PowerPC machines, except that the Intel release dropped support for the Classic environment. Mac OS 10.4.4 was built separately for the two different processors. The PowerPC and Intel versions of 10.4.4 shipped as two separate installers, and you couldn't install the PowerPC version of the OS onto an Intel-based Mac.

Retail

Apple opened 35 stores in 2006 for a total of 170 and again increased its international presence with three new stores in Canada, two in the United Kingdom, and one in Japan.

2007—IPHONE, APPLE TV, ALL NEW IPODS

On January 9, 2007, at Macworld Expo in San Francisco, Steve Jobs introduced the revolutionary iPhone; revealed the Apple TV, which was originally called by its code name *iTV*; and announced that Apple Computer Inc. had officially dropped *Computer* from its corporate name, switching to just *Apple Inc.*, reflecting the company's ongoing expansion into the consumer electronics market in addition to its traditional focus on personal computers.

For more on iPhone and Apple TV, see Chapter 4, "Strategies and Innovations."

Hardware

After completing its ambitious transition to Intel processors in all Macs in 2006, Apple continued its tradition of updating most of its hardware with speed-bumps every 9 to 12 months with some exceptions and new designs replacing old every two to four years.

Apple TV

On January 9, 2007, at Macworld Expo in San Francisco, Apple announced the Apple TV, a new $299 40GB set-top appliance that was first announced at a special press event in San Francisco on September 12, 2006. Apple TV was designed to play iTunes content (music, television shows, movies, etc.) from any computer (Mac or Windows) connected to the local network and could be connected to any widescreen TV with either HDMI or component video.

Released two months later, the Apple TV was Apple's first official foray into the set-top market (although prototypes of a never-released PPC 603-based set-top box from the late 1990s surface from time to time).

Apple TV can be a media playback device or a digital media receiver. It runs a closed, custom build of Mac OS 10.4.7 that allows it to stream audio and video from any iTunes-equipped computer on the local network. It uses a Front Row–style software application to play iTunes content from any computer in a household. The first Apple TV could also play movie trailers from the Apple Web site and select YouTube videos that were reencoded in h.264 format. The 40GB model sold for $299 and a second version with a larger 160GB hard disk started shipping on May 31, 2007.

While definitely a revolutionary device for Apple, critics had three issues with the Apple TV:

1. Apple TV can only stream content that's in your iTunes library and photos from iPhoto. This means that other content (including DVDs, DiVX, .AVI, .WMV, etc.) will not be able to be streamed to Apple TV—unless you convert them to something that plays in iTunes first. This was a deal-breaker for many people. Also, users of Apple's professional photo application Aperture weren't able to sync their libraries to Apple TV.
2. Apple TV only connects to TVs that have either HDMI (digital) or component video (analog) inputs. Component video inputs are (R)ed (G)reen and (B)lue and are not to be confused with the yellow RCA cable, which is composite video (also known as *S-video*). RGB was never popular in North America for consumer

electronics, as S-video was considered good enough. This effectively limits the Apple TV to consumers that own a relatively modern TV set.

3. Apple TV requires a widescreen set. According to Apple's system requirements, you need: enhanced-definition or high-definition widescreen TVs capable of 1080i 60/50Hz, 720p 60/50Hz, 576p 50Hz (PAL format), or 480p 60Hz. While many people are upgrading to widescreen sets, a large percentage of the TV-owning public didn't own either an Enhanced Definition (ED) or High Definition (HD) set, excluding them from using Apple TV.[20]

iPhone

At Macworld Expo in January 2007, Apple announced one of its most significant products since the iPod and arguably since the Mac and the original Apple I: iPhone. During his keynote address, Steve Jobs told attendees that Apple was announcing three revolutionary products. Then, interrupting the cheers, he said that all three were actually one product: iPhone. The caption on his slide read: "Apple reinvents the phone."

iPhone was Apple's first mobile phone and marked its entry into an entirely new market. Its design was simple and very much in the Jonathan Ive ethos. It was entirely flat, all screen, and only had one button on the front. Unlike smart phones and PDAs before it, iPhone didn't require a stylus. "Who wants a stylus?" Jobs asked the crowd facetiously. His reasoning was that the best pointing device in the world is already attached to your hand—your finger. Jobs went on to compare the iPhone's touch screen to other revolutionary interfaces, including the iPod and the mouse.

iPhone is controlled using a variety of one- and two-finger gestures (called *Multi-Touch*) and includes a custom version of Apple's Safari Web browser that allows full browsing of any Web page. The iPod functionality was enhanced to take advantage of the 3.5-inch screen and featured CoverFlow, which was borrowed from iTunes. iPhone also featured dedicated YouTube and Google Maps applications and an iChat-like SMS text-messaging interface (although iChat itself was missing). iPhone also came with the standard suite of smart phone applications such as a calendar and address book that automatically synced with their desktop equivalents through iTunes. iPhone shipped on June 29, 2007, and was sold in two configurations: a 4GB model sold for $499, and an 8GB model for $599. In September 2007, Apple dropped the price of the 8GB iPhone from $599 to $399 and later issued a $100 credit for the Apple store to people who purchased the original iPhone.

On June 11, 2007, at the WWDC, Apple announced that iPhone would support third-party applications via the mobile Safari Web browser on the device. This was viewed by many as a compromise and was clearly announced as a result of criticism that iPhone couldn't run third-party software. As of June 2008, the iPhone has access to hundreds of applications via the App Store.

For more on iPhone, see Chapter 4, "Strategies and Innovations."

iPod

On September 5, 2007, at an event called "The Beat Goes On," Apple revamped the entire iPod lineup with three new form-factors.

iPod Touch

Building on the success of the iPhone, the iPod touch was essentially an iPhone without the phone. People had been clamoring for a touch screen iPod even before the iPhone was announced, but many didn't want a mobile phone because (1) they were locked in a contract with an existing carrier, or (2) they didn't want, couldn't afford, or were too young to buy a mobile phone. The iPhone touch addressed this market perfectly.

The iPod touch inherited the Multi-Touch screen, graphical user interface, and Cover Flow from the iPhone and shipped with 8, 16, or 32GB of flash memory. The touch was the first iPod that had wireless access to the iTunes Store, providing the ability to purchase music "Over the Air" (OTA) from a Wi-Fi connection. As of June 2008, the iPod touch also has access to the App Store.[21]

iPod Nano Third Generation

Apple updated the nano again with its third major redesign on September 5, 2007. The third-generation nano featured a 2-inch QVGA (320 × 240) screen and a shorter, wider, heavier design and new colors. The iPod nano 3G included a revamped user interface with more graphics throughout, Cover Flow, video playback, and support for iPod Games. The nano

---

What Is Product Red?

Product Red is a charitable initiative begun by U2's frontman Bono and Bobby Shriver of DATA (Debt, AIDS, Trade in Africa), to raise money for the Global Fund to Fight AIDS, Tuberculosis and Malaria. Bobby Shriver is the CEO and Bono is the public spokesperson for the Product Red brand. Participating companies create products with the Product Red logo and/or color (like the iPod nano and shuffle) and return a percentage of the profit to the Global Fund. In addition to Apple, the Product Red brand is licensed to American Express, Converse, Motorola, The Gap, Emporio Armani, Hallmark, Microsoft, and Dell.

---

was announced in a 4GB version for $149 in silver, and an 8GB version for $199 in silver, turquoise, mint green, black, and Product Red. The battery lasts for approximately 24 hours on audio playback and approximately five hours on video playback.

iPod Classic

At the same event on September 5, 2007, Apple retired the iconic, original white iPod design and launched its replacement, the sixth-generation iPod classic in 80 and 160GB sizes. The iPod classic is the only iPod to retain the original iPod's 1.8-inch internal hard drive, as all the other models became flash-based. The classic did away with the old iPod's polycarbonate front in favor of an aluminum skin that came in silver or black, a material now present on almost all of Apple's products.

The iPod classic featured improved battery life with up to 40 hours of music playback and up to 7 hours of video playback. The new iPod also featured an overhauled interface incorporating more graphics, especially on the right half of the screen and Cover Flow.

Mac Mini

The Mac mini was speed-bumped in August 2007 to include the Intel Core 2 Duo processor, larger hard drives, and 1GB of standard RAM. Prices and other specifications remained the same.

iMac

On August 7, 2007, the iMac got a redesign that was a clear reference to the iPhone, inheriting the aluminum skin first donned by the MacBook Pro notebook and the Mac Pro tower. Apple touted the switch to aluminum design materials as being ecologically friendly because aluminum and glass are "highly recyclable." The new iMac shipped in 20- and 24-inch configurations with 2.0 to 2.8GHz Core 2 Duo processors from $1,199 to $2,299. Under the hood, though, the new iMac was really just a speed-bump of the previous model.

Aluminum Keyboard

The new iMac included a new, ultrathin, anodized aluminum keyboard (which sells separately for $49), measuring just 0.33 inches at its front edge. The new keyboard includes special function keys for one-touch control of Mac features like iTunes playback and volume, Dashboard and Spaces. Some of the differences between the new keyboard and the one it replaces include:

- Volume controls were moved from above the numeric keypad to the F10, F11, and F12 keys.
- The Eject key is now directly above the delete key (like it is on the MacBook).

- The Help key has been replaced by a Function (*fn*) key.
- The Apple logo has been replaced by the word *Command*—a boon for support techs everywhere.
- New playback keys (back, play/pause, forward) have been added to F7, F8, and F9.
- Bright and Dim keys have been added to F1 and F2 (like the MacBook).
- Expose (F3) and Dashboard (F4) keys have been added.

A wireless, $79 Bluetooth version of the thin keyboard was also released that lacks a built-in numerical keypad and the additional function keys available in the wider USB version.

Mac Pro

In April 2007, Apple speed-bumped the Mac Pro with a pair of 3GHz quad-core Intel Xeon 5100 "Woodcrest" processors, less than a month after a Web site error leaked the new configuration. The basic Mac Pro costs $2,200 but if you upgrade to two quad-core chips, the price almost doubles to $3,997; adding 16GB RAM increases the price to $4,499.

MacBook

In May 2007, Apple speed-bumped the MacBook to faster 2.0 and 2.16GHz Intel Core 2 Duo processors, AirPort 802.11n, 1GB RAM standard, and larger hard drives. In November, the MacBook was revved again to 2.0 or 2.2GHz Intel Santa Rosa processor, a faster 800MHz system bus, 4GB maximum RAM, and a better Intel GMA X3100 graphics processor.

MacBook Pro

In June 2007, Apple released speed-bumped 15- and 17-inch MacBook Pros with 2.2 and 2.5GHz Intel Core 2 Duo Santa Rosa processors, NVIDIA GeForce 8600M GT graphics, and LED backlit screens. The new backlit LED screens were touted as more power efficient and environmentally friendly because they were mercury-free.

AirPort Extreme

The AirPort Extreme was updated on January 9, 2007, and changed from a tented-dome form-factor to more of a square, flat box like the Mac mini and Apple TV. The new AirPort Extreme supported 802.11a/b/g and draft-n protocols and added two LAN ports for a total of three. A new feature called AirPort Disk (also called Network Attached Storage or NAS) enabled owners to connect a USB hard drive to the AirPort Extreme that then could be mounted and used wireless when connected to that base station. As with previous AirPort base stations, users can also connect a

USB printer. On August 7, 2007, the AirPort Extreme began shipping with gigabit (1000BaseT) Ethernet ports. One of the few complaints about the AirPort Extreme is its lack of an external antenna port.

Mac OS 10.5

Mac OS 10.5 *Leopard* was released on October 26, 2007, and promoted as "the largest update of Mac OS X" with more than 300 new features.[22] Leopard supports both PowerPC- and Intel x86-based Macintosh computers, but support for the G3 processor was dropped. A single DVD installer can be used on all supported Macs. New features include improvements in Mail, iChat, the Finder, Time Machine, Spaces, Boot Camp, 64-bit, new security features, and an updated user interface.

Mac OS 10.5 was released later than originally announced by Apple's CEO Steve Jobs. In June 2005, Jobs stated that Apple intended to release Leopard at the end of 2006 or early 2007.[23] A year later, Leopard's launch date was moved back to "Spring 2007."[24] Then on April 12, 2007, Apple stated that its release would be delayed until October 2007 because of the development of the iPhone.[25]

Retail

Apple opened its 200th store on October 26, 2007, in Gilbert, Arizona, a little more than six years after opening its first store. Apple opened 33 stores in 2007 for a total of 203, including flagship stores in New York and Glasgow. In 2007, Apple also opened its first store in Italy in Rome.

2008—MACBOOK AIR

On January 15, 2008, at Macworld Expo in San Francisco, Steve Jobs introduced the MacBook Air as the world's thinnest notebook computer, Time Capsule for use with the Time Machine backup software in Mac OS 10.5 Leopard, a software update for the iPod touch, iTunes Movie Rentals, Apple TV Take 2 software, and that the iPhone/iPod touch SDK would be launching in late February.

MacBook Air

On January 15, 2008, Apple announced MacBook Air, the company's first-ever subnotebook and the world's thinnest notebook. MacBook Air measures 0.16 inches at its thinnest point and 0.76 inches at its thickest. It ships with either a 1.6 or 1.8GHz Intel Core 2 Duo processor, 2GB RAM, 80GB 1.8-inch hard drive or optional 64GB Solid State Drive (SSD), 13.3-inch LED-backlit screen, 802.11n Wi-Fi technology, Bluetooth 2.1, full-size and backlit keyboard, built-in iSight camera, and a large trackpad with multi-touch gesture support, allowing users to pinch, rotate, and swipe.

The MacBook Air was a revolutionary product for Apple, both because of its tiny size and full-feature set, but also because it was an entirely new category of notebook, a subnotebook that Apple had never created before. The MacBook Air was in a category all to itself.

The MacBook Air had to make several compromises to achieve its record-breaking size, however. It didn't ship with an optical drive, although an external USB SuperDrive was offered for $99. The Air only shipped with a tiny subset of ports on a traditional notebook and didn't have FireWire. It also was Apple's first notebook to ship with a fixed battery, meaning that it couldn't be removed and replaced on a long flight, for example.

Either way, the MacBook Air was one of Apple's most coveted yet most controversial products of all time.

For more on MacBook Air, see Chapter 4, "Strategies and Innovations."

Time Capsule

On January 15, 2008, Apple introduced Time Capsule, a backup appliance resembling the AirPort Extreme 802.11n that automatically backs up Leopard Macs on the local network. Backups are performed by Time Machine, which is included in Mac OS 10.5 Leopard.

Time Capsule combines an AirPort Extreme 802.11n base station with a server grade 500GB or 1TB hard drive. In addition to being used as a Time Machine repository, Time Capsule can operate as Network Attached Storage (NAS) that can be used by Macs on the local network with the proper privileges. Time Capsule comes in two models: a 500GB model for $299 and a 1TB model for $499.

Apple TV Take 2 and Movie Rentals

At Macworld Expo 2008, Apple announced a significant software update for the Apple TV called *Apple TV Take 2* and lowered the price of the hardware from $299 to $229.

At the All Things D conference on May 30, 2007, Steve Jobs called Apple TV a hobby, saying, "The reason I call it a hobby is a lot of people have tried and failed to make it a business. It's a business that's hundreds of thousands of units per year but it hasn't crested to be millions of units per year, but I think if we improve things we can crack that."[26]

With the Take 2 software update, Apple released what probably should have been the feature set in the original Apple TV release. Rather than forcing the device to be tethered to an iTunes computer, the update gave Apple TV the ability—finally—to purchase and rent movies in High Definition (HD) and purchase television programs and music directly over the Internet.

Movie rentals were another first for Apple. The software update allowed users to browse, preview, and rent movies directly from Apple

TV; it even included a recommendation system in rentals, like that found in Netflix. Apple partnered with all the major movie studios, including Touchstone, Miramax, Metro, Lions Gate, New Line, Fox, WB, Disney, Paramount, Universal, Sony/BMG. Apple offered 1,000 movie titles for rent by the end of February with more than 100 in High Definition (HD) and 5.1 Dolby Digital surround sound. DVD-quality iTunes movie rentals cost $2.99 for library titles and $3.99 for new releases. High Definition versions cost one dollar more.

Once a movie is rented, it starts downloading from the iTunes Store directly to Apple TV, and users with a fast Internet connection can start viewing the movie almost immediately—HD movies take significantly longer to download. Customers have up to 30 days to start watching their rental, and once a movie has been started, they have 24 hours to finish it. A movie can be watched multiple times in the 24-hour period after it has been started.

One unique feature is that purchases (not rentals) downloaded to Apple TV are automatically synced back to iTunes on the user's computer where they can be watched and synced to all modern iPods or iPhone.

Apple TV Take 2 had access to more than 600 television shows, 125,000 audio and video podcasts, 50 million YouTube video streams, 6 million songs, and 10,000 music videos at launch. Apple continues to add new content to the iTunes service on a regular basis.

Mac Pro

On January 8, 2008, at Macworld Expo in San Francisco, Apple speed-bumped the Xserve to 3.2GHz, 8-core Intel Xeon processors. The new Mac Pro combines two Intel 45 nanometer Quad-Core Xeon processors running up to 3.2GHz, new graphics, and up to 4TB of internal storage. The low-end 8-core configuration starts at $2,799.

iPhone

On March 6, 2008, Apple announced iPhone 2.0 software beta and venture capital firm Kleiner Perkins Caufield & Byers launched a $100 million fund for iPhone application developers, appropriately called *iFund*.

On June 9, 2008, at the WWDC in San Francisco, Steve Jobs announced the second-generation iPhone with 3G networking and iPhone software 2.0. The new 3G iPhone utilizes AT&T's HSDPA/HSUPA high-speed data network that is up to four times faster than the previous EDGE network.

Jobs also announced new features in the iPhone 3G, including real GPS functionality and the iTunes App Store, which offers software applications that can be purchased or downloaded Over the Air (OTA).

iPod Touch and Nano

On January 15, 2008, Apple announced a $20 software update for the iPod touch that includes Mail, Maps, Stocks, Notes, and Weather. iPod touches shipped after this date include the new applications for free. On January 22, 2008, Apple released a pink version of the 8GB iPod nano.

iPod Shuffle Second Generation

On February 19, 2008, Apple announced a price drop on the iPod shuffle to $49 and introduced a new 2GB model for $69.

Mac OS 10.5.3

On May 28, 2008, Apple released 10.5.3, a maintenance release to its Leopard operating system that was widely anticipated by users due to a number of problems, mostly with audio applications and hardware, that users experienced with 10.5.2.

Retail

As of this writing, Apple opened eight new retail stores in 2008 for a total of 211, and there were at least 28 more that are confirmed (and as many as 37 more unconfirmed) to be opened by 2011.

Chapter Seven

Macworld Expo

Each January, Mac faithful gather at the Apple lovefest known as Macworld Expo. It's the place where new products are announced, not only by Apple, but also by every accessory, peripheral, and related product manufacturer. Many companies attend Macworld Expo hoping that some of the extra limelight generated by Apple will spill over onto their products. Even manufacturers that don't exhibit at the Big Dance (as it is sometimes called) will release new products during Macworld Expo in order to capitalize on the attention generated by whatever Apple is doing.

The event is huge for Apple's employees, partners, and customers because it's the culmination of a 12-month, highly secretive, product development cycle since the last Expo. Employees can finally breathe a sigh of relief after shipping their product; many take extended vacations as soon as the show is over. Partners are also sworn to secrecy on most Apple products, so they're also elated to both ship and finally be able to talk about their new offerings. Customers get the most worked up because, unlike employees or partners, they have no idea what to expect and have to rely on rumors and speculation about what is going to be announced.

Apple customers and fans flock to the event in San Francisco from all over the globe. Hotel rooms close to the Moscone Center are sold out months in advance. User groups and clubs use the week of the event to hold their own gatherings, and larger vendors throw lavish parties. There's an entire party and event circuit, large and small, that begins the minute the show floor closes and proceeds into the wee hours of the morning. The party circuit has grown so large that it even has its own unofficial online guide that's a bible of most attendees. People have proposed and been married at Macworld Expo.

For more on Apple's fans, see the "Culture" section in Chapter 3, "Historical Context."

THE KEYNOTE ADDRESS

Apple's annual Macworld Expo conference kicks off with a keynote presentation by Steve Jobs that's more like a rock concert than a technology presentation. Tickets to the "Stevenote" are coveted and difficult to get. They're only given in advance to people that purchase the most expensive all-inclusive conference passes, and even the media list is closely scrutinized.

Depending on the year and the amount of preshow speculation, the energy level in the building is palpable. Electricity fills the air, fueled by suspense that's built up over the past year and the murmur of attendees wondering what new products will come out of the event. Jobs plays prekeynote music at intolerably high levels from his personal playlist of favorites, including the Beatles, Dylan, and the Grateful Dead, which further builds anticipation.

JOBS THE SHOWMAN

When he eventually takes the stage, Jobs is greeted enthusiastically by the adoring crowd. Jobs typically wears his iconic uniform for Macworld: a black mock turtleneck and faded jeans, a dress code that he's only deviated from a couple of times. At Macworld Expo Tokyo in 2001, Jobs dispensed with his trademark jeans and black turtleneck for a business suit. The media buzzed. Why the departure? Did he have a big meeting that day? An interview? Jobs's change of clothes made more of an impression than the Dalmatian blue and flower power iMacs he introduced. At Macworld Expo Tokyo 2000, Jobs wore bright green Prada shoes that probably got more attention themselves than other CEOs' entire presentations.

Even the jaded members of the media who've been to all of Jobs's keynotes can't help but get swept up in the excitement. Jobs uses a methodical approach in his keynote presentations, beginning with a relatively benign recap of the past year that includes sales figures, milestones, and highlights. Then come the product announcements. Jobs likes to start small and work his way up to the big stuff. He'll usually begin with software, then speed-bumps to existing models, and finally, anything that's brand new or earth-shattering.

The entire time Jobs peppers his presentation with product demonstrations by top Apple executives. He also brings up the top brass from companies making significant announcements at the show and gives them a few minutes to speak. They usually speak in glowing terms about Apple and its new products while Jobs gets to rest his voice for a few minutes. Jobs plays his latest television commercials for the audience, which, in addition to giving him a break, provide valuable focus group testing. Imagine, for a second, a keynote address—with commercials. No other company could pull that off.

As he works his way through the winding, but carefully choreographed, keynote, he builds anticipation to a final and dramatic crescendo. At a concert, it would be the encore. After the bulk of the presentation, when it appears that he's finished, Jobs is famous for turning to the crowd to tell them that he has "One more thing." That one thing is usually the most exciting announcement of the entire keynote address.

Chapter Eight

Apple Leadership

There have been only six CEOs at the helm of Apple, and each left his own unique mark on the company—for better or for worse. Following are the CEOs and some of their notable accomplishments.

CEOS

1. 1977–1981: Michael "Scotty" Scott
2. 1981–1983: A. C. "Mike" Markkula
3. 1983–1993: John Sculley
4. 1993–1996: Michael Spindler
5. 1996–1997: Gil Amelio
6. 1997–present: Steve Jobs (interim CEO 1997–2000)

ORIGINAL LEADERS

Apple was founded on April 1, 1976, by Steve Jobs, Steve Wozniak, and Ronald Wayne to sell the Apple I personal computer kit. The kits were built in the living room of Jobs's parents' home. Apple Computer Inc. was incorporated January 3, 1977, by Jobs and Wozniak. Wayne sold his share of the company back to Jobs and Wozniak.

An internal power struggle between Steve Jobs and new Apple CEO John Sculley developed in 1985. The Apple board sided with Sculley, and Jobs was removed from managerial duties. Jobs later resigned and went on to found NeXT Inc. He also purchased the visual effects house, Pixar.

For more on the History of Apple, see Chapter 1, "Origins and History."

MICHAEL "SCOTTY" SCOTT

Michael "Scotty" Scott was Apple's first CEO and served from February 1977 to March 1981. A veteran of National Semiconductor, Scott was asked by Mike Markkula to become CEO because both Steve Jobs and Steve Wozniak weren't sufficiently experienced for the job. Scott was famous for his "no typewriters at Apple" mantra.

In 1979 and 1980, the Macintosh project consisted of four people and wasn't considered important within Apple. It was almost cancelled a couple of times. When Apple had another major reorganization in the fall of 1980, it was terminated again, but project leader Jef Raskin pleaded with Scott and Markkula for more time, and was granted a three-month stay of execution.[1]

On February 25, 1981, Scott fired 40 Apple employees, including half of the Apple II team, and later assembled the remaining employees to explain the firings by saying, "I used to say that when being CEO at Apple wasn't fun anymore, I'd quit. But now I've changed my mind—when it isn't fun any more, I'll fire people until it's fun again."[2] Afterward Scott became vice chairman and Mike Markkula replaced him.

A. C. "MIKE" MARKKULA

Armas Clifford "Mike" Markkula provided essential business expertise and co-signed for a much-needed $250,000 bank loan during the formation of Apple in 1977, for which he was given a one-third share of the company. Markkula brought in Apple's first CEO, Michael Scott, and replaced him in 1981 to become Apple's second CEO. Steve Wozniak gives Markkula a majority of the credit for Apple's success, even though he was replaced by John Sculley in 1983.

Jean-Louis Gassée

Jean-Louis Gassée worked for Hewlett-Packard before becoming head of Apple France. Apple CEO John Sculley appointed Gassée to be head of Macintosh development—Steve Jobs's old position. Gassée was an executive at Apple from 1981 to 1990 and introduced several Mac products in the late 1980s, including the Mac Portable and the Mac IIfx.

He's known for his sense of humor and unique sense of style. Gassée wore tailored suits when necessary, but preferred wearing a black leather jacket and a diamond-stud earring. Gassée later went on to found Be Inc., creators of the BeOS computer operating system. After leaving Be, he became Chairman of PalmSource Inc. in November 2004.

JOHN SCULLEY

The departure of Steve Jobs from Apple after a dispute with new CEO John Sculley ushered in a new era of management at Apple. Apple was no longer under the control of its original founders, and professional management was recruited to take Apple to the next level. Unfortunately, things don't always turn out as planned.

John Sculley was named PepsiCo's youngest president in 1977 and was hand-recruited by Jobs to become CEO of Apple on April 8, 1983. Sculley was the third and longest-serving CEO of Apple. Sculley's mission was to apply his marketing skills from Pepsi, a major consumer brand, to the personal computer market, especially the Macintosh.

Sculley raised the initial price of the Macintosh to $2,495 from the originally planned $1,995, using the extra money for better profits and more advertising.[3] Apple responded to the IBM PC with the Performa, Centris, and Quadra product lines, but they were marketed poorly. Part of Sculley's strategy was to release dozens of major models with hundreds of configurations. Apple released too many Macs that were too similar with a dizzying array of confusing model numbers, which didn't fit with Apple's reputation for simplicity.

During the Sculley years, Microsoft threatened to discontinue the popular Mac version of the Microsoft Office suite if Apple didn't license parts of the Macintosh graphical user interface to Microsoft. Sculley reluctantly agreed, forever changing the course of computer history.

Sculley was the driving force behind Apple's Newton MessagePad project. Newton wasn't originally intended to be a Personal Digital Assistant (PDA), though. It was designed to suit architects. The Newton project missed deadlines, and there was a fear that it would cannibalize Macintosh sales. Newton was reincarnated as a PDA, a term coined by Apple's Sculley[4] relatively late in the development cycle. Newton was repackaged as a device that would complement the Mac instead of competing with it. After costing the company more than $500 million in R&D, the Newton was eventually cancelled.

Sculley was removed by Apple's board in 1993. His tenure is regarded by many as unsuccessful, beginning the company's decline that was only reversed by Jobs when he returned to the company many years later.

MICHAEL SPINDLER

In June 1993, Michael Spindler replaced John Sculley as the fourth CEO of Apple, although Sculley remained on board for a while as chairman. Spindler was originally president of Apple Europe and came to Apple when it had a 10% market share of the global computer market, second only to the world's largest computer maker, IBM. Apple sold 4.7 million Macs that year, a company record, and Spindler presided over the introduction and rollout of the Power PC processor.

During the Spindler era, the Mac operating system and ROM were licensed to third-party manufacturers Power Computing, Motorola, Radius, APS Technologies, DayStar Digital, and UMAX for the first time in

Apple history. The problem is that cloning strategy didn't work. Instead of expanding Apple's market share as planned, it stagnated and clone sales slowly chipped away at Apple's bottom line.

Spindler presided over several failed initiatives, including Newton and Copland. He also entertained takeover discussions by IBM, Sun Microsystems, and Philips, which never came to fruition. In the first quarter of 1996, Apple reported a loss of $69 million and laid off 1,300 staff. On February 2, 1996, Apple's board fired Spindler and appointed Gil Amelio as the new CEO.

GIL AMELIO

Gilbert F. Amelio, a veteran of National Semiconductor and widely regarded turnaround artist, was named the fifth CEO of Apple in February 1996. During his short, 18-month tenure, Amelio identified several reasons why he thought that Apple was doing poorly, including poor cash flow, hardware, software, corporate culture, and a general lack of focus. In an attempt to turn Apple around, Amelio laid off a third the Apple staff, canceled a number of money-losing projects, discontinued the Copland operating system, and expedited the development of Mac OS 8.

Amelio was also responsible for negotiating with Steve Jobs's new company NeXT and eventually negotiated its purchase. Price aside, NeXT Inc.'s NEXTSTEP operating system would eventually become the foundation for Mac OS X, which became a runaway success and a key to Apple's recovery, renaissance, and resurgence. The meeting with NeXT was a fluke, though. Amelio was in discussions with former Apple executive Jean Louis Gassée to purchase BeOS when a NeXT salesman called Apple out of the blue suggesting that it look at NeXT.

Despite his minor successes, Apple's stock hit a 12-year low under Amelio's watch and market share continued to plummet due to quality problems and confusion about the product line. During this period, Amelio was criticized for his $7 million benefits package. He lavishly redecorated the executive suite, had $26 million in stock, and negotiated a severance package worth about $7 million.

In the second quarter of 1997, Amelio announced a $740 million loss and on July 9, 1997, he was removed as CEO by the Apple board after the company suffered crippling financial losses while he was at the helm.

STEVE JOBS

After Gil Amelio negotiated the purchase of NeXT on December 20, 1996, Steve Jobs returned to Apple as a "special advisor" to Amelio to aid in the transition. It was the first time Jobs had been back to the Apple campus in nearly 11 years. Jobs was reluctant to come back to Apple; he had turned the page on Apple in his mind. He was CEO of Pixar now and was enjoying the success of its first film, *Toy Story*.

Jobs was leery of returning to the fast-paced computer industry where computers were obsolete before they were released. He had gotten used to the slower pace of the movie business, telling *Time:*

> I don't think that you'll be able to boot up any computer today in 20 years. [But] *Snow White* has sold 28 million copies, and it's a 60-year-old production. People don't read Herodotus or Homer to their kids any more, but everybody watches movies. These are our myths today. Disney puts those myths into our culture, and hopefully Pixar will, too.[5]

Jobs was so skeptical of Apple, in fact, that he wanted his compensation for the Pixar deal in cash—which was declined by Amelio. Still, Jobs immediately sold Apple the $1.5 million in stock he got from the Pixar deal at bargain-basement prices, retaining just one share. After firing Amelio, the Apple board asked Jobs to be CEO, but he would only agree to be "interim CEO" for a period of six months, while he helped seek a permanent CEO.

During this time, Jobs began a much-needed restructuring of the company. The first thing he did was to replace most of the Apple board with his friends, including Larry Ellison of Oracle and a series of his captains from NeXT: David Manovich (sales), Jon Rubinstein (hardware), and Avadis "Avie" Tevanian (software). Jobs only kept one original board member, Fred Anderson, the CFO who'd recently been hired by Amelio.

Jobs then cut a deal with Microsoft whereby Apple would drop its user interface copyright infringement lawsuit against Microsoft and make Internet Explorer the default Web browser in exchange for Microsoft's commitment to continue to develop Office for the Mac for a period of five years and an investment of $150 million in Apple. Jobs also hired TBWA/Chiat/Day as Apple's advertising agency of record and effectively terminated Apple's agreements with the Apple clone makers.

Jobs proceeded to cancel hundreds of software and hardware products, including printers, monitors, and the beloved Newton. The most important change Jobs made was to simplify Apple's product line down from dozens of SKUs to a simple quadrant of four major market segments. The new simplicity made development and marketing much easier and also made it easier for customers to chose and purchase a Mac.

RECENT LEADERSHIP

Several of Apple's current executives have made an impact on Apple as a company such that their whims create trends, style, and have the ability to chart the course of society. Probably, none has changed the world more than Jonathan Ive.

Jonathan Ive

One of the most influential people in the recovery, renaissance, and resurgence periods of Apple is Jonathan Ive. The man credited as the principal designer of the iMac, iPod, and iPhone is internationally renowned, yet he remains humble, modest, and private. When asked to autograph his book *Apple Design* at a signing in Japan, he wouldn't sign his name "because it was a team effort" and instead autographed the book "Apple Design Team."

The London-born designer has been referred to as Apple's forgotten savior,[6] but Apple prefers to call him Senior Vice President of Industrial Design.[7]

Ive was raised in East London by his father, a silversmith, and studied industrial design at Newcastle Polytechnic in 1985, where he received a Bachelor of Arts and an honorary doctorate degree. He graduated with honors, having created a pebble-shaped concept for a product to replace cash and credit cards as his final-year project.

At London design agency Tangerine, Ive created products ranging from combs to power tools to televisions and ceramics. One of the agency's largest clients was a bathroom and plumbing company called Ideal Standard for whom Ive designed toilets—with inspiration from marine biology books.

Ive moved to the United States in 1992 to pursue his career at Apple. While at Apple, he designed computers with a goal to complete the user experience. His primary design principles are ease and simplicity, which are a perfect fit for Apple. "People talk about how design is important but that's such a partial truth. It's good design that is important."[8]

He ascended to Senior Vice President of Industrial Design in 1997, when Steve Jobs returned to Apple, and reports directly to Jobs. Ive and his team are responsible for the design of the iPod, iMac, and iPhone—three of the most influential products in computers, technology, and arguably, popular culture.

Ive has been recognized with numerous design awards, including being named Designer of the Year by the Design Museum London in 2003 and given the title Royal Designer for Industry by the Royal Society of Arts. Apple products have become celebrated design icons featured in the permanent collections of museums worldwide, including MOMA in New York and the Pompidou in Paris.

Apple's leadership at publication time consisted of the following:

Current Executives: 2008

- Steve Jobs, CEO and Co-founder, Apple Inc.
- Timothy D. Cook, Chief Operating Officer

- Daniel Cooperman, Senior Vice President, General Counsel and Secretary
- Tony Fadell, Senior Vice President, iPod Division
- Jonathan Ive, Senior Vice President, Industrial Design
- Ron Johnson, Senior Vice President, Retail Division
- Peter Oppenheimer, Chief Financial Officer
- Philip W. Schiller, Senior Vice President, Worldwide Product Marketing
- Bertrand Serlet, Senior Vice President, Software Engineering
- Sina Tamaddon, Senior Vice President, Applications Division

Current Board of Directors: 2008

- William V. Campbell, Chairman, Intuit Inc.
- Millard S. Drexler, Chairman and CEO, J. Crew
- Albert Gore, Jr., Former Vice President of the United States
- Steve Jobs, CEO and Co-founder, Apple Inc.
- Andrea Jung, Chairman and CEO, Avon Products Inc.
- Arthur D. Levinson, Ph.D., Chairman and CEO, Genentech Inc.
- Dr. Eric Schmidt, CEO, Google
- Jerome B. York, Chief Executive Officer, Harwinton Capital Corporation

Chapter Nine

Competition

Critics have written Apple off time and again, yet it rose from the ashes to astound the critics and delight its customers. That's not luck or happenstance—it's vision, dedication, and persistence. Everyone loves an underdog and Apple is a classic example, but now that Apple's the lead dog in several markets, will customers treat it differently? Will the competition?

In the late 1980s, Apple's chief competition was the Amiga and Atari ST platforms. But by the 1990s, clones of the IBM PC had become more popular than all three, thanks to Windows 3.0, a competing graphical user interface to the Mac OS.

Apple's response to the PC tidal wave was to flood the market with new Mac models, including Quadra, Centris, and Performa. The problem was that there were too many choices and confusing model names and numbers (Performa 6117CD, anyone?). Even employees couldn't differentiate between them, and they were all very close in specifications, often only deviating by a few megs here or there. The litany of confusing products names, numbers, and specs was a lethal combination that frightened customers away.

Apple's retail sales partners, like Sears and CompUSA, became its worst enemies. They were often incapable of demonstrating or even *displaying* Macs that they had in stock. Pricing only made matters worse. Stripped, bare bones PCs looked cheap on the price tag, but by the time you added basic features that the Macs came with, standard, they cost more. Still the perception was that the Mac cost more, so people bought PCs.

In 1994, Apple surprised its loyal flock by doing a deal with its longtime competitor IBM. Apple joined the AIM (Apple, Motorola, IBM) alliance to create a new hardware platform, known as PReP, short for PowerPC Reference Platform. The goal was to use IBM and Motorola hardware and Apple software to dominate the Windows-powered PC market. The Power Mac line, which utilized IBM's PowerPC processor, was the first step to this end in 1994. While it was good for users because it meant faster Macs, Power PC didn't even put a dent into Windows PC sales. In fact, PC sales increased.

Apple eventually ceded the low end of the market to the IBM clones, realizing that it was a race for the bottom, and not a market that Apple wanted to be in. Jobs smartly decided to let the commodity PC vendors like Dell, HP, and Compaq duke it out for the low-margin, cheapest machines while Apple would focus on higher-margin luxury machines targeting artists and professionals.

INTEL

When you can't beat 'em, join 'em. What was left to do? Dump IBM and Motorola and switch to Intel chips. The old expression, "keep your friends close and your enemies closer," may have factored into Apple's thinking. IBM and Motorola were small players in the mass-market chip game and subject to delivery problems, which made Macs ship late as a result. Plus, there was a 3.0GHz ceiling that the AIM troika was having trouble breaking, which bugged Jobs to no end. To make matters worse, it was becoming increasingly clear that neither IBM nor Motorola was capable of delivering a G5 chip that was small and cool enough for use in Apple's PowerBook. The desktop chip required nine fans to cool in the Power Mac G5 and that just wasn't possible in a notebook, so Jobs dumped IBM and Motorola for Intel.

In June 2005, Jobs announced that Apple was switching to Intel as its primary chip supplier. Apple began producing Intel-based Macs in 2006 and completed the transition to Intel by the end of the year—a year ahead of schedule.

It was another astonishing turn for Apple. First it jumped into IBM, its archrival in the 1990s, now it was going to use Intel chips? Blasphemy. What next? Would Apple cut a deal with Microsoft and take cash to drop its lawsuit? Jobs did that too.

Once Apple switched to Intel and got on par with the competition, the landscape suddenly changed. Now that Apple was using Intel chips, had a native operating system, and was even capable of virtualizing Windows at full speed (thanks to tools like Boot Camp, Parallels, and VMWare), the playing field was truly leveled. In fact, Macs could run Windows faster than some PCs could. Now Apple was able to compete with just about any computer on the market.

COMPUTER COMPETITORS

Apple's biggest competitors on computer hardware are all the big guys: Dell, Compaq, and HP. The switch to Intel forced Apple to be more competitive on price and when it did, sales climbed. For the first time, Windows users were defecting to the Mac platform en masse. Apple had built a compelling computer platform that was fast, stable, and gorgeous, and customers ate it up. On the software side, Apple's chief competitor is still Microsoft. With Apple slowly chipping away at Microsoft's golden goose—Windows—Microsoft was forced to make its latest operating system, Vista, more visually appealing and easier to use with the myriad of electronic gadgets that people were buying. Competition has arguable been good for both camps.

RISE OF THE CLONES?

An entirely new class of competitor emerged when Apple switched to the Intel platform in 2006: clones. Almost 10 years after Steve Jobs ripped up Apple's contracts with cloners, they had returned. This time was different. The clones of 2006 were unauthorized by Apple. Creative PC builders were able to build a Mac clone from off-the-shelf PC parts and a creative installation of Mac OS X. Dubbed Hackintosh, these Frankenmacs were being built almost as soon as OS X was available for Intel chips. One daring vendor, Psystar, tempted fate in early 2008 and even began shipping a low-cost Mac clone, with Mac OS 10.5 Leopard pre-installed. Apple was tolerating the practice as of this writing, but the conventional wisdom is that Apple won't allow the company to pre-install Mac OS on the new generation of clones for very long.

SOFTWARE COMPETITORS

In addition to the perennial competition from Windows on the desktop level, there's also the free alternative—Linux. Low-cost computers can be assembled that run a totally free collection of software. Everything from the operating system (Linux) to the office suite (Open Office) to photo editing software (GIMP) can be downloaded totally free and installed on a moderately powerful computer that costs between $200 and $300. While not necessarily a direct competitor to Apple, Linux is the only other operating system that has a fan base almost as passionate as Mac users. Intel Macs can also boot Linux, in addition to Windows and other OSes, giving Mac users more platform choices than ever. But as long as you buy the hardware from Apple, Cupertino doesn't mind which OS you run on it.

MEDIA PLAYER COMPETITORS

The advent of the iPod in 2001 put Apple in competition with an entirely new raft of companies. Sony's venerable Walkman lost several years of competition when it got mired in its proprietary DRM system called ATRAC. Unlike Apple, though, its early music players couldn't play MP3 files, dooming them to certain failure.

In an attempt to capitalize on the success of the portable media player market, Dell jumped into the fray with a hard drive player call the DJ. Microsoft, never being one to sit on the sidelines, released an iPod-like device called Zune. SanDisk also makes a whole line of players, as do Samsung, Archos, Creative Labs, e.Digital, Philips, and RCA. Each has its own slightly different take on the concept, but they all pretty much do the same thing.

Apple got off to such an early and strong start with iPod that it still dominates the field. The top five MP3 players as of February 2008 were Apple with 72.3%, SanDisk with 9.7%, Creative Labs with 2.7%, Samsung with 2.5%, and Microsoft with 4%.[1]

MEDIA CENTER, MOVIE RENTAL, SET-TOP BOX COMPETITORS

When Apple launched the Apple TV set-top box in January 2007, it jumped into yet another mature market with companies that have been doing it for a lot longer. Apple's 40GB set-top appliance originally sold for $299 but was later dropped to $229 and allowed users to stream digital content from a Mac OS X or Windows computer running iTunes to a widescreen television. A later software update allowed Apple TV to purchase and rent movies in High Definition (HD) and purchase television programs and music directly to the device without requiring a computer.

Comparisons between Apple TV and Microsoft's Xbox 360 game console were inevitable because the 360 has media center capabilities via Vista's Windows Media Extender that allows it to work with the Xbox 360. Microsoft has been at it longer than Apple and is sometimes given an edge over Apple; the reviews seem to be pretty evenly split.

In addition to the classic Apple versus Microsoft comparisons, there are also a number of other devices competing for attention in the set-top box category.

Netflix launched a set-top box with Rokuand, a $99 unlimited movie streaming service that's a formidable competitor to Apple. Netflix has the advantage of having a billing relationship with more than seven million subscribers who already rent their movies, which is tough to compete with. Its top-tier Web site and best-of-breed recommendation engine gives it a running start against all the other guys.

With digital television and movies being the next big prize in the digital revolution, Apple has more competitors in this field than any other. Content boxes are available from MovieBeam, Akimbo, and Myka. Digital media adapters from Netgear, D-Link, Buffalo, and Mvix. iPod docks are available from DLO, Griffin, and Keyspan. Convergent boxes from Pioneer, HP, TiVO, and PC services like MovieLink, Vongo, Orb, and Joost are also in the mix.

And don't forget that broadcast television networks like ABC and NBC are getting into the game, and traditional cable and telephone providers like Comcast, DirectTV, and Verizon are all placing big bets on time-shifting with DVRs and are keeping their eye on the emerging stream video market too.

If that wasn't enough, Apple also competes on a nontangible level as well. Apple has become a lifestyle brand that's much more than just hardware, software, and services. Apple is now a fashion accessory (iPod shuffle), clothing brand (its various iPod cases and MacBook bags), and a destination (Apple online and retail stores) that must compete for customers' most precious resource of all, their time.

Famous Flops

Apple III—Launched in May 1980, the Apple III ended up being a commercial failure for several reasons. For starters, at $4,340 to $7,800, it was far too expensive compared to competitors and its software catalog was limited. To make matters worse, Jobs wanted the Apple III to be designed without a cooling fan (or vents) so that it would operate silently. This turned out to be incorrect and the chassis wasn't able to adequately cool the system, and the Apple III became prone to overheating and crashing. Almost all the original Apple III computers were recalled and Apple had to replace as many as 14,000 of the first Apple IIIs for free.

Lisa—On January 19, 1983, Apple released the Lisa as one of the first commercial personal computers to have a Graphical User Interface (GUI) and a mouse. Although Lisa had advanced features like protected memory, cooperative multitasking, and a hard disk, it also came with an astronomical price tag of $9,995.

Taligent—This next-generation Apple operating system was supposed to replace the Mac OS. Taligent was developed in 1988 with IBM to compete with offerings from Microsoft and NeXT, but it never took off. By 1998 Taligent was dissolved.

Macintosh Portable—The Mac Portable was also announced in September 1989 and was Apple's first attempt at a portable Macintosh. The Mac Portable was nicknamed the "Mac luggable" because of its large size and weight. It became a commercial flop because it was enormous, heavy, slow, and the active matrix screen wasn't (initially) backlit. The $6,500 price tag helped cement the Mac Portable as one of Apple's biggest flops of all time.

Apple Newton—The Newton MessagePad was announced in August 1993 and was a completely new product for Apple and represented a brave step into the unfamiliar territory of Personal Digital Assistants (PDAs). The handwriting recognition was difficult to learn and would often suggest hilarious, but incorrect, phrases. The Newton's misrecognitions became the butt of many jokes in the national media. After it soaked up $500 million in R&D money, Apple discontinued the Newton in 1997 when Steve Jobs returned to Apple.

Macintosh TV—The limited edition Mac TV was announced in 1993 and was one of the few Macs that shipped in a black case. Only

10,000 Mac TVs were made, and it ultimately flopped because of poor graphic performance and because it couldn't display a TV feed in a desktop window. Oops.

eWorld—Introduced in 1994, eWorld was a joint effort of Apple and America Online that was designed as an easy-to-use online service that included applications for e-mail, news, shopping, and a bulletin board system. In 1996 eWorld was shut down after subscriptions failed to materialize as expected.

Pippin—In 1995, Apple's Pippin was another attempt at developing a multimedia platform. Powered by a 66MHz PowerPC 603e processor. Pippin suffered the same fate at the Mac TV and was silently killed after selling only 42,000 units.

Cyberdog—Introduced in February 1996, Apple's first attempt at a Web browser was anything but successful. Cyberdog included a browser, e-mail, news reader, and address book and was supposed to compete with Microsoft's Internet Explorer and Netscape Navigator. It was soon dropped in favor of Internet Explorer in May 1997.

Twentieth Anniversary Macintosh—In June 1997, Apple announced, appropriately enough, the Twentieth Anniversary Macintosh (or TAM for short) to mark the occasion. The system looked incredibly modern and had a tiny footprint thanks to a flat-screen monitor that was only found in notebooks at the time. Included in the astronomical price was a concierge service with personalized delivery and setup, but it had to be scrapped when sales didn't pan out.

Motorola ROKR—On September 7, 2005, Apple and Motorola released the ROKR E1, the first mobile phone to use iTunes. However, the announcement was buried in the iPod nano announcement and given less attention in the press conference than the nano. ROKR could only hold up to 100 songs, which in the era of the iPod, was perceived as too little, and it wasn't designed by the Apple design team, which was regarded as one of the top technology design groups in the world.

Chapter Ten

Finances

Apple was incorporated in California on January 3, 1977. Apple went public on December 12, 1980, and its Initial Public Offering (IPO) share price was $22.50. On a split-adjusted basis, Apple's Initial Public Offering stock price was $2.75. The Apple IPO generated more money than any IPO since Ford Motor Company in 1956 and created about 300 instant millionaires.

Apple doesn't pay its stockholders a dividend; it last paid dividends from June 1987 to December 1995. Apple had three 2-for-1 stock splits on June 15, 1987, June 20, 2000, and February 28, 2005. Apple's stock is traded under ticker symbol *AAPL* on the NASDAQ stock exchange. (On the Frankfurt Stock Exchange, Apple trades under the symbol *APCD*.)[1]

Over the course of five years, from January 2002 to January 2007, Apple's stock price ranged from $10.39 to $97.10 with a five-year average of $39.88. In 2006 (from January 2006 to January 2007), Apple's stock averaged $71.34.[2]

As of June 2008, APPL shares hit a 52-week high of $202.96 on December 27, 2007, and a 52-week low of $111.62 on August 16, 2007.

The returns for AAPL stock are:

- 1 Year + 58.92%
- 3 Year + 365.36%
- 5 Year + 2003.06%

Not bad. Even better would be purchasing Apple stock in February 1997, just before Jobs came back to Apple, when it was trading below $4 a share (split-adjusted). An investment of just $1,000 then would be worth $38,900 now.[3]

The bulls think that Apple stock still has a lot of growth potential. Piper Jaffray analyst Gene Munster predicts that the stock will hit $250 per share while Carl Howe of Blackfriars Communications, who follows Apple carefully (and owns Apple stock), predicts Apple shares will hit $300 in 2009.[4]

Table 10.1
Apple Financial Data

Period	Net Sales (M) Revenue	Net Profits (M)	Revenue Growth	Return on Sales
FY 1981	335	unknown	—	—
FY 1982	583	61	74%	10%
FY 1983	983	77	69%	8%
FY 1984	1.516	64	54%	4%
FY 1985	1.918	61	27%	3%
FY 1986	1.902	154	–1%	8%
FY 1987	2.661	218	40%	8%
FY 1988	4.071	400	53%	10%
FY 1989	5.284	454	30%	9%
FY 1990	5.558	475	5%	9%
FY 1991	7.977	310	44%	4%
FY 1992	7.087	530	–11%	7%
FY 1993	6.309	87	–11%	1%
FY 1994	9.189	310	46%	3%
FY 1995	11.602	424	20%	4%
FY 1996	9.833	–816	–11%	–8%
FY 1997	7.081	–1.045	–28%	–15%
FY 1998	5.941	309	–16%	5%
FY 1999	6.134	601	3%	10%
FY 2000	7.983	786	30%	10%
FY 2001	5.363	–25	–33%	0%
FY 2002	5.742	65	–2%	1%
FY 2003	6.207	57	18%	1%
FY 2004	8.279	266	33%	3%
FY 2005	13.931	1.328	68%	10%
FY 2006	19.315	1.989	39%	10%
FY 2007	24.006	3.496	24%	15%
Q1 2008	9.608	1.581	35%	16%
Q1 2008	7.512	1.045	43%	14%

One thing's for sure, Apple has consistently enriched shareholders since 2002. From a loss of $37 million in 2001, Apple has increased its revenues to $1.989 billion and its Earnings Per Share (EPS) from negative $.04 to a positive $2.27.

Apple uses a fiscal calendar so that year-end accounting work doesn't coincide with periods of traditionally high retail activity like the holiday shopping rush. Apple's fiscal year 2008 is as follows:

- First Quarter: October 1, 2007–December 31, 2007
- Second Quarter: January 1, 2008–March 31, 2008
- Third Quarter: April 1, 2008–June 30, 2008
- Fourth Quarter: July 1, 2008–September 30, 2008

Table 10.1 shows historical Apple financial data (all figures are in U.S. dollars).[5]

The following are some financial highlights (and lowlights) from Apple over the years. All years are fiscal years.

1997   In June, Apple CEO Gil Amelio announced a $740 million loss in the second quarter. By year's end, Apple turned a profit for the first year after losses through 1995 and 1996.[6] On August 6, Steve Jobs announced an alliance between Apple and Microsoft including a $150 million investment in Apple. In exchange, Apple includes Microsoft's Internet Explorer Web browser as the default Web browser on every Mac shipped.

1998   On January 7, Apple officially returned to profitability with Steve Jobs's announcement of a $47 million profit in the first quarter. The turnaround was complete. In July, Apple announced its third profitable quarter ($101 million) in a row.

2000   On April 19, Apple announced a $233 million profit in its third quarter. On September 29, Apple corrected its predicted earnings for the fourth quarter. The number was revised from $165 million down to $110 million, causing Apple stock to free fall from $53.50 to $29.13 (a 45% drop) overnight. On December 5, Apple announced an estimated loss of $259 million for the first quarter of 2001 ending on December 30, 2000. This was the first quarterly loss for Apple in three years.

2001   On April 18, Apple announced a quarterly profit of $43 million, with Mac OS X responsible for $19 million in sales. For the fiscal year ending September 9, Apple had $5.4 billion in revenue, a gross profit of $1,235 million, and a negative operating income of $344 million. It incurred a loss of $52 million before tax and after tax it was $37 million.[7]

2002 On January 16, Apple reported a profit of $38 million for the first quarter of 2002, shipping 746,000 Macs. On October 16, Apple announced a loss of $45 million in the fourth quarter of 2002, mainly because of low sales of the Power Mac and PowerBook line. For the year Apple had revenues of $5.7 billion, gross profit of $1.6 billion. Apple's income after tax for the fiscal year was $65 million.[8]

2003 In 2003, Apple's stock began an unprecedented climb. Between early 2003 and January 2006, the price of a share of Apple stock increased more than tenfold, from around $6 per share (split-adjusted) to more than $80 per share. For fiscal 2003, Apple increased its total revenue to $6.2 billion with a net profit of $57 million.

2004 Fiscal 2004 saw a considerable rise in operating expenses and revenues. Net income came in at $266 million—a whopping increase of 286% over 2003. In fiscal 2005 and 2006, Apple also experienced a tremendous rise in revenue.

2005 In Fiscal 2005, Apple reported net sales of $13.9 billion and $1.3 billion in net profits, breaking the one billion dollar profit mark for the first time. This was an astonishing increase in net profit of 399%.

2006 On January 13, Apple's market capitalization surpassed Dell's for the first time. Nearly 10 years prior, in 1997, Michael Dell, Dell's CEO, said that if he ran Apple, he would "shut it down and give the money back to the shareholders."[9] For Fiscal 2006, Apple reported net sales of $19.3 billion (a 39% increase) and a net profit of $2 billion, an increase of almost 50%.[10]

2007 During the third quarter of 2007, Apple grabbed 8.1% of U.S. market share, compared with just 6.2% during the year-earlier period.[11] For Fiscal 2007, Apple reported net sales of $24 billion (a 24% increase) and a net profit of $3.5 billion, an increase of almost 76%.

2008 In the first quarter of 2008, Apple posted revenue of $9.6 billion and a net quarterly profit of $1.6 billion. Gross margin was 34.7%, up from 31.2% in the year-ago quarter. International sales accounted for 45% of the quarter's revenue.

In the first quarter of 2008, Apple sold more than 2.3 million Macs—a growth rate that was more than 2.5 times that of the overall PC market, according to research firm IDC. Apple grabbed 6% of the U.S. personal computer market in the first quarter, according to IDC, up from 4.9% the year before.[12] Macs continue to gain market share against PCs, accounting for 6.5% of unit shipments in the first quarter compared with 5.2% in the year-earlier period, according to Worthen.[13]

In the second quarter of 2008, Apple posted revenue of $7.5 billion and a net quarterly profit of $1.1 billion. Gross margin was 32.9%, down from 35.1% in the year-ago quarter. International sales accounted for 44% of the quarter's revenue.

Chapter Eleven

Future Prospects

When you look at the history of Apple, it's pretty clear the company is on a major upswing. Revenue and profit are booming and so is the stock price, thanks to a strong product mix, excellent customer support, and an extremely loyal customer base. Apple has also made great progress with switchers, people that have switched from a Windows PC to a Mac, thanks in large part to the iPod's halo effect. Windows users start with an iPod, then switch to a Mac when they're due for a new machine.

In less than a decade, Apple has reinvented itself, removing the *Computer* from its name to be simply *Apple Inc.* This move speaks volumes about where Apple is headed. In January 2007, iPod sales made up almost half of Apple's quarterly revenue ($3.4 billion) and when you add items like iTunes, iPhone, and Apple TV to the bottom line, Apple is definitely making more money from things other than traditional computers. Hence the name change.

In 2001, Steve Jobs positioned the Mac as the digital hub to which you could connect your camera, music player, phone, etc. Today, Apple doesn't just want to be the hub—it wants to be the spokes and wheel too. Products like iPod and the iTunes Store allowed Apple to branch out into the uncharted waters of the music business, and it quickly became the captain of the high seas. Now Apple's doing the same thing with television and movies. Apple's got its sights set on the rest of the entertainment business, like it did with music, but it's going to take its time.

Apple's new modus operandi these days is to let other, well-funded companies take the first shot at a product, spend a lot of money, and make a lot of mistakes. Then once they've taken their licks, Apple enters the market with a product that works and looks better and reaps the rewards. It's not going to be easy, though; the iPod was a lot about having the right timing. Apple released the iPod in 2001 right after the halcyon days of Napster, when just about everyone was downloading music for free. As a result, people had accumulated massive libraries of digital music and needed something to play it on.

The music business got a lesson in digital technology at the hands of Apple and probably realizes in retrospect that it should have built it sooner, but it didn't and now it's forced to deal with the market leader— Apple. The movie studios and television networks won't go down as easy. They've been watching the iTunes era unfold with the intensity of someone whose livelihood depends on it, because it does.

As bandwidth increases, television and movies were the next logical target of file-sharing networks and the studios and networks are loath to get Napstered. By the same token, they're not about to let Apple call the shots in their business. Naturally, because of its huge market share, the television networks and movie studios want to distribute their content on iTunes, but they want to do it on *their* terms.

NBC is a perfect example of this. In August 2007, Apple announced that it wouldn't offer new fall seasons or shows from NBC on iTunes. Apple said it refused to agree to a cost hike NBC requested. NBC contended that it wanted a variety of pricing options but that Apple refused. NBC instead focused on its own digital streaming site, Hulu, and announced a deal with Microsoft to bring its television content to the Zune Marketplace. But NBC's posturing wasn't a total snub of Apple. In May 2008, the network began offering full episodes of two popular shows, *30 Rock* and *The Office*, to iPhone and iPod touch users to watch online for free.

The media center is the next frontier for Apple and digital content. Apple dipped its toe into the market with the Apple TV in January 2007, but it was an admittedly weak attempt. Apple fixed that with Apple TV Take 2 a year later, which featured a new interface, the ability to download TV shows, music, podcasts, and rent or download directly to the device. There are already many players in the crowded media center market and Apple will have to fight some established behemoths if it's going to establish a beachhead.

Apple's advantage is its commanding market leadership with iTunes and iPod. It can be expected to carefully observe the other players in the market, then slowly move in with an improved version, and its iPod army in tow.

Apple probably won't ever dominate the business computer market and it's probably fine with that. Although every company wants more sales, businesses are very price sensitive and Apple's perfectly happy to cede that market to low-cost Windows PCs. Apple would rather focus on its strengths and sell higher-end (and higher-margin) Macs to college students, creatives, and professionals.

"Apple's market share is bigger than BMW's or Mercedes's or Porsche's in the automotive market. What's wrong with being BMW or Mercedes?"[1]

With Apple's legendary secrecy in mind, it's difficult to predict anything from Cupertino with any accuracy. However, based on its success with iMac, iPod, iTunes, and iPhone, you can deduce that Apple will continue to grow and extend its products, as it continues to enhance and add digital content to its repertoire.

Apple's patent applications provide a veritable treasure trove of potential ideas that Apple is considering, including enhanced online shopping, Mac tablets, speech-recognition, handwriting-recognition, gaming consoles, digital video recorders, remote controls, docking stations, solar panels, and just about every kind of software that you can imagine.

Suffice it to say that Apple will continue to expand its number of spokes that are attached to the digital hub. It'll probably continue to build the rest of the wheel and eventually the whole "bicycle"—now *there's* an idea!

Glossary

AIX: Acronym for Advanced Interactive eXecutive. AIX was an IBM flavor of UNIX that Apple shipped with the Network Server 500 and 700 in February 1996. The Network Servers weren't commercially successful and were discontinued in April 1997.

APX: Acronym for Airport Extreme. A family of Apple products based on the IEEE 802.11g wireless communication specification.

A/UX: Acronym for Apple Unix (pronounced *ox*). A/UX was Apple's version of UNIX from 1988 to 1995, which was designed to run on the Mac II, Quadra, and Centris machines. A/UX was the first Mac system that allowed its users to access the command line interface.

BASIC: Acronym for Beginner's All-purpose Symbolic Instruction Code. BASIC was a simple programming language developed by John Kemeney and Thomas Kurtz in the mid-1960s at Dartmouth College.

BIT: Acronym for Binary digit. The smallest piece of data that a computer can recognize. A bit holds one of two values: 0 or 1.

Blue Box: An early phone-hacking tool that emulated phone company tones and signals that could be used to circumvent the phone company's billing system to make free telephone calls.

BPS: Acronym for Bits Per Second. A measurement of how fast the smallest piece of data that a computer can recognize (a 0 or 1) can be sent through a channel in one second.

BYTE: A string of 8 bits that represents a single character.

Cache: (pronounced *cash*). An area of high-speed memory, usually located close to the CPU, where data is copied when retrieved from RAM.

Combo Drive: An Apple DVD-ROM drive that supports writing to CD-R and CD-RW media and reading DVDs.

Cover Flow: A graphical user interface developed by Apple for visually browsing a digital music library by its cover art. Designed to simulate the experience of "flipping" through a stack of CDs or records.

CPU: Acronym for Central Processing Unit. The main part of a computer (a microprocessor or "chip") dedicated to executing instructions.

CRT: Acronym for Cathode Ray Tube. A common type of computer display or monitor, sometimes called a "picture tube."

DRM: Acronym for Digital Rights Management. An umbrella term for technology that is used to protect digital content and its copyright holders. Apple uses FairPlay DRM to protect tracks purchased from the iTunes Store.

DTP: Acronym for Desktop Publishing. The production on print collateral materials, brochures, flyers, and newsletters, on a desktop computer. Typically combined with a laser printer for proofs and final output.

DVD: Acronym for Digital Video Disk (also known as Digital Versatile Disk). An optical storage medium with 4.7GB, enough to hold a full-length movie.

DVR: Acronym for Digital Video Recorder (also known as Personal Video Recorder). A DVR or PVR records broadcast television content on a hard disk for playback at a later date.

Emulator: Software that allows one computer to act as another computer.

FireWire: A high-speed serial bus system developed between the late 1980s and 1995 by Apple, Digital Equipment Corporation (DEC), IBM, INMOS/SGS Thomson, Sony, and Texas Instruments as a replacement for the aging Small Computer Systems Interface (SCSI). FireWire is also known as IEEE 1394 and Sony's i.Link.

Flash Drive: A compact solid-state storage device that uses NAND flash memory rather than conventional spinning platters to store data.

Form-Factor: The shape and industrial design of a piece of computer hardware. Also used for peripherals.

FPU: Acronym for Floating Point Unit. A separate processor (or integral part of newer processors) designed to handle floating point calculations.

GUI: Acronym for Graphical User Interface. A front end to a computer invented at Xerox PARC during the 1970s, consisting of various widgets (windows, buttons, and icons) that perform a given task when activated either by mouse click or keystroke.

High Definition: Any video resolution over 1280 × 720 pixels. Almost exclusively utilizing a 16:9 aspect ratio.

Kernel: The central part of an operating system that manages resource allocation and hardware.

LAN: Acronym for Local Area Network. A means of connecting two or more machines in close proximity to each other.

Microprocessor: A complex integrated circuit usually manufactured from silicon that acts as the central processing unit of the computer. See CPU.

NAS: Acronym for Network Attached Storage. A disk or series of disks attached directly to a network rather than to a server on the network.

NeXTSTEP: An object-oriented, multitasking operating system developed by NeXT and launched on September 18, 1989.

OS: Acronym for Operating System. A software application that is loaded into memory by a boot program and manages all of the other software on a computer.

PASCAL: A computer programming language developed in 1970 by Niklaus Wirth based on Algorithmic Language (AL GOL). PASCAL got its name from the seventeenth-century mathematician Blaise Pascal who was responsible for building one of the first mechanical adding machines.

PDA: Acronym for Personal Digital Assistant. A handheld device used to store contacts and calendars. Newer models include Internet access.

Product Red: Product Red is a for-profit brand, which is licensed to partner companies such as Apple Inc., American Express, Converse, Motorola, The Gap, Emporio Armani, Hallmark, Microsoft, and Dell. Each partner company creates a product with the Product Red logo and/or color and returns a percentage of the profit to the Global Fund to Fight AIDS, Tuberculosis and Malaria.

RAID: Acronym for Redundant Array of Inexpensive Disks. A data storage technique that enables increased reliability and storage by using multiple hard drives.

R&D: Acronym for Research and Development. Activities undertaken while designing new and evolving existing products and services.

RAM: Acronym for Random-Access Memory. Memory that can be used by programs being processed to store data.

To RIP: Ripping (also referred to as digital audio extraction) refers to copying audio or video from one media form, such as CD or DVD, to a hard disk.

RISC: Acronym for Reduced Instruction Set Computer. A CPU design that increases arithmetic speed by decreasing the number of instructions and found in the PowerPC chip used by the Apple.

ROM: Acronym for Read Only Memory. A storage media that can be read but not written to.

Set-Top Box: A piece of computer hardware that connects to a TV to receive and play back digital audio and video content.

Speed-bump: An incremental upgrade to a piece of hardware. Typically some combination of upgraded CPU, graphics processor, optical drive, RAM, and hard drive.

SuperDrive: An Apple term used to refer to a high-density floppy drive and a combined CD/DVD reader and writer.

UNIX: An operating system co-created by AT&T researchers Dennis Ritchie and Ken Thompson known for its relative hardware independence.

USB: Acronym for Universal Serial Bus. A hardware interface that connects computers and peripherals.

Video Interlacing: A technique of improving the quality of a video signal, primarily on CRT devices, that divides each video frame into two fields to conserve bandwidth.

Notes

PREFACE

1. Apple Press Release, "Apple Introduces New iPod nano," September 9, 2008, http://www.apple.com/pr/library/2008/09/09nano.html.
2. Apple Press Release, "iTunes Store Tops Over Five Billion Songs Sold," June 19, 2008, http://www.apple.com/pr/library/2008/06/19itunes.html.

CHAPTER 1

1. Apple Confidential 2.0, p. 1, http://www.metromac.org/newsletter/express/march04/eden_bkrev.html, accessed April 21, 2008.
2. Mary Bellis, "Inventors of the Modern Computer, The First Hobby and Home Computers: Apple I, Apple II, Commodore PET, and TRS-80," http:/-240/inventors.about.com/library/weekly/aa121598.htm, accessed April 22, 2008.
3. S. G. Wozniak, with G. Smith, iWoz: From Computer Geek to Cult Icon: How I Invented the Personal Computer, Co-Founded Apple, and Had Fun Doing It (New York: W. W. Norton, 2006).
4. Andy Hertzfeld, "The Father of the Macintosh," Folklore.org, http://www.folklore.org/StoryView.py?story=The_Father_of_The_Macintosh.txt, accessed April 24, 2008.
5. Andy Hertzfeld, "Price Fight," Folklore.org, October 1983, http://folklore.org/StoryView.py?project=Macintosh&story=Price_Fight.txt&sortOrder=Sort%20by%20Date&detail=medium&search=John%20Sculley.
6. Brent Schlender, "Something's Rotting in Cupertino," *Fortune*, March 3, 1997, http://money.cnn.com/magazines/fortune/fortune_archive/1997/03/03/222710/index.htm.
7. Jerry Useem, "Apple: America's Best Retailer," *Fortune*, March 8, 2007, http://money.cnn.com/magazines/fortune/fortune_archive/2007/03/19/8402321/index.htm.

CHAPTER 2

1. "The World's Billionaires List 2008," *Forbes*, March 14, 2008, http://www.forbes.com/lists/2008/10/billionaires08_Steven-Jobs_HEDB.html.

2. Steve Jobs, "Stanford University Commencement Address 2005," http://news-service.stanford.edu/news/2005/june15/jobs-061505.html.

3. Jobs, "Stanford University Commencement Address 2005."

4. Michael Moritz, *The Little Kingdom: The Private Story of Apple Computer* (New York: William Morrow, 1984), p. 38.

5. David Sheff, "Playboy Interview: Steven Jobs," *Playboy*, February 1985, p. 176.

6. Owen W. Linzmayer, *Apple Confidential 2.0: The Definitive History of the World's Most Colorful Company* (San Francisco: No Starch Press, 2004).

7. Sheff, "Playboy Interview," p. 176.

8. Steve Jobs: The Journey Is the Reward. Jeffrey S. Young. Excerpt, http://www.jsyoung.com/jobs_journey_excerpt.htm.

9. Chris Foresman, "Steve Jobs's Cancer Went Unannounced for Nine Months," March 6, 2008, http://arstechnica.com/journals/apple.ars/2008/03/06/steve-jobss-cancer-went-unannounced-for-nine-months.

10. "America's 25 Most Fascinating Entrepreneurs," *Inc.*, April 1, 2004, http://www.inc.com/magazine/20040401/25jobs.html.

11. "Apple's Jobs Is Most Powerful Businessman," *Fortune*, November 27, 2007.

12. California Museum, "Jobs Inducted into California Hall of Fame," http://www.californiamuseum.org/Exhibits/Hall-of-Fame/inductees.html, accessed April 26, 2008.

13. R. Cringely, *Accidental Empires* (New York: Penguin, 1996).

14. S. G. Wozniak, with G. Smith, *iWoz: From Computer Geek to Cult Icon: How I Invented the Personal Computer, Co-Founded Apple, and Had Fun Doing It* (New York: W. W. Norton, 2006).

15. Linzmayer, *Apple Confidential 2.0*, p. 33.

16. "Short Bio for Steve Wozniak," http://www.woz.org/wozscape/wozbio.html, accessed April 27, 2008.

17. Andy Hertzfeld, "The Father of the Macintosh," Folklore.org, http://www.folklore.org/StoryView.py?story=The_Father_of_The_Macintosh.txt, accessed April 27, 2008.

18. http://www.kara.com/about/bio.html.

CHAPTER 3

1. "20 Most Profitable Tech Companies, 2008," *Fortune*, http://money.cnn.com/galleries/2008/fortune/0804/gallery.tech_profits.fortune/8.html, accessed May 3, 2008.

2. Adam C. Engst, "Apple Ranked Top Brand Worldwide," *TidBITS*, March 31, 2008, http://db.tidbits.com/article/9538.

3. Adam C. Engst, "Apple Tops *Fortune*'s Most Admired Companies List," *TidBITS*, March 5, 2008, http://db.tidbits.com/article/9488.

4. Jerry Useem, "Apple: America's Best Retailer," *Fortune*, March 8, 2007, http://money.cnn.com/magazines/fortune/fortune_archive/2007/03/19/8402321/index.htm.

5. Alan Deutschman, "The Second Coming of Steve Jobs," http://archive.salon.com/tech/books/2000/10/11/jobs_excerpt/.

6. U.S. Census Bureau, "Computer Use and Ownership, Current Population Survey (CPS) Reports," http://www.census.gov/population/www/socdemo/computer.html, accessed May 6, 2008.

7. "Mr. Morita, I Would Like a Walkman!," Sony History, http://www.sony. net/Fun/SH/1-18/h4.html, accessed May 7, 2008.

8. Kenji Hall, "Can Sony's New Walkman Run?," *BusinessWeek*, September 9, 2005, http://www.businessweek.com/technology/content/sep2005/tc2005099_6365_tc119.htm.

9. Robert Johnson, "The Fax Machine: Technology That Refuses to Die," *New York Times*, March 27, 2005, http://www.nytimes.com/2005/03/27/business/yourmoney/27fax.html.

10. Philip Elmer-DeWitt, "How to Grow the iPod as the MP3 Player Market Shrinks," *Fortune: Apple 2.0*, January 29, 2008, http://apple20.blogs.fortune.cnn.com/2008/01/29/beyond-the-incredible-shrinking-ipod-market/.

11. Jupiter Research, "US Cable and Satellite Households, 2006," http://www.boston.com/news/local/massachusetts/articles/2006/10/17/US_cable_and_satellite_households/, accessed May 9, 2008.

12. Tim Stevens, "82% of Americans Own Cell Phones," *Switched*, November 14, 2007, http://www.switched.com/2007/11/14/82-of-americans-own-cell-phones/.

13. "Gartner Says Worldwide Mobile Phone Sales Increased 16 Per Cent in 2007," February 27, 2008, http://www.gartner.com/it/page.jsp?id=612207.

14. "The Big Picture: Woodstock for Capitalists," *Sydney Morning Herald*, March 12, 2005, http://www.sharkisland.com.au/Woodstock/reviews.htm.

15. Leander Kahney, *The Cult of Mac* (San Francisco: No Starch Press), p. 2004.

CHAPTER 4

1. Jason D. O'Grady, "Apple Leads in Support—by Double Digits," *Consumer Reports*, May 6, 2008, http://blogs.zdnet.com/Apple/?p=1689.

2. Pamela Pfiffner, "The Birth of Desktop Publishing," *Macworld*, 2004, http://www.macworld.com/article/29180/2004/02/themacturns20.html, accessed May 14, 2008.

3. Bill Kincaid, "The True Story of SoundJam," Panic, http://www.panic.com/extras/audionstory/popup-sjstory.html, accessed May 14, 2008.

4. Cabel Sasser, "The True Story of Audion," Panic, http://www.panic.com/extras/audionstory/, accessed May 16, 2008.

5. "The iPod Has Landed," *Macworld*, October 2, 2001, http://www.macworld.com/article/7931/2001/10/ipod.html.

6. Steve Jobs, "Macworld Expo 2001 Keynote Address," January 9, 2001, http://www.stefanoparis.com/apple/macworld2001/macworld2001.html.

7. Leander Khaney, *Cult of iPod* (San Francisco: No Starch Press, 2005), p. 10.

8. Acaben, "Apple Introduces iPod, iTunes2," *MacSlash*, October 23, 2001, http://macslash.org/article.pl?sid=01/10/23/1732227&mode=thread.

9. Philip Elmer-DeWitt, "How to Grow the iPod as the MP3 Player Market Shrinks," *Fortune: Apple 2.0*, January 29, 2008, http://apple20.blogs.fortune.cnn.com/2008/01/29/beyond-the-incredible-shrinking-ipod-market/.

10. Apple Press Release, "Apple Unveils World's First 17-inch Notebook," January 7, 2003, http://www.apple.com/pr/library/2003/jan/07pbg4_17.html.

11. Mark Harris, "iTunes Store History—The History of the iTunes Store," About.com, http://mp3.about.com/od/history/p/iTunes_History.htm, accessed May 17, 2008.

12. "iTunes Store Top Music Retailer in the USA," Apple Inc., April 3, 2008.

13. Apple Press Release, "iTunes Store Tops over Five Billion Songs Sold," June 19, 2008, http://www.apple.com/pr/library/2008/06/19itunes.html, accessed May 22, 2008.

14. "Digital Developments Could Be Tipping Point for MP3," Reuters.com, http://www.reuters.com/article/musicNews/idUSN0132743320071203?pageNumber=3&virtualBrandChannel=0.

15. Apple Press Release, "Apple Unleashes the World's Fastest Personal Computer—the Power Mac G5," June 23, 2003, http://www.apple.com/pr/library/2003/jun/23pmg5.html.

16. "Number of Unlocked iPhones Reaches 250,000," Mobilewhack, October 30, 2007, http://www.mobilewhack.com/number-of-unlocked-iphones-reaches-250000/.

17. Rex Crum, "Apple CFO Upbeat about Unlocked iPhone's Impact," *Market-Watch*, March 5, 2008, http://www.marketwatch.com/news/story/apple-cfo-up beat-about-unlocked/story.aspx.

CHAPTER 6

1. Mary Bellis, "The First Spreadsheet—VisiCalc—Dan Bricklin and Bob Frankston," http://inventors.about.com/library/weekly/aa010199.htm, accessed June 2, 2008.

2. Jim Forbes, "Apple to Enhance System Software, Desktop Database," *PC Week*, April 12, 1988.

3. David Beaver, "Some Simpler Solutions to Making Macros (MacroMaker and AutoMac III Macro Recorders for the Macintosh)," *MacWEEK*, July 19, 1988.

4. Owen W. Linzmayer, *Apple Confidential 2.0: The Definitive History of the World's Most Colorful Company* (San Francisco: No Starch Press, 2004), p. 132.

5. Steve Jobs, "Macworld Expo 1997 Keynote Address: The Microsoft Deal."

6. Apple Press Release, "Apple Sells 1.2 Million Copies of Mac OS 8; Best Software Product Sales Ever in First Two Weeks of Availability," http://www.apple.com/ca/press/1997/08/MacOS8Sales.html, accessed June 16, 2008.

7. "Definition of: Apple," *PC* Magazine Encyclopedia, http://www.pcmag.com/encyclopedia_term/0,2542,t=Apple&i=37872,00.asp, accessed June 17, 2008.

8. Bryan Gardiner, "Learning from Failure: Apple's Most Notorious Flops," Wired.com, January 24, 2008, http://www.wired.com/gadgets/mac/multimedia/2008/01/gallery_apple_flops?slide=7&slideView=2.

9. Leander Kahney, "Apple Cube: Alive and Selling," Wired.com, http://www.wired.com/gadgets/mac/news/2003/07/59764, accessed June 17, 2008.

10. "The Ugliest Products in Tech History," *PC World*, http://tech.msn.com/products/slideshow.aspx?cp-documentid=5551551&imageindex=7, accessed June 18, 2008.

11. Bill Kincaid, "The True Story of SoundJam," *Panic*, http://www.panic.com/extras/audionstory/popup-sjstory.html, accessed June 19, 2008.

12. Cabel Sasser, "The True Story of Audion," *Panic*, http://www.panic.com/extras/audionstory/, accessed June 20, 2008.

13. Apple Press Release, "Apple Unveils World's First 17-inch Notebook," January 7, 2003, http://www.apple.com/pr/library/2003/jan/07pbg4_17.html, accessed June 20, 2008.

14. "iTunes Store Top Music Retailer in the USA," Apple Inc., April 3, 2008, http://www.apple.com/pr/library/2008/04/03itunes.html.

15. "Virginia Polytechnic Institute and State University: Cost-conscious Supercomputing," Apple.com Science Profile, http://www.apple.com/science/profiles/vatech/, accessed June 20, 2008.

16. Jacqui Cheng and Clint Ecker, "Dissecting Mighty Mouse," *Ars Technica*, August 3, 2005, http://arstechnica.com/articles/paedia/hardware/dissect.ars.

17. "WWDC 2007 Keynote," Apple Inc., June 11, 2007, http://events.apple.com.edgesuite.net/d7625zs/event/.

18. Apple Press Release, "Apple to Use Intel Microprocessors Beginning in 2006," June 6, 2005, http://www.apple.com/pr/library/2005/jun/06intel.html.

19. John Markoff and Steve Lohr, "Apple Plans to Switch from I.B.M. to Intel Chips," *New York Times*, June 6, 2005, http://nytimes.com/2005/06/06/technology/06apple.html (accessed May 4, 2006).

20. Jason D. O'Grady, "Theories on Apple TV," The Apple Core, February 19, 2007, http://blogs.zdnet.com/Apple/?p=440.

21. Pau Miller, "Apple Announces App Store for iPhone, iPod touch," Engadget, March 6, 2008, http://www.engadget.com/2008/03/06/apple-announces-app-store-for-iphone-ipod-touch/.

22. Apple Press Release, "Apple to Ship Mac OS X Leopard on October 26," October 16, 2007, http://www.apple.com/pr/library/2007/10/16leopard.html.

23. "Apple's Intel Switch: Jobs' Keynote Transcript," Cnet, June 15, 2005, http://www.news.com/Apples-Intel-switch-Jobs-keynote-transcript—page-2/2100–1047_3-5748045-2.html?tag=st.num.

24. Ryan Block, "Live from WWDC 2006: Steve Jobs' Keynote," Engadget, August 7, 2006, http://www.engadget.com/2006/08/07/live-from-wwdc-2006-steve-jobs-keynote/.

25. "Apple Statement," Press release, Yahoo! Finance, April 12, 2007, http://biz.yahoo.com/prnews/070412/sfth056.html?.v=87.

26. Ryan Block, "Steve Jobs Live from D 2007," Engadget, May 30, 2007, http://www.engadget.com/2007/05/30/steve-jobs-live-from-d-2007/.

CHAPTER 8

1. Andy Hertzfeld, "Macintosh Stories: Good Earth," Folklore.org, October 1980, http://folklore.org/StoryView.py?project=Macintosh&story=Good_Earth.txt&sortOrder=Sort%20by%20Date&detail=medium&search=Mike%20Scott.

2. Andy Hertzfeld, "Macintosh Stories: Black Wednesday," Folklore.org, February 1981, http://folklore.org/StoryView.py?project=Macintosh&story=Black_Wednesday.txt&sortOrder=Sort%20by%20Date&detail=medium&search=black%20wednesday.

3. Andy Hertzfeld, "Price Fight," Folklore.org, October 1983, http://folklore.org/StoryView.py?project=Macintosh&story=Price_Fight.txt&sortOrder=Sort%20by%20Date&detail=medium&search=John%20Sculley.

4. "Technology Milestone: Apple Newton 1993," *Ciber*, http://www.ciber.com/ciber/30years/more.cfm?dataid=174&id=90, accessed July 16, 2008.

5. Cathy Booth, "Steve Jobs: Restart Apple," *Time*, August 18, 1997, http://www.time.com/time/magazine/article/0,9171,986849,00.html.

6. "Jonathan Ive, Apple's Forgotten Saviour," *Cube*, May 19, 2007, http://cube1986.blogspot.com/2007/05/jonathon-ive-apples-forgotten-saviour.html.

7. Apple Public Relations, "Biography—Jonathan Ive," http://www.apple.com/pr/bios/ive.html, accessed July 18, 2008.

8. "Chingford Boy Is Mr Ive-Pod," *Sun,* January 11, 2007, http://www.thesun.co.uk/sol/homepage/news/article7632.ece.

CHAPTER 9

1. Eliot Van Buskirk, "Zune Eats Creative's Meager Lunch, Grabbing 4 Percent of MP3 Player Market," *Wired,* May 12, 2008, http://blog.wired.com/music/2008/05/ipod-loses-mark.html.

CHAPTER 10

1. Leander Kahney, "Apple Stock Crash Means It's Time to Go Long on AAPL," Wired, November 13, 2007, http://www.wired.com/gadgets/mac/commentary/cultofmac/2007/11/cultofmac_1114.

2. Bhaskar Chitraju, "Apple Financial Analysis," January 18, 2007, http://blogs.indews.com/financial_analysis/apple_financial_analysis.php.

3. Kahney, "Apple Stock Crash."

4. Connie Guglielmo, "Apple iPhone Fees Prompt Analysts to Revalue Earnings," *Bloomberg,* November 8, 2007, http://www.bloomberg.com/apps/news?pid=20601109&sid=aTTQICamfprA&refer=home.

5. "Apple Investor Relations Page," http://www.apple.com/investor/, accessed July 20, 2008.

6. Thomas Hormby, "NeXT, OpenStep, and the Triumphant Return of Steve Jobs," Low End Mac, November 15, 2005, http://lowendmac.com/orchard/05/1115.html.

7. Chitraju, "Apple Financial Analysis."

8. Chitraju, "Apple Financial Analysis."

9. Jal Singh, "Dell: Apple Should Close Shop," *CNET News,* October 6, 1997, http://www.news.com/Dell-Apple-should-close-shop/2100–1001_3–203937.html (accessed March 2, 2007).

10. Jeff Gamet, "Apple Passes Dell's Market Cap," *MacObserver,* January 16, 2006, http://www.macobserver.com/stockwatch/2006/01/16.1.shtml.

11. Brian Caulfield, "Leopard on the Prowl," *Forbes,* October 26, 2007, http://www.forbes.com/technology/2007/10/26/ipod-apple-jobs-tech-cx_bc_1026leopard.html.

12. Brian Caulfield, "Meet the Mac-Clone Mystery Man," *Forbes,* April 18, 2008, http://www.forbes.com/technology/2008/04/18/apple-mac-psystar-tech-cx_bc_0418macman.html.

13. Ben Worthen, "PayPal Bans Browsers; Mac Love; Cell Phone Bans," *Wall Street Journal,* April 18, 2008, http://blogs.wsj.com/biztech/2008/04/18/paypal-bans-browsers-mac-love-cell-phone-bans/.

CHAPTER 11

1. Jason Snell, "Steve Jobs on the Mac's 20th Anniversary," *Macworld,* February 2, 2004, http://www.macworld.com/article/29181/2004/02/themacturns20jobs.html.

Bibliography

Angelelli, Lee. *Steve Paul Jobs: Biography*. Department of Computer Science, Virginia Tech, 1994, http://ei.cs.vt.edu/~history/Jobs.html.

Butcher, Lee. *Accidental Millionaire: The Rise and Fall of Steve Jobs at Apple Computer*. New York: Paragon House, 1988.

Caddes, Carolyn. *Portraits of Success: Impressions of Silicon Valley Pioneers*. Palo Alto, CA: Tioga, 1986.

Carlton, Jim. *Apple: The Inside Story of Intrigue, Egomania, and Business Blunders*. New York: HarperBusiness, 1998.

Cringely, Robert X. *Accidental Empires: How the Boys of Silicon Valley Make Their Millions, Battle Foreign Competition, and Still Can't Get a Date*. New York: HarperCollins, 1996.

Denning, Peter J., and Karen A. Frenkel. "A Conversation with Steve Jobs." *Communications of the ACM* 32, no. 4 (April 1989): 437–43.

Deutschman, Alan. *The Second Coming of Steve Jobs*. New York: Broadway Books, 2000.

Hertzfeld, Andy. *Revolution in The Valley: The Insanely Great Story of How the Mac Was Made*. New York: O'Reilly Media, 2004.

Kahney, Leander. *The Cult of Mac*. San Francisco: No Starch Press, 2004.

———. *The Cult of iPod*. San Francisco: No Starch Press, 2005.

———. *Inside Steve's Brain*. New York: Portfolio, 2008.

Levy, Steven. *Hackers: Heroes of the Computer Revolution*. Garden City, NY: Anchor Press/Doubleday, 1984.

Linzmayer, Owen W. *Apple Confidential 2.0: The Definitive History of the World's Most Colorful Company*. San Francisco, CA: No Starch Press, 2004.

Malone, Michael S. *Infinite Loop*. New York: Currency/Doubleday, 1999.

Moritz, Michael. *The Little Kingdom: The Private Story of Apple Computer*. New York: William Morrow, 1984.

Sculley, John, and John A. Byrne. *Odyssey: Pepsi to Apple: A Journey of Adventure, Ideas, and the Future*. New York: Harper & Row, 1987.

Slater, Robert. *Portraits in Silicon*. Cambridge, MA: MIT Press, 1987.

Wozniak, Steve, with G. Smith. *iWoz: From Computer Geek to Cult Icon: How I Invented the Personal Computer, Co-Founded Apple, and Had Fun Doing It.* New York: W. W. Norton, 2006.

Young, Jeffrey S., and William L. Simon. *iCon: Steve Jobs—The Greatest Second Act in the History of Business.* Hoboken, NJ: John Wiley, 2005.

———. *Steve Jobs: The Journey Is the Reward.* Glenview, IL: Scott, Foresman, 1988.

Index

About the Author

JASON D. O'GRADY has written for many Macintosh trade magazines, including *MacWorld, MacWEEK,* and *MacPower* (Japan). He has also been interviewed on ABC, NPR, NBC, and BBC radio, and featured in the *New York Times, Wall Stree Journal,* and *USA Today.* O'Grady runs O'Grady's PowerPage.org, a Web site devoted to mobile applications related to Apple products.